MACHINE LEARNING

This book includes

Machine Learning for Beginners

Artificial Intelligence and Machine Learning for Business

Networking for beginners

Scott Chesterton

Table of Contents

Machine Learning for Beginners:

Artificial Intelligence and Machine Learning for Business:

Networking for beginners:

Machine Learning for Beginners

Machine Learning Basics for Absolute Beginners. Learn What ML Is and Why It Matters. Notes on Artificial Intelligence and Deep Learning are also included

Scott Chesterton

Introduction

Congratulations on downloading *Machine Learning for Beginners: Machine Learning Basics for Absolute Beginners,* and thank you for doing so.

The following chapters will discuss Machine Learning along with a lot of concepts that make you get a thorough understanding of machine learning with a lot of real-life examples that will help you understand the topic in detail.

Machine learning has been news in recent days for its extravaganza and phenomenon for its complex algorithms that run many applications. You might have already heard about IBM Watson, the famous supercomputer that uses Machine Learning for an infinite number of tasks it does.

There are plenty of books on this subject on the market, so thanks again for choosing this one! Every effort was made to ensure it is full of as much useful information as possible, please enjoy reading and learning!

Chapter 1: Introducing Machine Learning

Machine learning has prospered itself in the last few years for its amazing applications that changed the world, but its history dates back more than half a century. A. L. Samuel is known famously for coining this term. He conveyed that if a machine can learn itself without involving any programming, it can be called as Machine Learning. That has increased its effectiveness exponentially and had become one of the best human inventions to the world. Nowadays, every small thing that you don't observe keenly is linked with artificial intelligence and its corresponding fields that had penetrated deeply into society

There is a small story that needs to be said before discussing machine learning in detail. Long before, IBM has developed a checkers program that is self-learning and can gradually identify the good and bad pieces in the current game by analyzing a large number of games, thereby improving the game and quickly outplayed the famous Samuel's Checker Player. In 1956, he was invited by John Johan McCarthy, the father of artificial intelligence and the winner of the 1971 Turing Award, to present the work at the Dartmouth Conference, which marked the birth of the field of artificial intelligence. Samuel made sure that people understood the importance of machine learning and its huge scope of applications that can change mankind.

After the article of his study regarding the experience he had with machine learning was officially published in IRM Journal in 1959, Edward Feigenbaum, the father of Knowledge Engineering and the winner of the 1994 Turing Award, wrote his magnum opus Compilers, and in 1961, Samuel was invited to provide an example of the best game in the program. So, Samuel took the opportunity to challenge Connecticut's checkers champion, the then fourth best player in the United States. The program won, causing a sensation at the time in the tech industry and making people getting serious with artificial intelligence.

Samuel's checkers program had a major impact not only on artificial intelligence but also on the development of computer science as a whole. Early research in computer science suggested that computers could not perform tasks that were not explicitly programmed in advance, a hypothesis that Samuel's checkers program disproved. Also, this program was one of the first to perform non-numerical computing tasks on a computer. Its logic instruction design greatly influenced the instruction set of IBM Computer and was soon adopted by other computer designers.

Development of Machine Learning in Detail

Artificial intelligence research with a lot of collaboration of professors and scientists around the world had made Machine Learning prosper in very less time. In the 1950s and early 1970s, when artificial intelligence research was in its reasoning phase, it was assumed that machines could be intelligent if given the ability to reason logically. The representative work in this stage mainly has the Logic Theorist program of A. Newell and H. Simon's, and later, the General Problem Solver program and many other programs are designed which achieved encouraging results at that time. For example, the logical theoretician program proved 38 theorems in the famous mathematician Russell and Alfred North Whitehead's Principal Mathematics in 1952 and all 52 theorems in 1963. However, with the development of research, people gradually realized that artificial intelligence cannot be achieved only by logical reasoning. E. A. Feigenbaum and others believed that to make a machine intelligent, it must somehow know a lot of information and think like a human.

In their advocacy, from the mid-1970s, artificial intelligence research had moved into the knowledge period. In this period, a large number of expert systems have developed that are used in application areas which made a lot of results. E. A. Feigenbaum was awarded the Turing Award in 1994 as the father of knowledge engineering. However, people gradually realized that the expert system faced Knowledge Engineering Bottleneck. In short, it is very difficult for a human to sum up knowledge and then teach it to the computer. So some scholars thought that if only machines could learn on their own, there would be favorable results and great learning for the computers to think exactly like humans.

Definition of Machine Learning

In plain English, a computer learns from experience and gets better at something. From the definitions of pioneers and great minds of machine learning, we can summarize our understanding to get a valid expression of machine learning which learns itself without any valid instructions but with a lot of data that helps the machine to think just like a human.

From this understanding of the definition, we can conclude that the following are the most important aspects of Machine Learning:

- **Data:** Experience is ultimately transformed into data that a computer can understand so that it can learn from what it had understood. Whoever has the most data and the highest quality has the most leverage in machine learning and artificial intelligence. To use the human analogy, data is like our educational environment, and one of the most important aspects of being smart is being able to have a good education. So, in that sense, it is clear that an internet company like Google could develop machine learning programs that can perform well because they have access to vast amounts of data that they collect from their users.

- **Model:** That is, the Algorithm is the main important source or path for a machine learning application. Data can help us make a perfect model which we intended to. And when we use this infinite data to train it, there will be fruitful result which is an improvement in the machine. After training with a lot of data, that model becomes the core of machine learning, making the model the hub of decision making. A well-trained model, when inputting a new event, will make an appropriate response, producing high-quality output.

Explaining Machine Learning with Daily Life Examples

Half a century after its birth, machine learning has become more widely used, thanks to Moore's law, as computer performance improves and computing resources become cheaper. You may not see it, but your daily life has become filled with artificial intelligence, machine learning, and deep learning-based applications.

Now, we will look at a detailed example of how machine learning had interlinked with our lives. This will give you a brief understanding of the subject and its scope in larger detail.

When you wake up in the morning, turn on Siri on your iPhone or Google Assistant in your Android or Cortana in your Windows laptop, and ask what the weather today is like. Siri will automatically locate your current city and display weather information. This function is simple to use, but the system behind it is extremely complex. One is speech recognition, one of the earliest applications of machine learning, where Siri first converts what you say into words. As you know, speech is essentially a series of waves with different amplitudes. To transform speech into text, we need to design a model. First, we need to train the model through a lot of speech input. When the model is trained, we take speech as the input and the input can further process the information from various sources and gives you back the information that you asked for. Speech recognition has been studied since the 1950s, and its model is constantly evolving. This evolution is now using neural networks and other deep learning strategies to score a better result.

The other is natural language processing, which is another very important aspect of machine learning and artificial intelligence. After Siri converts a voice to text, the software needs to understand the words to give an accurate answer. It is not easy for a computer to understand words. First of all, there should be a large-scale Corpus. Secondly, there should be a corresponding language model, and then through the Corpus, you should be able to train the language model in a way that it can finally understand part of the text semantics. For natural language processing and search engine technology, you can refer books that can make Advanced Math easy to understand and fun to read.

Let's get back to the story of getting out of bed. While you are washing up, take a moment to look at the news on your phone, and you might have noticed that there is an ad for a camera below it. You have talked to your friend about buying a camera just a day before. Your phone had understood it automatically and had recommended an ad that you may be interested in. Click on it and it opens up a well-known e-commerce site. You look at the price and the reviews and then buy a cheap product. Then, browse the news; you can observe that the news appears like more and more human nature, automatically pointing you to your favorite news in the front page tempting you to read them. When you are finally ready to go to the office, you sit on the subway, turn on your music player, browse through your music library in Spotify, and find no songs you want to listen to, so you ask the system to recommend some songs to you. The system that recommended the song is quite reliable to you, which you have never heard and likes them in the first place when you listen to them.

In this description of the experience, the person behind it is the recommender system, which is an important application of machine learning. The core of the recommender system is to learn the user's usage habits, then draw a picture of the user, and according to the user's picture, it recommends songs, articles, products and any other source of information that the user can get hooked up with.

Then, you go to your workplace, and you get welcomed with a new face recognition system that detects your face and allows you to enter into the office. This face recognition system uses machine learning algorithms to detect your face in different expressions. The best thing is that it detects you automatically and greets you with sweet wishes according to the time. At present, most of the most advanced face recognition systems are based on the algorithm of the deep learning model that uses complex patterns to recognize the faces with accuracy.

Data Mining

Data mining is nowadays being used explicitly as a statistical world in a pejorative sense because traditional statistical research tends to focus on the beauty of theory rather than its utility. But that has changed recently as more and more list of statisticians focus on problems that are somehow linked with common experiences that people face which uses machine learning.

In fact, as the basic means of scientific research moves from the traditional "theory + experiment" to the present "theory + experiment + calculation", and even to the emergence of the phrase "data science", the importance of machine learning is increasing because the purpose of computation is data analysis; the core of data science is to gain value by analyzing data. To list the most active and high-profile branches of research in computer science and technology, Machine Learning must be one of them.

Why Machine Learning Matters with respect to Data Mining?

In 2006, Carnegie Mellon University announced the creation of the world's first Machine Learning Department, one of the founders of the field. After a few years, American presidential had shown interest in the development of machine learning, where Professor Mitchell became the first head of the department. The National Science Foundation launched an intensive program at the University of California, Berkeley. It emphasizes three key technologies for deep research and integration in the big data era: machine learning, cloud computing, and crowdsourcing. Machine learning is the essential core technology of the big data era, and the reason is simple: the purpose of collecting, storing, transferring, and managing big data is to "leverage" it, and without machine learning to analyze it, no use can be made of it.

The field of data mining came into being in the 1990s, and it was influenced by many fields, of which database, machine learning, and statistics were undoubtedly the most influential. Data mining is to mine knowledge from mass data, which involves the management and analysis of mass data. In general, research in the database provides data management techniques for data mining, while research in machine learning and statistics provides data analysis techniques for data mining.

In this sense, statistics mainly influence data mining through machine learning; the machine learning domain and the database domain are the two main supports of data mining. In this sense, statistics has a great influence on data mining through machine learning.

Today, machine learning is relevant to the lives of ordinary people. For example, in areas such as weather forecasting, energy exploration, and environmental monitoring, the effective use of machine learning techniques to analyze data from satellites and sensors is an efficient way for better forecasting and detection. Sales data can be deeply researched using machine learning, and customer information can not only help businesses optimize inventory and reduce costs but also help them design specific marketing strategies for their user base. Here are a few more examples:

As we all know, Google, Bing, and other Internet search engines have begun to change the way of human life. For example, many people have been accustomed to travel through the Internet before the search to understand the destination information, to find the right place.

If you want another example, car accidents are one of the deadliest killers of humanity, killing one million people a year worldwide and around 100,000 in our country alone. The ideal solution is for a computer to drive an autonomous car because the machine on the road can ensure that not only it is not a novice driver, fatigue driving, and drunk driving but it also has important military applications. The United States has been conducting research in this area since the 1980s. The biggest difficulty here is not being able to take into account, design, and program all the situations that a car will encounter on the road in a car factory. Instead, the information received by the onboard sensors can be taken as input, and the control behavior of direction, brake, and throttle can be taken as the output according to the situation encountered on the road. Then, the key problem here can just be abstracted as a machine learning task.

Machine learning has been the backbone of the Internet search ever since. Today, the objects and contents of the search are becoming more complex, and the influence of machine learning technology is more obvious. For example, both Google and Bing are using the latest machine learning technology when conducting "image search". Google, Bing, Facebook, Yahoo, and other companies have set up research teams specializing in machine learning technology.

Machine learning technology has even influenced the human's social and political life. During the 2012 election, Obama's machine learning team analyzed various election data to give him hints about what to do next. For example, they use machine learning to analyze social network data, determine which voters will turn after a presidential candidate's first debate, and develop personalized communications strategies based on that analysis. Google can come up with one of the most compelling reasons for each voter to stay: they are based on machine learning models.

It's worth noting that machine learning has gained a lot of attention certainly because it has become a source of innovation in intelligent data analytics. However, there is another important aspect of machine learning research that can't be ignored, which is to promote our understanding of how humans learn by building computational models of learning. For example, when P. Kanerva proposed his Sparse Distributed Memory model (Kanerva, 1988) in the mid-1980s, it did not deliberately mimic the physiological structure of the brain, but neuroscience research found later that the sparse encoding mechanism of SDM exists widely in the cortex of visual, auditory, and olfactory functions. The driving force of natural science research can be summed up as man's curiosity about the origin of the universe, the essence of everything, the nature of life, and self-consciousness. Machine learning conquers itself with natural and biomedical sciences along with every other study that can be learned with a practice.

Types of Machine Learning

After innumerable research and a lot of experiments, computer scientists decided to divide machine learning into two categories for a better understanding and fast research. They are as follows:

- **Supervised Learning**: It is the process by which a computer learns laws from a large number of known input-output pairs of data, enabling it to make reasonable output predictions for new input. In our existing data, we have different characteristics (area, location, orientation, developer, etc.) of the house price data. By learning these data, we can predict the price of a known feature of the house, and this approach is called Regression learning, which is the output is a specific value and its prediction model is a continuous function. Another example is that we have a large number of emails, each of which has been flagged as spam. By studying the tagged email data, a model is developed that can accurately determine whether the email is spam or not for a new email. This is called Classification learning, where the output is discrete. Either output 1 is spam or output 0 is not spam.

- **Unsupervised Learning:** It can be understood implicitly as learning from undistinguished data to analyze its intrinsic characteristics and structure. Corporate companies like Amazon have huge access to customer data, and we use that data to analyze the different categories of customers that shop with them. How many categories can we end up with in response to this question? What are the characteristics of each category? We didn't know about it. This is called Clustering. There is a distinction to be made between categories in supervised learning where we already know which categories exist, and clustering is a process where we don't know which categories exist until we analyze the data. That is, the classification problem is to choose one of the known answers, while the answer to the clustering problem is unknown, and the Algorithm is needed to mine the characteristics and structure of the data.

The biggest difference between the two types of machine learning is that training data with supervised learning has known results to monitor, while training data with unsupervised learning has no known results to monitor.

Explaining Machine Learning Concepts with a House Price Evaluation System

This section deals with a clear-cut explanation of simple concepts of machine learning with a simple example that anyone can link within their real life. Suppose we want to develop a house price evaluation system, the goal of the system is a known characteristic of the house price evaluation forecast. Establishing such a system requires the following steps:

1. Training Samples

We need a large number of different characteristics of the house and the corresponding price information. You can directly get this information from the Property Assessment Center to obtain information about the house, such as the size of the house, geographical location, orientation, price, and so on. There are other kinds of information that may or may not be available in a real estate appraisal center, such as a nearby school where the house is located, a characteristic that often affects the price of the house, and at this point, the data needs to be collected through other means. These data are called training samples, or data sets. The size, location, and so on of a house are called features. In the data acquisition phase, many features of the possible requirements need to be collected. The more complete the feature set, the more data and the more accurate the trained model will be and the more accurate results we will get.

The cost of data acquisition can also be felt through this process. Machine learning can be used to analyze your previous transactions from various sources and give you a credit score according to your payments and debts. This credit score is very important for banks to get known with potential risk frauds and thus making the financial transactions more transparent.

2. Data Tagging

In the case of the home appraisal system, our home price information is obtained from the home appraisal center, which may not be accurate. Sometimes, to avoid taxes, the appraisal price of the house is much lower than the actual transaction price of the house. At this point, the actual transaction price of the house needs to be collected by a process called data tagging. Markers can be artificial, such as asking a real estate agent for the actual price of a house one by one or they can be automated, such as by analyzing data by finding out the Real Estate Assessment Center to assess the price of the house and the true price of the match, and then directly calculated by various complex algorithms. Data tagging is necessary for supervised learning methods. For example, for a spam filtering system, our training sample must contain flag data on whether the message is spam or not. Data is very important for machine learning. If there is no sufficient or reliable data the results will be absurd and far away from reality.

3. Data Cleansing

Suppose we collect data on the size of the house, there are often represented by square meters. You need to collect this data and apply it to your house. This process is called data cleansing. Data cleansing also involves removing duplicate and noisy data and giving it a structured character that can be easily used as input to machine learning algorithms. Suppose we collect hundred house features, and by analyzing these features one by one, we finally select thirty features as input. This process is called feature selection. One of the methods of feature selection is manual selection, that is, people analyze each feature, and then select the appropriate feature set to another requirement. Another approach is to do it automatically through models, such as the PCA Algorithm.

This example is linked to the first category of machine learning, which deals with the simplest linear equation to simulate. Which model we need to choose is related to the problem domain, data volume, training time, accuracy of the model, and so on.

4. Training Data Sets

There are two types of data sets mostly one belongs to training, whereas the other deals with testing, which are usually divided into 8:2 or 7:3 ratio, and then the training data sets can be improvised and used in such a way that they can help increase the effectiveness of the model. And soon after the training, this can be tested to check the valid accuracy of the model. Why should a separate test data set be tested? The answer is to make sure the test is accurate, that is, the model is tested with data it hasn't seen before, not with the data used to train the model. In theory, the more logical way to partition a dataset is to divide it into three, plus a cross-validation dataset. When the model comes out, there needs to be a process where we can check different conditions and make a thorough checklist of the performance. Performance evaluation includes many aspects, as follows.

The training duration is how long it takes to train the model. For some big data machine learning applications, it may take a month or more to train a model, at which point, the algorithm's performance becomes important. Also, it is necessary to judge whether there are enough data sets. Generally speaking, the larger the training data set is, the better for the system with complex features. Then, there is a need to determine the accuracy of the model, whether new data can be accurately predicted. Finally, we need to determine whether the model can meet the performance requirements of the application scenario. If it cannot meet the requirements, we need to optimize the model, and then continue to train and evaluate the model or change to other models.

The trained model can save the parameters and load them directly when the next time it is used. Generally speaking, model training needs a lot of computation and a long time to train because a good model parameter needs to be trained on a large data set. However, when the model is used, the computational load is relatively small. Generally, the new sample is used as the input, and then the model is invoked to get the prediction result.

Scope of Machine Learning

April 2013 was a phenomenal day in the history of machine learning because the concept of Industry 4.0 strategy was first proposed. Industry 4.0 refers to intelligent manufacturing dominated information revolution or revolutionary production methods. The strategy is aimed at achieving the goals of the Millennium Development with faster technological advancement using different machine learning, deep learning, and artificial intelligence techniques. The combination of a virtual system and information physics system will transform the manufacturing industry into intelligence. Based on future trends in intelligent technologies such as machine learning, 4.0 is a future trend that consists of various advanced technologies like intelligent systems, distributed computing, Pentagon Resources, facial recognition with accurate prediction, OCR recognition with machine translation, and image manipulation with preciseness along with Internet of Things that are believed to be available soon in few years.

In September 2015, Major General Steve Jones, commander of the U. S. Army Medical Center, told a U. S. army conference that intelligent robots could replace humans on the battlefield to transport the wounded. The US military has even made a high profile announcement that soldiers may not be the ones to be rescued on the battlefield in the future but rather robots because the army of intelligent robots will replace humans.

Until the 21st century, the idea of a "Big Bang" for artificial intelligence seemed like a pipe dream for science fiction writers. Today, more and more people are beginning to think seriously about what will happen to humanity when the technological singularity arrives?

In the exponential growth of science and technology, the human defense during the war seems imminent. The university, founded with the support of Google, Autodesk, and Genentech, has three programs covering robotics, medicine, biotechnology, data science, and corporate governance. Cloud computing brings powerful computing power, and big data algorithms are widely used, although they are not enough to make computers smarter. They create the strong AI necessary for big data to enable machines to learn from vast amounts of information, and cloud computing has cheap and powerful computing power close to the human brain.

Shortly, machine learning will move into the strong AI, where there will be real intelligent machines capable of reasoning and problem-solving. These machines will have consciousness and self-awareness with the same level of intelligence as humans.

The Applications of Machine Learning

Machine learning is widely used; there are opportunities for machine learning algorithms to be deployed in both military and civilian contexts.

- **Data Analysis and Mining**

  Data mining and data analysis are often mentioned in the same breath and in many cases are considered interchangeable terms. Data analysis refers to the use of appropriate statistical methods to collect a large number of primary source and second-hand information analysis; it is to extract useful information and form conclusions on the data for detailed study and summary process. Whether data analysis or data mining, it is to help people collect and analyze data, make it into information, and make judgments.

Data analysis and mining technology is the result of the machine learning algorithm and data access technology using statistical analysis, knowledge discovery, and other tools provided by machine learning to analyze large numbers. At the same time, the data access mechanism is used to achieve efficient data reading and writing. Machine learning is irreplaceable in data analysis and mining, and the 2012 entry of Hadoop into machine learning made this better.

In 2012, Cloudera bought Myrrix to co-create Big Learning, and since then, the machine learning club has a co-partner called Hadoop. Cheap hardware makes big data analytics easier, and as hard drives and CPUs become cheaper and open-source databases and computing frameworks mature, startups and even individuals can perform terabytes of complex computing. Myrrix, which evolved from the Apache Mahout project, is a real-time, scalable clustering and recommendation system based on machine learning.

Other big companies are also using machine learning to analyze data to improve the quality of their products and services. Microsoft officially launched the Azure Machine learning platform, which is already available for Xbox and Bing and supports R, Python, Hadoop, Spark, and more. Ford uses AI to schedule its work and solve the scheduling problems that come with a growing number of employees. Certain companies use deep learning from neural networks to virtual drug screening in an attempt to replace or improve the computational methods used in high throughput screening. Yahoo uses machine learning algorithms to mine data from 16 billion emails, and researchers at the lab studied 16 billion emails between 2 million people.

- **To Analyze User Behavior**

PayPal uses machine learning to fight fraud, also machine learning and statistical models to identify fraud and more sophisticated algorithms to filter transactions. AWS has opened up the machine learning service to European developers, which can be used through the Dublin AWS region, and the company expects that Amazon's machine learning will help solve the limitation problem and that all the analysis and prediction will be done with data from Europe and never leave the area.

- **Pattern Recognition**

The combination of pattern recognition, which originated in engineering, and machine learning, which originated in computer science, has led to the adjustment and development of pattern recognition. Pattern recognition research mainly focuses on two aspects: one is to study how organisms (including humans) perceive objects, which belongs to the field of cognitive science, and the other is how to use computers under given tasks.

Pattern recognition is one of the pioneering applications of machine learning and can be used to detect images, text, fonts, calligraphy, and a lot of other things that are impossible on other way by humans. Moreover, systems are improving day by day and are believed to understand any pattern by 2050. Pattern recognition is applied in many fields, including computer vision, medical image analysis, optical character recognition, natural language processing, speech recognition, handwriting recognition, and biometrics. Others such as file classification, search engines, and so on are also areas where machine learning is well-established.

- **Wider Areas**

2015 is the year of machine learning, and the time has come for a revolution in machine learning to transform human society. Not only are big companies such as Google, Amazon, Accenture, Toyota, Tesla, and Johnson & Johnson are adopting machine learning on a massive scale, but startups are also getting in on the artificial intelligence for fast growth.

The machine learning revolution is on par with the big companies. Startups have already announced innovative applications for machine learning, and investors have expressed a strong interest in startups. More than 170 startups have gone into AI, and big tech companies like Google and IBM have invested heavily in AI.

The use of machine learning in all walks of life around the world has entered its peak; the news is everywhere. Google DeepMind researchers have successfully turned computers into masters of Atari Video Games using machine learning. Google has teamed up with Johnson & Johnson to AI surgical robots that can help surgeons reduce injuries to patients.

The current wave of machine learning platform GraphLab is an open-source project—renamed it Dato—which raised $18.5 million in new financing. It was designed to help machines analyze images. Microsoft has built chat for Microsoft Cortana, and ML has enabled Microsoft Cortana not only to recognize jokes and predict sports events but also to tell you to get to meetings early (for example, because of traffic). Intel's 18-core Xeon chip, adapted specifically for machine learning and designed for the fast-changing services market, is six times faster than the new chip as the company claims. Airbnb has unveiled Aerosolve, a machine learning package that

Airbnb believes will work better with humans and machines in symbiosis than with humans or machines alone. Machine learning is also featured in Gartner's 2015 Hype Cycle report, which shows only digital technologies and mainly those that Gartner considers having a significant impact, and humanism is the first technology to appear in the report.

Chapter 2: Basics of Machine Learning

Machine learning is one such discipline that focuses on how to improve the performance of systems through computation, experience, and a little more experience. In computer systems, an experience usually exists in the form of data. Therefore, the main content of the machine learning algorithm is an algorithm for generating a model from data on a computer. With the learning algorithm, we provide empirical data to it, and it can generate models based on that data; in the face of a new situation, the model will give us corresponding judgments. If computer science is the study of programs, machine learning is the study of algorithms.

Dataset

To do machine learning, you need data. Suppose we collect a collection of data on watermelons, such as (green in color; curled at the base; dull tapping), (dark in color; slightly curled at the base; dull tapping), (pale in color; stiff at the base; crisp tapping). Each pair of parentheses contains a record.

This collection of records is called a dataset, where each record is a description of an event or object called an instance or sample. Something that reflects the behavior or nature of an event or object in some way such as color, root, and tap are called attribute or feature. Values on attributes such as green and black are called attribute values. The spaces where attributes are stretched are called attribute space, sample space, or input space. Since each point in space corresponds to a coordinate vector, we also refer to it as a feature vector.

Hypothesis

The process of learning a model from data is called learning or training and is accomplished by performing a learning algorithm. The data used in the training process is called training data, where each sample is called a training sample, and the set of training samples is called the training set. The learning model corresponds to an underlying law of data and is therefore called a hypothesis; the underlying law itself is called a "truth" or "ground-truth", and the learning process is designed to find or approximate the truth. The model is sometimes referred to as a learner, an instantiation of a learning algorithm on a given data and parameter space.

If you want to learn a model that can help you decide if it is a good result, the sample data are not enough. To establish such a "prediction" model, we need to obtain the "result" information of the training sample, such as (color green; curling; ringing)

Classification

If we want to predict discrete values, such as "good melon" and "bad melon", this type of learning task is called "classification". If you want to predict a continuous value, such as watermelon maturity 0.95 or 0.37, this type of learning task is called regression. For a "binary classification" task involving only two classes, one is usually called a "positive class" and the other a "negative class"; when multiple classes are involved, it is called a "multi-class classification" task.

Testing

After learning the model, the process of using it to make predictions is called testing, and the predicted samples are called sample testing. For example, after learning, the test case can get its prediction mark.

We can also "cluster" watermelons, which will be divided into several groups, each group called a "cluster"; these automatically formed clusters may correspond to some of the underlying concepts, such as "light-colored", "dark-colored", or even "local". This learning process can help us understand the inherent law of data and establish the basis for further analysis of data. It should be noted that the concepts of "light-colored melon" and "native melon" are unknown to us in cluster learning, and the training samples used in the learning process usually do not possess the labeled information.

As said before, after a careful understanding of all the resources available in detail, you can interpret whether a model uses supervised learning or unsupervised learning by a little brainstorming. Classification and regression are the representatives of the former, while clustering is the representatives of the latter.

Note that the goal of machine learning is to make the learned model work well with "new samples" and not just training samples; even for unsupervised learning tasks such as clustering, we also hope that the cluster partition can be applied to the samples, not in the training set. The reason why training samples can work well in the whole sample space is that it has generalizability. Generalizability is defined as the ability to use the mastered model in new samples. The beauty of machine learning is, even though training set being a small sample, it can reflect its characteristics quite well in the sample space. Thus, generalizability is an important concept that leads machine learning to a new trend with its simplicity in complexness. It is usually assumed that all samples in the sample space are subject to an unknown "distribution" D, and each sample we obtain is independently sampled from that distribution, i. e. independent and identically distributed (IID). In general, the more training samples we have, the more information we get about.

Induction and Deduction

Induction and deduction are two basic means of scientific reasoning. The "generalization" process from the special to the general, that is, from the concrete facts to the general law, and the latter is the "specialization" process from the general to the special, that is, to deduce the concrete situation from the basic principles. For example, in a mathematical axiom system, it is deductive to derive a theorem corresponding to it based on a set of axioms and inference rules, while "learning from examples" is an inductive process; hence it is also called "inductive learning".

Inductive learning can be divided into a narrow sense and a broad sense, which is roughly equivalent to learning from a sample, while a narrow sense requires learning concepts from training data, which is also called "concept learning" or "concept formation". It is very difficult to learn the concept with good generalization performance and clear semantic meaning. However, an understanding of concept learning helps to understand some of the basic ideas of machine learning. The most basic concept learning is Bourg concept learning, that is, learning the target concepts such as "yes" and "no", which can be expressed as 0/1 Boolean values.

Learning is known for hypothesis amidst of all discover and model analysis that goes on the background. The goal of the search is to find the fit hypothesis, that is, the correct one. Once the representation of a hypothesis is established, the size of the hypothetical space and its size are determined.

There are many strategies for searching this assumption space such as top-down, general to special, or bottom-up. During the search process, you can continuously delete the hypothesis inconsistent with the positive example and/or the hypothesis consistent with the negative example. Eventually, we will get the same assumption as the training set that all the training samples are correctly judged, and this is what we learn.

Inductive Preference

Any effective machine learning algorithm must have its inductive preference; otherwise, it will be confused by the hypothesis of "equivalent" in the training set in the hypothesis space and cannot produce definite learning results. It is conceivable that, if there were no preferences, our watermelon learning algorithm would generate a model that randomly selects the equivalent assumptions on the training set each time it makes prediction Learning models, which sometimes tell us it is good and sometimes bad do not make sense.

Inductive preferences correspond to the learning algorithm's assumptions about what model is better. In practical problems, whether this assumption is true or not, that is, whether the algorithm's inductive preference matches the problem itself most of the time, directly determines whether the algorithm can achieve good performance.

Due to its complex patterns dealing with deep learning, it is easy to "over-fit" if there are few data samples; such a complex model, such as large data sample, cannot be solved without powerful computing equipment. It is accurate because humans have entered the "big data era"; data storage and computing devices have developed, making connectionism learning technology spring again. Interestingly, neural networks became popular in the mid-1980s. It is related to the increase of computing power and data access efficiency caused by the wide application of Intel X86 microprocessor and memory strip technology.

Deep learning in this situation is very similar to the neural networks of that time. In the past two decades, the ability of human beings to collect, store, transmit, and process data has increased rapidly, and huge amounts of data have accumulated in every corner of human society. There is an urgent need for computer algorithms that can effectively analyze and utilize data. Machine learning has responded to this urgent need of the Great Age, so it is natural that the field has grown enormously and gained widespread attention.

Computer science has excelled in this decade exponentially due to a large number of researchers voluntarily dedicating their valuable time to academia. Apart from that, machine learning has also helped researchers to speed up their research process. Now, machine learning is almost in every nook and corner of the world with its infinite number of applications that are serving mankind. From facial recognition to autopilot cars to Internet marketing to bioinformatics that uses protein synthesis. A lot of fields are now actively involved in the development of artificial intelligence with all their strength. In coming years, it is believed that machine learning will expand its horizons in a way that no one ever imagined.

Bioinformatics research involves the whole process from "life phenomena" to "law discovery", which necessarily includes data acquisition, data management, data analysis, simulation experiments, and so on. Data analysis is the arena for machine learning, where machine learning technologies are already thriving. Machine learning provides data analytics capabilities. Cloud computing provides data processing capabilities. Crowdsourcing provides data tagging capabilities.

Overfitting and Underfitting

In the process of model evaluation and adjustment, we often encounter "overfitting" or "underfitting" situation. How to effectively identify the "overfitting" and "underfitting" phenomena and adjust the model is the key to improve the machine learning model. Especially in the actual project, it is the domain knowledge that the algorithm engineer should have to adopt many methods to reduce the risk of "overfitting" and "underfitting".

When trying to define these two, remember that if a model fits with the training samples well but gives a very bad percentage of accuracy, it is called overfitting. On the other hand, if the training sample did not fit well in the model and if was not accurate too in effect to the prediction, it is called underfitting.

The cost is an index to measure the conformity between the model and the training sample. Simply put, the cost is for all the training samples, the model fit out of the true value of the training samples of the average error. And the cost function is the function relation between the cost and the model parameter. The process of model training is to find the appropriate model parameters to minimize the value of the cost function. The cost function is recorded as j (), representing the model parameters.

The cost of the test data set, Jtest (), is the most intuitive indicator of the accuracy of the model. The smaller the Jtest () value means the smaller the difference between the predicted value and the actual value of the model, and the better the prediction accuracy of the new data. Special attention is needed due to the fact that the test data set used to test the accuracy of the model must be "unheard of" data for the model.

Ways to Reduce the Risk of Overfitting

1. Start with the data and get more training data.

    Using more training data is the most effective way to solve the overfitting problem because more samples can make the model learn more effective features and reduce the impact of noise. Of course, it is usually difficult to add experimental data directly, but some rules can be adapted to expand training data. For example, in the problem of image classification, the data can be expanded by means of image translation, rotation, scaling, and so on.

2. Reduce model complexity.

    The main factor of overfitting is that the model is too complex when the data is less. Reducing the model complexity properly can avoid too much sampling noise. For example, the network layer and the number of neurons are reduced in the neural network model, and the depth of the tree is reduced and the tree is pruned in the decision tree model.

3. Integrate learning method.

    Ensemble learning is the integration of multiple models to reduce the overfitting risk of a single model, such as bagging method.

Ways to Reduce Risk of Underfitting

1. Add new features.

   When the feature is not enough or the correlation between the existing feature and the sample label is not strong, the model is easy to be underfitted. By mining new features such as "context feature", "ID class feature" and "combination feature", better results can be obtained. In the deep learning trend, there are many models that can help to complete feature engineering, such as factorization machine, gradient lifting decision tree, deep-crossing, etc.

2. Increase model complexity.

   The learning ability of the simple model is poor, and the model has a stronger fitting ability by increasing the complexity of the model. For example, the linear model adds higher order terms in the neural network model to increase the number of network layer or the number of neurons.

3. Reduce the regularization coefficient.

   Regularization is used to prevent overfitting; but when the model appears underfitting, it is necessary to reduce the regularization coefficient.

Datasets and Examples

It is generally accepted that machine learning is the main way to realize artificial intelligence, which is gradually realized by human beings based on machine learning and a huge amount of data, and deep learning is a branch of machine learning. If the three ranges are represented by concentric circles, then AI is the outermost circle and deep learning is the innermost circle. Artificial intelligence is the ability of machines to make decisions that humans can make in less than a second, and those machines can make decisions that one hundred thousand people can make in a second at the same time.

There are so many concepts in machine learning, from supervised to unsupervised, from clustering to regression, from shallow to deep learning, from accuracy to recall. What do they all mean? This chapter introduces some of the most important concepts. Many machine learning beginners, even veteran drivers in the industry, have been struggling to find the right training data and test data, and processing the data has taken a lot of manpower and resources. How exactly does one convert the various physical objects around us into digital features that machines can understand? This chapter will introduce the dataset acquisition and feature extraction scheme.

The datasets introduced in this chapter include KDD 99, SEA, ADFA-LD, and so on. The emphasis is put on how to extract features from both digital and textual data and how to read common data. Finally, how to verify the results of machine learning is introduced.

Learning from training samples with concept markers (classifications) to label (classify) the data outside the training sample set as far as possible. Here, all the tags (classifications) are known. Therefore, the ambiguity of training samples is low. Learn a training sample without conceptual markers (classifications) to discover the structural knowledge in the training sample set. Here, all the tags (classifications) are unknown. Therefore, the ambiguity of training samples is high. Clustering is typical unsupervised learning.

- **Accuracy and Recall**

  Two basic indexes are said to be important in the information retrieval and other processes like recognition. These indexes are important for a better understanding of the topic.

  In the problem that goes on with the accuracy and recall, there are four scenarios that can be used. Out of which the first one is true positive, which means an instance is perfectly true. The second one is called false positive, meaning it is not true but been predicted as true by the machine. The third one is called true negative, which means it is absolutely false and the system has guessed it right. The last one is called false negative that is not false but predicted as false by the machine for various reasons that need to be monitored.

- **Datasets**

Datasets and algorithms are as essential as butter and bread, and in many cases, data is more important than algorithms. The examples in this book are primarily based on open-source datasets collected over many years and partially desensitized test data.

- **HTTP Dataset:** The HTTP dataset CSIC 2010 contains a large number of labeled 36,000 normal requests for web services and 25,000 requests for attacks of SQL injection, buffer overflow, information leakage, file containment, XSS, etc. It is widely used in the functional evaluation of WAF products.

- **Alexa Dataset:** Alexa is a website that publishes world rankings. Founded by search engine, Alexa in April 1996 (USA), it aims to enable Internet users to share virtual world resources and participate more in the organization of Internet resources. Alexa collects more than 1,000 GB of information on the web every day, not only giving links to as many as one billion websites but also ranking each one of them. It can be said that Alexa currently has the largest number of URLs, ranking the most detailed information published website. Alexa rankings are one of the most frequently cited metrics used to measure the number of visits to a website. Alexa rankings are based on users who download and install the Alexa tools bar embedded in browsers such as IE and Firefox to monitor the websites they visit, so their ranking data is not necessarily authoritative. But it provides a comprehensive ranking, visitors ranking, page traffic ranking, and other evaluation index information; it is difficult to have more scientific and reasonable evaluation reference. Alexa offers download of the TOP one million web domains in the world in CSV format.

- **Movie Review Dataset:** The movie review dataset contains different movie-related data that can be used for various analysis and testing purposes. This is widely used all around the world due to its simple implementation and easy instructions.

Text Data Extraction

In machine learning, feature extraction is considered as a kind of manual work. Some people call it "feature engineering", which shows how much work it takes. In feature extraction, digital and text feature extraction is the most common. Digital features can be used as features directly, but for a multi-dimensional feature, the range of values of one feature is very large, which may lead to the influence of other features on the results being ignored. At this time, we need to pre-process the digital features.

Text data extraction features are much more complex than digital features. They are essentially word segmentation. Different words are used as a new feature.

Word set model: A set of words in which each element has only one word, that is, each word in the word set has only one word.

Word bag model: If a word appears more than once in a document, count the number of times it appears (frequency).

The essential difference between the two is that the word bag increases the frequency dimension based on the word set: the word set only concerns with and without, and the word bag also concerns with several. When processing data, CSV is the most common format, with each line of the file recording a vector, with the last column marked. TensorFlow provides a very convenient way to read data sets from CSV files.

Chapter 3: Machine Learning Algorithms

This chapter describes the famous algorithm models used in machine learning. Use this as a resource to improve your knowledge of the basics of machine learning. A few real-life examples are given for your better understanding of the topic

K-Nearest Neighbors Algorithm

When you Google a question or product, you will find recommended products on the left side. For letting people know similar items, search engines or websites like YouTube use k-nearest neighbors algorithm. It is also one of the most famous classification algorithms in machine learning. Although its principle is very simple, it is widely used in many fields.

Suppose we have a labeled dataset in which we already know the category to which each sample in the dataset belongs. At this point, there is an unlabeled data sample, and our task is to predict which category the data sample belongs to. The principle of the k-nearest neighbors algorithm is to calculate the distance between the data sample to be marked and each sample in the data set and to take the nearest k samples. The nearest k samples vote for the category to which the labeled data sample belongs.

Assuming X is the data sample to be labeled and x is the labeled data set, the algorithm works as follows:

Sort the distance array, take the nearest k points, and mark them as X. Count the number of each category in x, that is, class0 has several samples in x, class1 has several samples in x, and so on.

K-nearest neighbor algorithm is famous and all of together a lazy learning algorithm. It had adapted abundant examples in real life due to its nonlinear nature.

Sometimes, streaming websites like Netflix and Hotstar may recommend you movies that people in your demographics watched before. There is no certainty that you may like it, but you may certainly see it in your newsfeed due to being the nearest sample in the dataset. There are quite disadvantages due to its non-parametric and non-feasible nature.

Several bank websites and credit card companies use k-nearest neighbor algorithm to predict or decide whether a viable customer seeking for a loan is a correct fit for their financial organization or not.

Advantages: High accuracy, high tolerance to outliers and noise.

Disadvantages: A large amount of computing. Memory requirements are also larger. From the principle of the algorithm, we can see that every time we classify an unlabeled sample, we need to calculate the distance all over again.

Decision Tree

Decision tree and random forest are common classification algorithms, especially the decision tree. The logic of judgment is very close to human thinking in many cases. You can draw a decision tree as your decision logic.

Decision tree is one of the most classical machine learning models. Its forecast result is easy to understand, easy to explain to the business department, forecast speed, and can handle type data and continuous data. The decision tree is one of the interviewer's favorite interview questions in machine learning data mining job interviews.

As the most basic and common supervised learning model, the decision tree is often used to classify problems and regression problems, especially in the fields of marketing and biomedicine mainly because the tree structure and sales, diagnosis, and other scenarios under the decision-making process are very similar. Applying the idea of ensemble learning to the decision tree, we can get the models of stochastic forest and gradient lifting decision tree.

We know that the goal of the decision tree is to establish a tree-like classification structure from a set of sample data according to different characteristics and attributes. We hope that it can fit training data and achieve good classification results, and at the same time, we also hope to control its complexity, so that the model has some generalization ability. For a particular problem, there may be many choices for the decision tree. For example, in a scenario description, if a girl takes the ability to write code into account at the root node, a simple tree structure might be required to complete the classification.

Decision tree is a very strange machine learning algorithm when compared with others due to its huge applications in spite of being slow and less predictiveness. This is due to its ability to filter a lot of nonlinear data effectively in a short time. For example, Hubble telescope, a famous instrument and a lifesaver from astronomical scientists that delivers thousands of images every day, uses decision tree to clear the noise in its pictures. Decision tree can be used to predict medical diagnosis after a divide and conquer method of differential diagnosis from a lot of cumulative data it has access to. Applications like VisualDx, a famous differential diagnosis tool for physicians use decision tree to automatically decide a diagnosis with the given patient data. Decision trees are easy to read and create a hypothesis, unlike other machine learning algorithms that are often confusing when represented. With a lot of historical data for example of sales or credit score, decision trees can be used to decide the next strategy to approach people with their next product. Decision trees can be used as a great marketing tool if a lot of data is available that can be used to interpret customer traits and expectations from the product.

Random Forest

Random forest algorithm is quite similar to the decision tree strategy but deals with a lot more questions, decisions, and predictive analysis. An example can help you understand this complex algorithm easily. Let us assume that you are trying to go on a vacation with your newly married wife. You are confused about where to go due to your overwhelming behavior. So you ask your married friend for suggestions on where to visit for a vacation. Your friend asks you a lot of questions like your wife habits, tastes, as well as yours to let him decide a good place for your vacation that you both may like. He gives you a place that he believes that would be great for you and your wife for your first vacation. But you are not convinced that he may be right, so you ask your other friends and they ask different questions and recommend you a place. Now, with a lot of options, you decide to visit a place with a high number of votes. This is in detail how a random forest algorithm in machine learning works. Random forest algorithm is extensively used in banking applications like PayPal to decide fraudulent customers that are likely spamming the system. It can also be used in medical applications to likely decide an over abusive drug.

Naive Bayes Algorithm

The Naive Bayes algorithm is probably the most famous algorithm in machine learning, and anyone who knows anything about IT will know that early spam algorithms used Naive Bayes. More than 200 years ago, scientists put it forward and gave a mathematical proof, and Naive Bayes English abbreviation is very eye-catching: NB algorithm, is not a special NB feeling. This section will introduce the basic concept of Naive Bayes algorithm and will give the basic use, including how to use Naive Bayes algorithm to detect abnormal operations in a web environment.

Spam can be said to be the most controversial by-product of the Internet to human beings; its flooding has made the entire Internet overburdened, and it has seriously affected people's daily work and life. Usually, enterprises and large mail service providers will provide the ability to intercept spam. One of the most common algorithms is based on Naive Bayes text classification algorithm. The general idea is to train a text classification model with Naive Bayes by learning a lot of spam and normal email samples.

Bayes classification is the general term for a series of classification algorithms, all of which are based on Bayes' theorem and are therefore collectively called Bayes classification. The NB algorithm is a classification method based on the independent hypothesis of Bayes theorem and characteristic conditions. The algorithm invented more than 250 years ago by British mathematician Bayes holds an unrivaled position in the field of information. NB is based on a simple assumption: attributes are conditionally independent of each other for a given target value.

At the same time, the estimated parameters of NB are very few, and the algorithm is simple. An example that relates to real life can give you a thorough explanation of the Naive Bayes algorithm.

Normally, entertainment websites like Hulu collect data from customers as feedback to help improve their services. All positive data collected from customers can be studied, trained to deliver an all-new recommender system that will help to increase the trust with the user. Naive Bayes algorithm can also be used for an automatic document classification using the data that is present. OCR detection and machine translation highly depend on this algorithm for accuracy and high-level prediction.

Logistic Regression Algorithms

Logistic regression is arguably the most basic and most commonly used model in the field of machine learning, and the derivation and extension of the principles of logistic regression are almost essential skills for an algorithmic engineer. Medical pathology diagnosis, bank personal credit assessment, and mailbox classification spam reflect the sophisticated and extensive application of logistic regression.

When we open a browser to visit a web page, we often see familiar ads in the corner of the page which seem to be related to recent topics and browsing content. It is an application of logistic regression, where ad services automatically predict which ads you will click on based on your history, content, topics, and so on.

Logistic regression, also known as regression analysis, is one of the classifications and prediction algorithms. Logistic regression predicts the probability of future results by the representation of historical data. The dependent variable is the result that we hope to obtain. The independent variable is the latent factor that affects the result; it may have one or many. Regression analysis with only one independent variable is called unitary regression analysis. Suppose we have a football game, we have all the players of the two teams, the historical results, the time of the game, the home and away games, the referee, and the weather information, based on which the team wins or loses. Suppose the game result is y, the winning mark is 1, and the loss mark is 0. This is a typical binary classification problem which can be solved by a logistic regression algorithm.

When talking about logistic regression there is a necessity to talk about linear regression as there is a huge chance of getting confused between both the terms. Linear regression is often said to be straight on point with a target of the constant variable. That is in simple terms all applications of linear regression try to find out a single variable data with high precision. For example, estimating the number of kidnaps that could happen in a region in a year or number of votes a party candidature can get in the next elections. Whereas logistic regression differs from it by a margin by trying to detect a result using categorical questions that may lead to two or other levels. For example, logistic regression is used in healthcare to analysis a sudden epidemic like Ebola.

Support Vector Machine

Support vector machine is believed to be one of the easiest machine learning algorithms that can be implemented and is used in many areas of life, basically all classification problems, especially binary classification problems. You can try it out first, and many machine learning textbooks introduce support vector machine as the first algorithm, showing how important it is.

About SVM, there is a story about the angel and the devil. Legend has it that the devil and the angel played a game in which the devil placed two colored balls on the table. The devil told the angels to use a stick to separate them. That seems too easy for an angel. The angel did it without thinking. The devil has added more balls. As the number of balls increases, it seems that some balls can no longer be properly separated by the original stick.

The SVM is actually trying to find the best place for the angels to put the sticks so that the balls on both sides are far enough away from the sticks separating them. According to the position of the stick chosen by SVM for the angel, the stick can separate the two kinds of balls very well even if the devil continues to add new balls in the way just now.

Seeing that the angels have solved the problem of dividing the ball linearly with a stick, the devil presents the angel with a new challenge. The way the balls are arranged, there doesn't seem to be a single stick in the world that can pull them apart perfectly; but the angel had power. As soon as he hit the table, he sent the balls into the air, and with psychokinesis, he grabbed a piece of paper and stuck it between the balls. From the devil's point of view, the balls appear to be cut perfectly by a curve.

Later, "bored" scientists called the balls "data", called the stick a "classification surface", called the process of finding the position of the largest spaced-out stick an "optimization", and the power of hitting a table to send the ball into the air was called "nuclear mapping". The paper separating the spheres in the air is called a "classified hyperplane". This is the fairy tale of SVM. In the field of real-world machine learning, SVM covers all aspects of knowledge and is a common basic model in interview questions.

Support vector machine is used mainly for face detection and handwriting recognition in real life. It distinguishes a face and gives a positive variable if it is a face, and negative if it is not. Famous supercomputers like Watson use SVM to detect plants and animal species that exist around the world. Google Goggles' much anticipated Google creation decades back has used support vector machine to detect objects surrounding the phone camera. Google Lens is also said to be using support vector machine to detect a different type of text writings for handwriting recognition, an excellent resource for researchers performing excavations around ancient historical sites.

K-Means

K-means and DBSCAN are the first unsupervised algorithms we have introduced; they require less work in data processing than supervised learning, which requires human tagging.

Once upon a time, there was a group of monkeys who lived a simple, happy life. One day, two of the monkeys are at daggers drawn because of a trivial quarrel, so they were divided into different groups and finally out of control. In the first group, the leader ruled smoothly. In the second group, another monkey rose up suddenly and defeated the original monkey king to become the new king. Eventually, the group's actions and management were stabilized and divided into two groups, completing the clustering. This is a small story to explain the k-means algorithm.

In the above example, a large group is divided into smaller and smaller groups whatever the reason may be. This significant process is called clustering, and by using this method to divide, the data into significant smaller details can help you understand a lot about user dynamics and importance. For example, the k-means algorithm can be used in fantasy league teams to get a thorough understanding of the players that you have assigned. Sometimes, telecommunication companies can analyze the call record data available to get a thorough understanding of the caller dynamics for improvement of their service. K-means algorithm can help researchers to pinpoint an area in data for research instead of dealing with a lot of unusable data.

DBSCAN Algorithm Overview

Let us explain DBSCAN using the previous example. Again, this time there is no limit to the number of small groups and to the number of the original monkey king, only the minimum number of members of the group. As long as the monkeys are capable, they can gather enough followers that can make themselves a king. So, after several rounds of fighting, the formation of several groups of small monkeys, each group has its monkey king. This is DBSCAN doing clustering.

DBSCAN stands for Density-based Clustering of Applications with Noise. In contrast to the k-means method, DBSCAN can find clusters of any shape and identify noise points without knowing the number of clusters to be formed. Usually, clustering algorithms are used in astronomy, medicine, pharmacy, and e-commerce applications. Especially e-commerce websites like Amazon and eBay use DBSCAN algorithm to help their customers to choose the products. Didn't get it? Here is a simple example. Suppose you are trying to buy an Amazon Kindle, an e-reader device from Amazon, and when you are trying to buy it, Amazon system will recommend you an all-new Amazon Kindle case and a touchscreen pen along with it. This is where DB clustering comes into real-life application. Amazon analyzes its abundant data and finds patterns based on DB clustering to determine what other users have brought along with Amazon Kindle. When you think about it in layman terms, you may understand a lot about clustering algorithms.

Apriori Algorithm

Association rule mining is usually unsupervised learning. By analyzing data sets, potential association rules can be mined. The most typical example is the story of diapers and beer. According to legend, Wal-Mart's data analysts have found that a significant proportion of consumers buy diapers and beer at the same time, and they sell them side by side, increasing both sales. The result of the association rule analysis is an objective phenomenon:

some obvious, such as buying salmon and mustard at the same time; some plausible, such as diapers and beer; and some bizarre, such as lighters and cheese. The most famous association algorithm is the Apriori algorithm. This can be used to find associations between similar items to get a better understanding of customer dynamics. Apriori algorithm is also used extensively in medical diagnosis application to get a detailed symptom of a certain disease after an analysis of thousands of patients' records for better and efficient parent care.

Firstly, three basic concepts are introduced: support, confidence, and frequent k-item sets. We will explain these three important concepts with an imaginable example for a better understanding. Apriori algorithm has substantial use in online grocery stores, so we will go with an example of a grocery store.

Support: This determines which product or item is famous among the customers. For example, when people buy groceries in bulk as they usually do, salt has been brought by more than five customers in a group of ten. This explains that salt has good support among the other. Just see this as a layman example rather than a theoretical concept.

Confidence: This determines with salt which item is brought frequently. For example, four of six people who had brought salt brought chilies. Confidence can help us decide to deliver a recommender system in a grocery store or another e-commerce application.

Frequent: This will give a clear example and determines if a product can be recommended or not. If the frequency is less than 1, it is not recommended.

Apriori algorithm is to mine association rules that satisfy both the minimum support threshold and minimum confidence threshold. Finally, strong rules are found in all frequent sets, that is, association rules of interest to users are generated.

There is very little support for Apriori in mainstream ML libraries, but Apriori is easy to implement; there are a lot of resources online, suggested by Peter Harrington in his book the practice of machine learning. Shopify uses Apriori algorithm to determine recommended stores for their customers. It can also be used to detect adverse drug reactions by using complex algorithms.

FP-Growth Algorithm

FP-Growth after a lot of researches had been proved to give better performance than Apriori algorithm. Both perform the same associative mapping to find the frequent sets. FP-Growth is known to be used by airplane booking websites to find similar flights with different destinations. It also uses the same frequent, confidence, and support parameters to get a thorough understanding of the frequent item sets.

Markov Algorithm

In the field of network security, time series data also exist widely, such as the order of website visits, the order of system calls, the operator's operation command, etc. In the real world, there are problems with obvious timing, such as traffic lights at intersections, days of changing the weather, and the context in which we speak. Markovian, the Russian mathematician, proposed the famous Markov chain. Hidden Markov Model (HMM) is based on the assumption that the state of a continuous time series is determined by the events in front of it, and the corresponding time series can be called the n-order Markov chain.

Assuming that today's haze is determined only by the previous day and yesterday, a second-order Markov chain is formed. If it was sunny yesterday and the day before yesterday, the probability that it will be sunny today is 90%.

To complicate things a bit, suppose you want to know about the smog in a city 2,000 kilometers away but you can't go directly to the local area to see the air. You only have the local wind, which means the air is hidden. Wind conditions are observable, and hidden sequences are inferred from observable sequences.

Because the wind has a significant effect on haze conditions, even assuming that 90% of the time is sunny when the wind is strong, it is possible to infer hidden sequences from previous observation sequences by learning from samples. This is the implicit Markov model.

The greatest example to determine Markov model in real life is Google page rank. Every web page has links, and if there are links from a high domain rank page, there is a huge chance for you to get into Google page rank. That is unlikely if there is a link from high domain authority your chance to be in Google page rank one increases. Almost famous web applications like Facebook, Twitter, and YouTube use Markov chain and its model to determine most trending content.

Graph Algorithm

Graph algorithm is a very simple and effective machine learning algorithm; the idea of the algorithm is very easy to understand. It is widely used in the fields where there are a lot of unstructured network data, such as social network, finance, traffic, search, etc. The network security field in the wind control and threat intelligence also has a lot of unstructured network data, so we will use the graph algorithm.

In the real world, some relationships are hard to express in a database table structure, such as fan relationships on Weibo, love handles on idol shows, registration relationships between multiple domains, and so on. This old data structure comes in handy. In a directed graph, the edges associated with a node have an outgoing edge and an incoming edge, and the two points associated with a directed edge have a beginning and an end. In contrast, a graph with no direction to its edges is called an undirected graph while the lateral is a directed graph.

Cab apps like Uber use graph algorithms to determine the shortest path the driver can take to go to your destination. Facebook implemented a graph search to determine your mutual friends easily. There are an abundant number of examples when it comes to graph algorithms.

Knowledge Mapping

When you search Google for famous football players, you will see a direct introduction to the Wikipedia entry of Ronaldo. This is because Baidu searches through the knowledge map between the establishment of entities and relations, lets the search engine more understand the user's intentions, and directly answers the user's doubts.

When you pick up your phone and search for a coffee cafe, it will automatically show you the location of the coffee store near you. This is because of Google search with the help of knowledge atlas combined with user behavior information to provide users with more in line with the current situation of the search results. When you search for "Harry Potter" on Google, in addition to displaying information about Harry Potter, Ron, and Hermione, it also automatically display other characters and works that Rowling has done in her lifetime. This is because Google search used the knowledge map to establish the relationship between things, expand user search results, and find more content.

A search for "Amazon" (Amazon River), for example, usually returns the most relevant information about Amazon. Amazon, for example, has the most information about it online, but Amazon isn't just a website, it's the most trafficked Amazon River in the world.

If history is any guide, it may still be the name of the Greek Warrior Women. These results will be presented in the "knowledge map" of Google search in the future. Google's "Knowledge Atlas" will not only get professional information from Freebase, Wikipedia, or global overview but also increase the depth and breadth of search results through large-scale information search analysis. There are now more than 500 million things in Google's database and more than 3.5 billion relationships between different things. It integrates various kinds of data on the Internet and further excavates the potential connection and value of data.

The application of knowledge mapping in the field of security can explore the potential connections between data, and the combination of these potential connections can greatly expand our thinking on data analysis.

In recent years, threat intelligence is very popular in the field of information security. Threat intelligence is based on massive data analysis. It excavates the potential correlation and provides formidable data intelligence support for other security product. At present, it has emerged the massive start-up enterprise to invest in the threat intelligence domain.

This is the age of connectivity where attack portals are ubiquitous and defenses based solely on vulnerabilities or critical assets are out of reach. Therefore, if enterprises want to carry out their business safely, they must take a more comprehensive and efficient defensive approach. The emergence of threat intelligence has made up for this deficiency and has brought an effective complement to the traditional defense methods. Threat intelligence, based on the attacker's perspective, relies on its broad visibility and comprehensive understanding of the risks and threats across the Internet to help us better understand the threat, including possible targets, tools, and methods used, as well as their knowledge of the Internet infrastructure through which weapons are transmitted, enabling them to act accurately and efficiently in the event of a threat. The 2016 RSA conference featured 10 threat intelligence companies, including established security firms Symantec and Dell Security.

Neural Network Algorithms

In general, SVM, KNN, and other previously introduced algorithms are understood as shallow learning, and the recognition ability of the model depends more on the effectiveness of feature selection. Shallow learning and use need to spend at least half of the time on data cleaning and feature extraction. Some people vividly called these steps "feature engineering", which is a description of its huge workload.

The human brain is a complex network of millions of neurons. A neuron is a cell with a long process, consisting of a cell body, an axon, and a dendrite. Each neuron can have one or more dendrites that can receive stimuli and transmit excitation to the cell body. Each neuron has only one axon, which carries excitement from the cell body to another neuron or other tissue, such as a muscle or gland.

Neural network algorithm is to simulate the working principle of human neurons, multiple input parameters with their respective weights after the excitation function processing, which is the output. The output can then be connected to the input of the next stage of the neural network, thus forming a more complex neural network.

Biological nerve cells in the brain are interconnected with other nerve cells. To create an artificial neural network, artificial nerve cells have to connect in the same way. There are many different kinds of connections, and one of the most understandable and widely used is to connect nerve cells layer by layer. This type of neural network is called a feedforward network.

If you punish the wrong neurons, you can fix the problem by looking up at the wrong neurons from the output layer and fine-tuning the weights of those neurons. An algorithm like this is called backpropagation.

Recurrent Neural Network Algorithm

It has even been implemented to let recurrent neural networks learn and then automatically generate code and write poems and drawings.

As the ancients learned from the past, we tend to analyze things in conjunction with our previous experiences and try to remember how we solved similar situations in the past, even in situations we have never seen before. This is actually in line with the idea of recurrent neural networks.

Recurrent neural networks are used extensively in machine translation. For example, Google Translate, a famous machine translator, translates a poem from French to English. It uses a recurrent neural network algorithm to check its syntactical structure after translating every word from a lot of data it has to access it. It analyzes the syntactical structure and grammatical rules to get a clear translation, although difficult to implement for high power it uses.

It is also used in speech recognition and photo recognition apps where it determines colors and items to the user. Pandora uses recurrent neural network algorithm to determine the song after listening from its huge database of songs where it searches for the syntactical analysis of a song.

Convolutional Neural Network

The convolutional neural network algorithm is widely used in image processing. It has the unique ability of convolution processing and pooling. It can automatically extract advanced features from image data without complicated preprocessing and then analyze them further at the same time. The computational complexity is reduced exponentially. How does convolutional neural network fare in the security arena?

Image recognition technologies such as face recognition are changing people's lives. Looking back on previous MNIST datasets, the success rate of image recognition numbers hovered around 95%. So what kind of technology has enabled image recognition to take off? The answer is a convolutional neural network.

In a fully connected neural network algorithm such as DNN, each node in the previous layer of the hidden layer needs to be connected to each node in the next layer. It is almost impossible to complete the training process in a limited hardware environment.

To solve the problem of a huge amount of computation caused by full connection in the field of image processing, the local connection is proposed. Its theoretical basis is based on the assumption that the biological image recognition (the understanding of the image only needs to deal with local data) does not need a comprehensive analysis of all images that can be processed. This hypothesis has been widely used in the field of image processing, which proves that it is simple and effective.

This is the first time in this chapter that we are discussing a deep learning algorithm. Deep learning is a significant branch under machine learning that is developing with tremendous growth due to its scope that can be used for many applications mostly in robotics and image recognition.

Image recognition has been the latest fad among the tech arena. Apple has unveiled its face lock, where the iPhone determines your face using certain algorithms. Although Apple doesn't say about how it has done it, enthusiastic researchers had reasoned that convolutional neural network algorithms are the ones that did this magic. Deep learning and facial recognition in the coming years augmented reality and virtual reality generations. Although being difficult to program and implement, convolutional algorithms are going through deep research.

Linear Models

Linear models are known to be used in many real-life applications due to its easy implementation and a rather fast interpretation by the machines due to its simplistic nature. Amazon gift card uses linear models for its implementation. Linear models can be further improvised for higher order applications like protein synthesis.

- Linear Regression: Given a data set, it attempts to learn a linear model to predict real-value output markers as accurately as possible.

Multi-Category Learning

In reality, we often encounter multi-classification learning tasks. Some binary classification learning methods can be directly extended to multi-classification, but in more cases, we solve multi-classification problems by using binary classification learners based on some basic strategies.

The basic idea of multi-classification learning is without loss of generality, which divides multi-classification tasks into several binary-classification tasks. Specifically, a classifier is trained for each binary classification task, and the prediction results of these classifiers are integrated to obtain the final multi-classification results. The key here is how to split multi-classification tasks and how to integrate multiple classifiers.

Practical Applications of Machine Learning and Deep Learning Algorithms

Captcha Detection

Captcha is a public, fully automated program that can tell a computer from a person. The original design is to prevent malicious password cracking, swiping, and forum irrigation. In fact, with a captcha, it is now a common way for many sites. The basic assumption of captcha is that because the computer can't answer the question, the user who answers the question is considered human. Attack and defense are complementary for the emergence of a large number of captcha cracking technology; the reader can refer to the captcha security and other things.

An MNIST dataset can be used as an example to introduce the recognition of digital captcha and the feature extraction methods used in the captcha, including one-dimensional vector, two-dimensional vector, the model used, and the corresponding verification results. This includes k-nearest neighbor, support vector machine, and deep learning.

Spam Detection

As one of the most controversial by-products of the Internet, the first impact of spam on corporate email users is to place an additional burden on the day-to-day office and email managers. According to incomplete statistics, in an efficient anti-spam environment, there are still 80% of users need to spend about 10 minutes per week to deal with spam, and for most of China's enterprise email application is still in an inefficient anti-spam environment, the proportion is showing dozens of growth— China's total spam has reached the world's third largest. For the enterprise mail service providers, the malicious delivery of spam, but also a large number of network resources making the mail server 85% of the system resources used to deal with the identification of spam. Not only resource waste is extremely serious, it may even lead to network congestion paralysis, affecting the normal business mail communication.

The more serious spam problem affects the efficiency of the enterprise or even the whole server. Because the enterprise mail platform often has better communication quality and is more easily accepted by the white list of the international anti-spam platform, it becomes the target of spammers and even network hackers. By hijacking these corporate mailboxes, spammers can greatly increase the rate of spam delivery. This will not only encounter enterprise e-mail users' unpredictable impact but also may encounter anti-spam organizations and recipients of "hero broken wrist". International anti-spam organizations and recipient services add spam addresses to the international spam database so that the host cannot communicate with other countries where the expansion of the overseas business of the enterprise is seriously affected.

Because spam is so harmful, many domestic small and medium enterprises from the past independent construction services have low-cost small service providers who set up a mail system to 163 and QQ Enterprise Mailbox as the only major professional mail service provider. It is more beneficial to cooperate with many anti-spam organizations and mail service providers at home and abroad to set up a comprehensive anti-spam platform to block the spread of spam by sharing real-time rejection lists. Large enterprises often choose to build their email systems. To protect themselves from spam, they often use commercial email security solutions. Common foreign vendors include CISCO, Blue Coat, Websense, Zscaler, and McAfee.

We use Enron dataset to detect emails of huge data for spam detection. Datasets can be used to create a training model that can categorize spam qualities and malicious email content. As we already know, training is directly proportional to better performance in machine learning. Usually, spam can be identified using a lot of deep learning and machine learning algorithms. But after certain experiments, it is proved that the Bayes algorithm is the best fit for spam detection, and Gmail uses its better performance. The convolutional neural network can be used too but takes a bigger implementation and larger dataset.

It is worth mentioning that in the Naive Bayes experiment, we found that not only the number of words in the word bag extraction and spam recognition probability but there is also a middle point to achieve the best effect. And the TF-IDF combined word bag model will improve the detection capability. We will use the combination of both later chapters.

The methods mentioned above have a large number of parameters that can be adjusted, such as the number of neural network layers, the length of the sample text, etc. Besides, for the English environment, there is room for improvement in feature extraction, such as the different tenses of verbs, the normalization of singular and plural nouns, and the processing of common pause words.

Negative Review Identification

Speaking of negative reviews, let us talk about the water army first. Just as the name implies, the water army refers to a large number of people in the forum; they are employed by the network public relations company to post a reply as the main means. It is for the employer to promote the network staff. There are full-time and part-time. Generally speaking, it often takes a hundred thousand people to create a thread-writing campaign, and those who temporarily solicit posts from the Internet are known in the industry as the "online water army".

In December 2009, CCTV reported that the network water army is an emerging phenomenon. By community-wide attention, many long-term online netizens have joined the network water army group. The prevalence of the water army has seriously affected public opinion, especially the defamation and attack against public figures and enterprises in an organized way, causing serious social impact. Large social media and well-known forums hired a large number of operational support staff to manually identify processing. Can machine learning be used to automate the process of identifying negative comments to some degree? We have tried to do this with the accumulation of spam detection techniques.

IMDB dataset can be taken as an example to introduce the technology of negative reviews identification. The datasets used to identify negative comments and the feature extraction methods used are introduced, including word bag and TF-IDF model, vocabulary model, and Word2Vec and Doc2Vec models. It introduces the models used and the corresponding validation results, including naive Bayes, support vector machine, and deep learning.

Harassing Phone Calls Detection

Nowadays, harassing phone calls and text messages have become more and more intense. The survey found that at present, citizens personal information is involved in many aspects, such as applying for a license, applying for a card, shopping online, seeing a doctor, and so on. Many businesses come in a variety of names to obtain personal information of citizens, and many citizens on personal information protection awareness have weak, random access. Same goes with SMS. Surely most people's text messages are filled with junk messages like selling houses, selling cars, offering discounts, even issuing invoices, and taking out loans. Some of them are from mobile phones, while the vast majority are "106" business numbers. Over 90% of these texts are "received".

In addition to advertising, many spam messages are also in the name of winning the fraud, so that some wait for the "pie in the sky". Lottery SMS fraud is often cross-provincial or even cross-border; it is very difficult to detect. For example, many students rent a house, and some scam messages ask for the rent to be paid on a card in the name of the landlord. Some students received this type of text message without verification on the ransom money. In addition to students, some middle-aged and elderly people are also vulnerable groups. For example, swindlers will say "Your Bankcard is used to launder money, please transfer money to a safe account." Some elderly people who lack social experience falls into the trap of swindlers. Such fraudulent SMS or phone calls have often no designated target of the "mass"; the fraudster do it through a wide-spread way to "catch" the dupe.

SMS Spam Collection dataset is an example to introduce the technology of identifying harassing SMS messages. This introduces the feature extraction methods for identifying the use of harassing short messages, including word bag and TF-IDF model, vocabulary model, and Word2Vec and Doc2Vec model, and introduces the models used and the corresponding verification results. These include Naive Bayes, support-vector machine, XGBoost, and MLP algorithms.

We use ADFA-LD dataset as an example to introduce Linux backdoor detection. Feature extraction methods are 2-Gram and TF-IDF. Classification algorithms include Naive Bayes, XGBoost, and multilayer perceptron.

Linux Backdoor Detection

Linux is an operating system that is open-sourced and is used mainly by network and security professionals for a better maintenance of network and a lot of web-based applications. Linux systems are often vulnerable due to their implementation and can be a headache for enterprise system network professionals to notice every small attack. Although intrusion detection systems are said to work well, they are often straightforward and cannot detect complex attacks that malicious hackers use. So, machine learning can be a better alternative for attack study and intrusion detection. There are several data sources that can be used to train systems for a better understanding of the Linux backdoor detection.

Although several security products, including data leak prevention (DLP), have been added to enterprise network security strategies, ensuring the security of confidential data and assets remains a challenge for enterprises and organizations. According to a 2015 survey by the Inside Job, most of the most costly cybercrime cases are caused by people inside companies. Then, there are denial-of-service attacks and web-based attacks.

The inside job of people inside a company is an abnormal behavior of employees, and it is dangerous. At about 23:00 on January 31, 2017, a system administrator tried to delete an empty directory in a state of extreme fatigue. The instructions were sent to the command window of another server, and when he came to his senses, 27 minutes passed. It was too late to terminate the deletion operation, and only about 4.5 GB of data remained, about 300 GB or so. The gitlab.com lost 6 hours of database data. On April 5, 2017, a well-known VPS provider, DigitalOcean, experienced an incident in which it deleted its production database.

The deletion caused the DigitalOcean control panel and API to fail for up to 4 hours and 56 minutes. They began to receive alerts that public services were not functioning. In the first 3 minutes of the alert, they discovered that the primary database had been deleted. After 4 minutes, they started to recover from a delayed copy of the database. For the next 4 hours, they copied and restored the data to the master backup copy. The main reason for the long outage was the time-consuming process of restoring data from the replica to an online server. The root cause of the accident was a configuration error by the engineer. There is a program for automated testing that uses certificates from the production environment by mistake. So an apology was written by the chief of DigitalOcean.

The abnormal operations performed by malicious internal personnel and internal staff are collectively referred to as malicious operations. Detecting such malicious activity requires advanced technologies, such as User Behavior Analysis (Uba), an emerging technology that provides data protection and fraud detection capabilities that were previously missed. Combined with the user's daily operation of the system, UBA uses a special security analysis algorithm that can not only focus on the initial login operation but also track the user's every move. The UBA has two main functions: it helps to establish a baseline for normal activities performed by users, and it quickly identifies abnormal behavior that deviates from normal behavior so that security analysts can carry out investigations. Some of the unusual behavior may not appear malicious at first glance, but it requires further investigation by security analysts to determine whether it is legitimate or malicious.

Web Shell Detection

Web shell is a command execution environment in the form of ASP, PHP, JSP, or CGI, which can also be called a web back door. Web shell is often used by intruders to gain some degree of operation permission to the web server through the web service port.

Web shell detection is a booming area for vulnerability testing platforms. There are a lot of scanners that automatically detect web shells by using different machine learning and deep learning strategies. If you are good at programming, it is possible that you can create your own vulnerability testing scanner for a better understanding of lot of topics related to web security.

There are several common web shell detection methods:

- Static detection: done by matching the characteristic code, the characteristic value, and the dangerous operation function to find the method of web shell.

- Dynamic detection: detection of the performance of the characteristics of time, such as database operations, sensitive file reading, and so on.

- Grammar detection: according to the way of PHP language scan compilation, it carries on the stripping code and the annotation through the analysis variable, the function, the string, the language structure way. It realizes the key danger function capture. This will solve the problem of underreporting perfectly. But there are still problems with false positives.

Chapter 4: Machine Learning Software

Getting Started with Machine Learning

The application of machine learning is based on computation, which is the main part of scientific computation. These problems used to be very difficult to solve with ordinary computing tools, but now they are very easy to solve with computers. At present, there are two main types of mathematical computations which are more frequently performed by computers.

The first one is the numerical calculation, which takes a numerical array as the operation object and gives the numerical solution. Error accumulation may occur in the course of calculation, which affects the accuracy of calculation results.

The second type is a symbolic evaluation, which takes symbolic objects and symbolic expressions as pairs. The operation is not affected by the problem of accumulation of calculation error.

The numerical calculation method has become an important means of scientific calculation. It studies how to use computational tools to solve numerical solutions of mathematical problems. The objects of numerical calculation are calculus, linear algebra, interpolation and approximation, least square fitting, and numerical integrals.

Mathematical problems, such as eigenvalues and eigenvectors of matrices, roots of a system of linear equations and nonlinear equations, and numerical solutions of a differential equation, are the mathematics to be applied in machine learning areas such as pattern recognition, data analysis, and automated manufacturing.

Symbolic computation is the mathematics that should be applied in the machine learning field such as an expert system. In symbolic computation, the data processed by a computer and the results obtained by computer are both symbols. Symbols used as a letter and formula can also be a numerical value. Its operation is carried out in the way of reasoning and analysis; it is not bothered by the problem of accumulation of calculation error. The result of the calculation is a completely correct closed solution or arbitrary precision numerical solution, which means that the result of the symbolic computation can avoid problems caused by rounding errors. More branches of mathematics are moving into machine learning, where complex mathematical computations require powerful scientific platforms. The scientific computing platform provides low-level support for the application of machine learning algorithms.

Overview of Scientific Computing Software Platforms

There are three main methods of modern scientific research: theoretical argumentation, scientific experiment, and scientific calculation. In recent years, scientific computing has gradually become the mainstream method of scientific research and has been widely used in financial engineering, information retrieval, gene research, environmental simulation, numerical calculation, data analysis, decision support, and other fields. Because of the development of computer technology and the popularization and deepening of its application in various fields of technology and science, these fields of application, regardless of their background and meaning, all need to use computers for scientific calculation and must establish corresponding mathematical models. The calculation method suitable for computer programming is also studied. The scientific computing platform has become a necessary foundation platform for scientific research, which has promoted the development of scientific research and the progress of engineering technology.

Machine learning applications need scientific computing. Most scientific computing applications in the field require machine learning algorithms, and the relationship between scientific computing platforms and machine learning is like the relationship between fish and water. The research and application of modern machine learning have been inseparable from the scientific computing platform; the scientific computing platform has entered a new era of contention because of the rapid development of machine learning.

Popular Scientific Computing Software

There are several types of popular scientific computing software:

MATLAB

If you are in the computer science industry, you might have already known how famous MATLAB is for the machine learning industry. Almost all complex programming problems that involve numerical calculations can be solved by MATLAB, which is a licensed program with great performance. MATLAB uses various algorithms for better performance when compared to other open-source licensed software like GNU Octave. Also, MATLAB has separate packages for a better implementation of machine learning algorithms, although good practice should be present for better utilization of MATLAB. So, before trying to experiment with MATLAB, get a good overview of all options available. This will be your forever loving tool if you know how to use it properly.

GNU Octave

Similar to MATLAB, GNU Octave is a free redistribute software developed by the Free Software Foundation, with the help of John W. Eaton, led by a group of volunteers who developed a high-level language called GNU Octave, which is compatible with

MATLAB and is primarily used for numerical calculations. It also provides a convenient command line way to numerically solve lines and nonlinear problems, and do some numerical simulations.

Mathematica

Mathematica is a powerful system developed by Wolfram Research. It is a computer math system. It provides a wide range of mathematical computing functions that are supported in various fields. People working in fields do all kinds of calculations in the course of scientific research. It is an integrated computer software system whose main functions include symbolic calculus, numerical calculation, and graphics. It can help people to solve the more complicated theoretical and practical problems of symbolic and numerical computation in various fields.

Maple

In September 1980, a research group on symbolic computation at the University of Waterloo in Canada developed a computer algebra system called Maple, which has evolved into excellent mathematical software. It has good use of the environment, powerful symbol computing capacity, and high accuracy. Its features are also digital computing, flexible graphics display, and efficient programmable functions. Maple has powerful functions in symbolic computation. Symbolic formulas can be directly given as input and output in mathematical form, which is intuitive and convenient.

SPSS

SPSS predictive analytics is an IBM product that provides statistical analysis, data and text mining, prediction mode, and decision optimization. IBM claims to have five major advantages with SPSS: business intelligence; powerful and simple analytics to control data explosions; meet organizational needs for flexible deployment of business intelligence; raise user expectations; and performance management, which guides management strategies. Making it the most profitable and provide timely and accurate data, scenario modeling, easy-to-understand reports, etc.

R

R language is mainly used for statistical analysis, mapping language, and operating environment. Right now, developed by the "R core team", it is a GNU project based on the S language; the language method comes from Scheme so it can also be used as an implementation of the S language, although R is primarily used statistical analysis or the development of statistical-related software, but can also be used for matrix calculations, its analysis. It is as fast as GNU Octave or even MATLAB. R is primarily a command-line operation on the Internet.

There are also several graphical user interfaces available for download. R language is built in a variety of statistical and numerical analysis work. Yes, it can also be enhanced through packages. Python scientific computing platforms such as NumPy, SciPy, and Matplotlib can be used.

Python

Python is an object-oriented, dynamic programming language with a very concise and clear syntax, which can not only be used for rapid development of program scripts but also the development of large-scale software, making it perfect for high-level missions. NumPy is a fundamental science package that includes a powerful N-dimensional array of objects that encapsulates C++ and Fortran tools, linear algebra, Fourier transforms, and random number generator functions, among other complex functions. SCIPY is open-source math, science, and engineering computing package that performs optimizations, linear algebra, integrals, interpolation, and special function number, fast Fourier transform, signal processing, image processing, ordinary differential equation, etc. Matplotlib, Python's most famous drawing library, provides a complete set of command APIs similar to MATLAB, which is ideal for interactive charting and can be easily used as a drawing control to embed in GUI applications.

MATLAB, Mathematica, Maple, SPSS, and other software features have a complete friendly interface while containing a variety of powerful software packages, but they are expensive as they are commercial software. For open-source software and free engineering computing platform, the GNU Octave, R, and Python scientific computing packages would be good choices.

Successful single machine learning algorithms can be applied to large scale distributed computing with a few modifications. Because Python has so many advantages, it is often used internally by Google. The R language contains a large number of statistical analysis packages; it can access part of the system functions. The core is to explain the implementation of the language, most user-visible R functions written by the R language itself. For the principle of efficiency, computationally intensive tasks are accomplished by linking and calling C, C++, and Fortran code at runtime. Also, RCPP can combine a rich environment with C/C++ and encapsulate R's API and data object into class and class's method for External C++ program to call.

OpenSOC Project

Machine learning algorithms and training data are the basis for solving data mining problems, and to make data mining work, it requires an engineering framework. OpenSOC was an open-source project that Cisco announced in 2014; however, it did not open-source its source code but just released its technical framework. OpenSOC is deployed entirely with open-source software, Hadoop for storage, Elasticsearch for real-time indexing, and Storm for online real-time analysis, so OpenSOC is a combination of open-source big data architecture and security analysis tools.

OpenSOC is composed of a data source system, data collection layer, message system layer, real-time processing layer, storage layer, and analysis processing layer. From a data processing point of view, OpenSOC's data sources can include raw network traffic, NetFlow, Syslog, and so on. Combined with external threat intelligence, OpenSOC can identify various security issues through offline and online analysis and mining. OpenSOC has joined the Apache project and changed its name to Apache Metron, but the system architecture has not changed much.

Here are the main functions of OpenSOC:

- Extensible receiver and analyzer capable of monitoring common data sources

- Supports exception detection and rule-based real-time alerts for data streams

- Supports the use of Elasticsearch to automate real-time indexed data flows

- Supports HIVE using SQL queries to store data in Hadoop

- Compatibility with ODBC/JDBC and inheritance of existing analysis tools

- Has a wealth of analytical applications and can integrate existing analytical tools

- Supports to automatically generate reports and exception alerts

- Supports the original network packet capture, storage, reorganization.

Data Source Systems

The data source system refers to the data used in data analysis, it also can be understood as the data format supported by the system. Common data sources include network traffic, files, syslog, SNMP, and databases.

Network Traffic

Network traffic is one of the most common data sources, mainly divided into full network traffic and NetFlow. Full network traffic contains complete network data, including TCP/IP stack data, such as Mac header, IP header, TCP header, HTTP header, and HTTP payload data, which is very helpful in analyzing attacks in the network.

There are three common ways to get total network traffic: switch mirror, splitter, and network splitter. Switch mirroring is a low-cost and easy-to-operate method, widely used in network troubleshooting, simple traffic analysis and monitoring.

The optical splitter is a widely used means of traffic replication. The basic principle of the optical splitter is to divide a beam of light into two beams from the physical level through a precise optical fiber production process to achieve the goal of flow replication.

Because of its low cost and stable performance, the optical splitter is the first choice for traffic replication in large networks. But there are limitations, such as not being able to use it when the light decays too much. Also, if there is a certain interface link in the network, it is also unable to use the spectrometer for traffic replication. This is where you need to use your dedicated traffic replication device, network TAP.

NetFlow provides a session-level view of network traffic, recording information for each TCP/IP transaction. It may not provide a complete record of network traffic like full traffic mirroring, but when aggregated, it is much easier to manage and read.

There are some differences between different versions of NetFlow traffic statistics. Common versions include dataflow timestamps, source and destination IP addresses, source and destination port numbers, input and output interface numbers, next hop IP addresses, total bytes in the stream, and the number of packets in the stream.

Documents

The file is the most basic form of saving data. There are common CSV, XML, JSON, spreadsheets, and various kinds of log files, such as Linux system log, Apache access log, and so on.

Syslog

Syslog is a standard for forwarding system log information over a network. Developed by the Berkeley Software Distribution Research Center, syslog is now an industry standard protocol for logging devices. Syslog records any event in the system, and an administrator can keep track of the system by viewing the system records. It logs the system events through the syslog process and can also log the application operational events. With proper configuration, you can also implement communication between machines running the syslog protocol. By analyzing these network behavior logs, you can track and keep track of equipment and network-related situations.

Syslog is a master-slave protocol that sends a small text message (less than 1024 bytes) to the syslog receiver. Common network devices, security devices, and Linux distributions have default support for sending logs in the form of syslog.

SNMP

SNMP is a network management standard based on the TCP/IP family. It is a standard protocol to manage network nodes (such as server, workstation, router, switch, etc.) in the network. SNMP enables a network administrator to improve network management effectiveness, identify and resolve network problems promptly, and plan for network growth. The network administrator can also receive notification messages from network nodes and alert event reports to keep track of problems on the network.

A network managed by SNMP consists of three main parts: SNMP agent, managed equipment, and network management system (NMS).

Every managed device on the network has a management information base for collecting and storing management information. The NMS can access this information through the

SNMP. Managed devices, also known as network units or nodes, can be routers, switches, servers, or hosts that support the SNMP. An SNMP agent is a network management software module on a managed device that holds relevant management information for the local device and can convert it into an SNMP-compatible format to be passed to the NMS. NMS runs applications to monitor managed devices. Also, NMS provides a large number of processors and necessary storage resources for network management.

Database

When data is stored in a database and can change at any time, it is necessary to synchronize the data from the database on a regular or even real-time basis, usually based on JDBC (Java Database Connectivity) to accomplish these tasks. JDBC is a Java API for executing SQL statements that provide uniform access to multiple relational databases. It consists of a set of classes and interfaces written in the Java language. JDBC provides a benchmark against which to build more advanced tools and interfaces that enable database developers to write database applications. With JDBC, it is easy to send SQL statements to a variety of relational data. In other words, with the JDBC API, you don't have to write a program specifically for accessing Sybase databases, another program specifically for accessing Oracle databases, another program specifically for accessing Informix databases, and so on. All a programmer needs to do is write a program using the JDBC API that sends an SQL call to the appropriate database.

Reptilian

When the data is stored in the third-party business system, the data may change at any time and cannot be accessed directly to the database; the crawler can be used to access the data by accessing the API or directly grabbing the web pages and files. For example, in order to eliminate the false report caused by the employee's business trip or field trip, it is necessary to synchronize the employee's travel status and the employee's punch card status in the access control system from ERP. This requires the use of crawlers to crawl data from ERP and access control system APIS.

Data Collection Layer

The data collection layer collects and initially processes the acquired data into a specified format. Common applications for the data collection layer include Logstash and Flume, full network traffic collection, and Bro. Logstash and Flume do the same thing just pick one, and this chapter covers only Logstash.

Logstash

Logstash is a powerful data processing tool for data transfer, format processing, formatted output, and powerful plug-ins, often used for log processing. Logstash consists mainly of three parts, including Inputs, Filters, and Outputs

Inputs are the data input side and support a wide variety of data formats, commonly listed as follows:

- **CloudWatch:** supports fetching data from the Amazon Web Services CloudWatch API

- **Event log:** supports reading event log from the Window system

- **File**: supports reading files

- **JDBC**: supports reading data from a database

- **Syslog**: supports receiving data in the form of Syslog. Filters are the data transfer layer that handles formatting, data type conversion, data filtering, field addition, modification, and more. The most common filter is Grok, which resolves and structures any text through regular parsing and structuring for most of their needs.

Outputs are the last phase of Logstash's work and are responsible for outputting data to a specific location. Common outputs are as follows:

- **Elasticsearch:** sends event data to Elasticsearch

- **File:** writes the event data to a disk file. Kafka writes event data to Kafka

Bro

Bro is a passive open-source traffic analyzer, mainly for the link of all the deep-level suspicious behavior of traffic security monitoring. Network traffic analysis provides a comprehensive platform with special emphasis on semantic security monitoring. Although it is often compared to traditional intrusion detection/prevention systems, Bro takes a completely different approach, providing users with a flexible framework, customizable tools, and in-depth monitoring that goes well beyond the capabilities of traditional systems. Bro's goal is to search for attack activity and provide background information and usage patterns. It can organize devices in the network into a visual graph, deep into the network traffic and can check network packets. In the ML framework, Bro is responsible for analyzing the network's full flow mirror, restoring the network protocol, and sending data to the Kafka cluster through the Kafka plug-in.

Messaging Layer

Messaging systems are the information superhighway of the whole ML framework on which data flows in and out. The most commonly used messaging system is Kafka. Kafka is a high-throughput distributed publish-subscribe messaging system with the following features:

- The persistence of messages is provided by the O (1) disk data structure, which is stable over long periods for even terabytes of message storage.

- High throughput, even very common hardware, can support millions of messages per second

- Support for partitioning messages through the Kafka server and consumer cluster.

The Kafka swystem consists of the following components:

- The Kafka cluster contains one or more servers, which are referred to as a **broker**.

- **Topic**, which has a category for every message posted to the Kafka Cluster. Physically, messages of different topics are stored separately. Logically, messages of a topic are stored on one or more broker, but users simply specify the topic of the message to produce or consume data regardless of where the data is stored.

- **Partition** is a physical concept, and each topic contains one or more partitions.

- **Producer**, the message producer, is responsible for releasing the message to the Kafka Broker.

- **Consumer**, the message consumer, is the client that reads the message to the Kafka Broker.

- The **consumer group**, where each consumer belongs to a specific consumer group (the group name can be specified for each consumer or the default group if no group name is specified).

Real-Time Processing Layer

The real-time processing layer uses Storm, a free, open-source, distributed, and fault-tolerant real-time computing system. Storm makes continuous stream computing easy, making up for real-time requirements that Hadoop batch processing cannot meet. Storm is often used in the areas of real-time analysis, online machine learning, continuous computing, distributed remote invocation, and ETL. Storm's deployment management is very simple and its performance is excellent compared to other similar streaming computing tools.

Storage Layer

HDFS

The distributed data store is designed to be suitable for a distributed data store running on general purpose hardware. It has a lot in common with the existing distributed data store, but it is also very different from other distributed data stores. HDFS is a highly fault-tolerant system suitable for deployment on inexpensive machines. HDFS provides high throughput data access and is ideal for applications on large data sets.

HDFS is designed to make it easy to migrate between platforms, which will push applications that require large datasets to use HDFS more widely as a platform. HDFS is a master-slave structure, and an HDFS cluster has a name node, which is a master server that manages the file namespace and coordinates client access to files. And, of course, there are data nodes (data node), usually one node, one machine, that manage the storage of the corresponding node. HDFS opens the file namespace to the public and allows user data to be stored and accessed as files. The internal mechanism is to split a file into one or more blocks, which are stored in a set of data nodes.

A file or directory operation is used to manipulate a file namespace, such as opening, closing, renaming, and so on, that determines the mapping of the block to the data node. The data node is responsible for reading and writing requests from the file system customer. The data node also performs block creation, deletion, and block copy instructions from the name node. Both the name node and the data node are software running on ordinary machines, typically GNU/Linux.

HDFS is written in Java, and any Java-enabled machine can run name or data nodes. The ultra-portability of the Java language makes it easy to deploy HDFS to a wide range of machines. A typical deployment is for a dedicated machine to run the name node software, and each other machine in the cluster to run a data node instance. The architecture does not preclude running instances of multiple data nodes on a single machine, but actual deployment does not recommend such use. Having only one name node in the cluster greatly simplifies the system architecture. The name node is the repository of the arbiter and all HDFS metadata, and the user's actual data is read and written without the name node.

HBASE

HBASE is a highly reliable, high-performance, column-oriented, and scalable distributed storage system. A large-scale structured storage cluster can be built on low-cost PC server using HBase technology. Hbase is an open-source implementation of Google Bigtable, similar to Google Bigtable using GFS as its file storage system and HBase using Hadoop HDFS as its file storage system. Google runs MapReduce to process the massive amounts of data in Bigtable, and HBase uses Hadoop MapReduce to process the massive amounts of data in HBase. Also, Pig and Hive provide high-level language support for HBase, which makes it very easy to do statistics on HBase. Sqoop provides a convenient RDBMS data import function for HBase, which makes it very convenient to migrate traditional database data to Hbase.

Elasticsearch

Elasticsearch is a Lucene-based search service that provides a distributed multi-user full-text search engine based on a RESTful web interface. Elasticsearch, developed in Java and released as open source under the Apache license, is a popular enterprise search engine. Elasticsearch is designed for real-time search in cloud computing. It is stable, reliable, fast, easy to install and use. The only requirement for installing Elasticsearch is to install the official new version of Java.

Installing Marvel

Marvel is a management and monitoring tool for Elasticsearch and is available for free in a development environment. It includes an interactive console called Sense, which allows users to interact directly with Elasticsearch through the browser. Many of the sample code in the Elasticsearch online documentation comes with a link to view in Sense. Clicking on it will open the corresponding instance in the Sense console. Installing Marvel is not required, but it can increase the book's interactivity by running sample code in your local Elasticsearch cluster. Marvel is a plug-in that can be downloaded and installed by running the following command in the Elasticsearch directory.

Analytical Processing Layer

Apache Spark is a fast and versatile computing engine designed for large-scale data processing. Spark is a general-purpose parallel framework for Hadoop-like MapReduce open source at UC Berkeley AMP lab. Spark has the advantage of Hadoop MapReduce, but unlike MapReduce, the intermediate job output can be stored in memory, eliminating the need to read and write HDFS so Spark can be better suited to the Iteractive MapReduce algorithms of data mining and machine learning. Spark is an open-source clustered computing environment similar to Hadoop, but there are some useful differences between the two that make Spark better at performing certain workloads. In other words, Spark enables memory-distributed datasets to optimize iterative workloads in addition to providing interactive queries. Spark is implemented in the Scala language, which uses Scala as its application framework. Unlike Hadoop, Spark and Scala are tightly integrated, where Scala can manipulate distributed datasets as easily as local collection objects.

Spark has a unique advantage in machine learning, mainly because machine learning algorithms generally have many steps of iterative computing process. ML calculations need to be done with a small enough error or enough convergence after many iterations, such as when using Hadoop's MapReduce computing framework, where each computation requires a read/write to disk and a task start. This results in very high I/O and CPU consumption. Spark's memory-based computing model is inherently good at iterative computing, where multiple steps are performed directly in memory, and disks and networks are manipulated only when necessary, so Spark is an ideal platform for ML. MLB (machine learning lib) is Spark's implementation library of commonly used machine learning algorithms, including related tests and data generator. MLB currently supports four common ML problems: classification, regression, clustering, and collaborative filtering. MLlib, based on RDD, is designed to seamlessly integrate with Spark SQL, GraphX, and Spark Streaming.

TensorFlow

TensorFlow is an open-source software library that uses data flow diagrams for numerical computation. The nodes represent mathematical operations in the diagram, and the lines in the diagram represent a multidimensional array of data associated with the nodes, known as a tensor. Its flexible architecture allows you to spread computing across multiple platforms, such as one or more CPUs (or GPUs) in a desktop computer, servers, mobile devices, and more. TensorFlow was originally developed by researchers and engineers at the Google Brain group (part of Google's machine intelligence research institute) for machine learning and deep neural networks. But the versatility of the system allows it to be widely used in other computing fields as well.

Although machine learning has been around for decades, two relatively recent trends have led to its widespread use: massive training data and powerful and efficient parallel computing. Here are two examples of powerful and efficient parallel computing:

- **GPU**
  Called the graphics processing unit (GPU), it was originally designed for computer graphics rendering and has tens of thousands of computing units for parallel computing. Floating-point and parallel computing, in particular, can be tens or even hundreds of times better than CPU performance.

  Industrial and academic data scientists have used GPUs for machine learning to achieve groundbreaking improvements in applications, such as image classification, video analysis, speech recognition, and natural language, processing the GPU on the driverless vehicle.

Deep learning, in particular, has been an area of intense investment and research. Deep learning is the use of complex multi-level depth neural networks to build systems; these systems can be from the huge amount of training data to mark the detection of features.

The GPU is used to train these deep neural networks, which uses a much larger training set, takes much less time, and consumes much less data center infrastructure. GPUS are also used to run these ML training models for classification and prediction in the cloud, enabling far greater data volumes and throughput with less power and infrastructure. Early users of GPU accelerators for machine learning included many large-scale web and social media companies, as well as leading research institutions in data science and machine learning. Prerecorded speech or multimedia content was transcribed three times faster using the GPU in a test of a machine learning application. Compared with CPU only, GPU has thousands of computing cores and can achieve 10~100 times application throughput, so GPU has become a must for data scientists to deal with big data.

- **TPU**

It is a chip developed by Google specifically to speed up deep neural network computing power. It greatly improves computing power by optimizing off-chip memory access, using low computational accuracy and using pulsating data streams 15-30 times faster than GPU/CPU combination.

TPU chips use up to 24 MB of local memory, 6 MB of accumulator memory, and memory for docking with the master processor, accounting for a total of 37% of the chip area. This means that Google is fully aware that off-chip memory access is a major cause of the GPU's low energy efficiency ratio and so has put a huge amount of memory on the chip at great cost.

TPU's high performance also stems from its tolerance for low computational accuracy. The research results show that the loss of algorithm accuracy caused by the low precision operation is very small, but it can bring great convenience in hardware implementation These include lower power consumption, higher speed, the smaller footprint of the chip, smaller memory bandwidth requirements, and so on. TPU uses 8-bit low-precision computing, meaning that it will require fewer transistors per step. With the total capacity of the transistors unchanged, more operations can be performed per unit time on these transistors, allowing more complex and powerful machine learning algorithms to be used to achieve faster and more intelligent results.

It takes a lot of time for the GPU to fetch instructions and data from memory. The TPU does not even fetch commands. Instead, the main processor provides it with its current instructions. This enables TPU to achieve higher computing efficiency. In matrix multiplication and convolution, many data can be reused, and the same data must be multiplied by many different weights to get the final result.

Therefore, at different times, only one or two new data need to be taken from outside, the other data is just the shift of the last time. In this case, it is very inefficient to Flush all the data on the chip and then fetch the new data. Based on this computing feature, TPU adds support for pulsating data streams, shifting data every clock cycle and retrieving new data. This maximizes data reuse and reduces memory access times, reducing memory bandwidth pressure while also reducing memory access energy consumption.

Chapter 5: Artificial Intelligence and Its Importance

Definition

Artificial intelligence is the ability of machines to do things that people don't think they can do—a very subjective definition, but also a very interesting one. Whether a computer program is artificial intelligence is entirely defined by whether or not the program is doing something that is mind boggling. This kind of empiricism definition obviously lacks consistency and will apply different standards according to different times, different backgrounds, and different judges' experiences. But this definition often reflects the way most ordinary people think about AI in an era: every time a new AI hot spot comes up, the news media and the public always use their own experience to judge the value of artificial intelligence technology, whether or not it is "intelligent" in nature.

Artificial intelligence generally refers to the technology that makes machines have human intelligence. The goal of this technology is to enable machines to perceive, think, do, and solve problems as humans do. Artificial intelligence is a broad area of technology that includes natural language understanding, computer vision, robotics, logic, and planning. It can be viewed as a subfield of computer science, except for computers. It also intersects with psychology, cognitive science, and sociology.

Machine Learning

Machine learning is when a computer learns, self-updates, and advances by observing and interacting with its environment. We all know what a computer program is, a program is a series of instructions that a computer can execute, such as printing a picture. So, what is the essential difference between machine learning and programs we know? You can imagine a program is written by a machine, not by a programmer. So, how does the machine know how to write this program? This machine learns from a huge amount of data.

Simply put, most machine learning algorithms can be divided into two steps, training and testing, which can overlap. Training, in general, requires training data, which tells the machine what previous humans have learned, such as what a cat is, what a dog is, and what to stop for when you see it. The result of the training can be thought of as a program written by a machine or stored data called a model. In general, there are two types of training: supervised learning and unsupervised learning. Having supervision is like having a teacher telling you the right answer; having no supervision is like watching and learning. The machine looks for patterns and features in the data itself. Deep learning is a method of machine learning. It is based on a neural network, and it is suitable for audio, video, language understanding, and so on.

Deep Learning

Deep learning is originated from neural networks, but it has now surpassed this framework. So far, several deep learning frameworks, such as deep neural networks, convolutional neural networks and deep belief networks, and recurrent neural networks, have been applied in the fields of computer vision, speech recognition, natural language processing, audio recognition, and bioinformatics.

The motivation for deep learning is to build a neural network that simulates the human brain for analytical learning. It mimics the mechanisms of the human brain to interpret data such as images, text, and sound. By learning a deep nonlinear network structure, a simple network structure can be used to achieve the approximation of complex functions and to demonstrate the powerful ability to learn the essential features of data sets from a large number of unlabeled samples. Deep learning can obtain features that better represent data, and because the level of the model is deep (usually there are 5 layers, 6 layers, or even 10 layers of hidden layer nodes, the advantage of "deep" is that you can control the number of hidden layer nodes. It is a polynomial multiple of the number of input nodes, not as many as exponential times, and has strong expressive power, so it has the ability to represent large-scale data.

History of Artificial Intelligence

Let us take a brief look at the three waves of artificial intelligence. What are their characteristics? What difference does it make? How do they relate to each other and on the previous one? The first wave of artificial intelligence came around the 1950s. In 1956, at a conference on artificial intelligence at Dartmouth, John McCarthy officially introduced the concept of "artificial intelligence", which is recognized as the beginning of the modern subject of artificial intelligence. Joseph McCarthy and the Marvin Lee Minsky are known as "fathers of artificial intelligence".

In the early days of the invention of computers, many computer scientists thought and talked seriously about how the machine invented by human beings was fundamentally different from human beings. The Turing machine and the Turing test are one of the most typical results of this thinking. The original group of experts thinking about artificial intelligence, from the thought and theory of a very cutting-edge, expert early on saw the potential of computers. They asked questions: what is reasoning and how does a machine reason; what is understanding, and how does a machine understand; what is knowledge, and how does a machine acquire and express knowledge; and when we cannot tell the difference between a machine and a person. This stage produced a lot of basic theories, not only the basic theory of artificial intelligence but also the cornerstone of computer science.

Technically speaking, the first big advances in artificial intelligence were primarily based on logic. In 1958, Joseph McCarthy came up with the logical language LISP. From the 1950s to the 1980s, researchers demonstrated that computers could play games and have some degree of natural language understanding. In the lab, robots can make logical decisions and build blocks; robot mice can make decisions about different paths and obstacles, and cars can drive themselves in limited environments. Researchers have created neural networks that can do simple language comprehension and object recognition.

In the first 20 or 30 years of AI, however, though it was a fruitful field of research, it was of little practical use. In the early 1980s, artificial intelligence entered the "winter" due to a lack of application. By the late 1980s and early 1990s, artificial intelligence scientists decided to take a different approach, moving away from solving big, pervasive intelligence problems and toward solving single problems in certain fields. The concept of an "expert system" was proposed, which allowed these to findings to find their first possible commercial outlet.

With the development of computer technology in the past 30 years or so, data storage and application have a certain foundation. Researchers see the possibility of combining artificial intelligence with data, and the best combination of applications is "expert systems". If we could tell a machine all the data from a certain industry, for example, all the data on heart disease, and give it some logic, wouldn't that make the machine a "cardiologist" if we wanted to see a doctor, is it okay to ask it?

Expert systems for medical care, weather forecasting, and so on, sounded very promising and meaningful, and they did have practical applications, so there was a boom in artificial intelligence in academia. What's interesting, though, is that when we tried to use these expert systems to make smart diagnoses, we found that the problem wasn't how to make a diagnosis, but that most of the data were not digitized at the time. The patient's diagnostic history was written by a doctor who could not read it. Some of that information, even if it is being digitized, is in some form or some disconnected machine, out of reach or out of use.

So, instead, the people who wanted to do automated diagnostics did some basic work. The basic job, in a word, is to digitize all the information in the world. At a time when several people are working to make every book, every map, and every prescription in the world available electronically, the widespread use of the Internet is connecting all this information into real big data. In the meantime, the increase in computational performance predicted by Moore's law has been at work. As computing power grows exponentially, applications that can only be implemented in the labor limited scenarios are getting closer to the real world. As computing power improves, it is only a matter of time before machines beat humans at these single, goal-setting tasks.

The third wave of AI is based on two other big developments, one in computing power and the other in data. Huge computing power comes from the development of hardware, distributed systems, and cloud computing. Recently, neural-network-based computing has given another boost to the integration of artificial intelligence hardware and software. Massive amounts of data come from the accumulation of data and the development of the Internet technology in the previous decades. For example, the GPS, which as launched in 2001, brought an unprecedented amount of travel data; smart phones brought an unprecedented amount of data about people's habits, and so on. The combination of computational power and data promotes and catalyzes the leap of machine learning algorithms.

The AI wave began nearly a decade ago. The rapid development of technology has brought unprecedented possibilities of application. The most fundamental difference between this latest wave of AI and the last two is its pervasive use and impact on ordinary people's lives. In other words, artificial intelligence left the academic laboratory, really into the public field of vision.

First, for the first time in history, computers outperformed or were about to outperform humans on complex tasks such as image recognition, video understanding, machine translation, driving cars, playing go, and so on. These are easily understood tasks that have always been done by humans. So, the replacement of humans by artificial intelligence is starting to make headlines.

In fact, in a single technology, much computing-related technology has long been beyond human capacity and is widely used, such as navigation, search, map search, and stock trading.

Many people are used to using voice to give simple instructions to operate. However, these relatively simple technologies are mainly "to complete a task"; the computer is not too much involved in human perception, thinking, complex judgments, and even emotions.

In recent years, however, machines have come closer to humans in terms of complexity and form. For example, machine learning based self-driving technology has matured to revolutionize not only the way people travel but also the way they build cities, consume, and live. People may no longer need to own a car or know how to drive one. People are both excited and frightened by the rapid arrival of these new technologies, enjoying their convenience while at the same time being at a loss for what to do if the change happens too quickly.

Also, the self-learning ability of the computer is increasing. The development of modern machine learning algorithms, especially deep learning type machine learning algorithms, has made machines behave not as relatively predictable "programs" or "logic" but more like "black box thinking". With an almost human capacity for inexplicable though.

On closer inspection, however, while AI has made great strides in several specific areas, it is still a long way from the general purpose intelligence that the fathers of AI were working on in the first wave. That is fact number two. The machine is still put in a specific situation to do a specific task, but the task is more complex. Machines still lack some basic human intelligence, such as common sense. AI still cannot understand even simple emotions like fear.

The third fact is that the scenarios for AI and machine learning are very broad. With the rapid development of artificial intelligence and machine learning applications in recent years, this once academic research concept has suddenly entered the public domain and become an inevitable topic related to the future. Computer vision, deep learning, robotics, and natural language understanding, are all referred to as the application layer.

The application of algorithm class goes out of academic circles, penetrates every corner of society, and infiltrates every aspect of people's life. We are familiar with face recognition, automatic driving, medical diagnosis, machine assistant, smart city, new media, games, education, etc. There is also less talked about things like the automation of agricultural production, the care of the elderly and children, the operation of hazardous situations, traffic dispatch, and so on. It is hard to imagine any part of society not being affected by this wave.

Both at home and abroad, the media industry has been at the forefront of artificial intelligence applications because media tend to reach tens of millions or even hundreds of millions of users. There are ever-changing users of daily content, such as news, sports, and movies; rich content and user integration scenarios; and there are also rich and creative business opportunities.

Apple's Siri, Baidu's Secret Service, Google Allo, Microsoft's Little Ice, Amazon's Alexa, and other smart assistant and smart chat apps are trying to revolutionize the way you interact with your phone, turning it into a smart little secretary. News headlines and other popular news apps rely on artificial intelligence to feed you the stories that work best for you, and many of today's press releases are written by artificial intelligence programs. Google Photos uses artificial intelligence technology to quickly identify people, animals, landscapes, and places, which quickly help users organize and retrieve images. Meituxiu uses artificial intelligence technology to automatically beautify photo images and video applications such as Prisma, and Philm create intelligent "art" based on photos or videos. We take search engines such as Google and Baidu who have already advanced to a new level of intelligent question answering, intelligent assistant, and intelligent search. Machine translation technology, represented by Google translation, is developing rapidly with the help of deep learning. When traveling with Didi or Uber, AI agorithms will not only help drivers choose routes and plan vehicle schedules, but in the near future, autonomous driving will redefine smart mobility, smart transportation, and smart cities. When shopping on your mobile phone, e-commerce sites like Taobao and Amazon use artificial intelligence to recommend products that are best for you. Advanced warehouse robots, logistics robots, and logistics drones are helping e-commerce companies distribute goods efficiently and safely.

It is something many people do every day to watch the hot news on their mobile phone. The popularity of news apps, such as News Reader, is largely due to the use of artificial intelligence, the ability of apps to intelligently sum up the different habits and interests of everyone watching the news recommend different news content to different users. If an app with smart recommendations works well, users will feel that the more often they use it, the more the machine will know what is on their minds, and over time, the app will become nothing less than a tailor-made news steward.

Face recognition, which is the most widely used machine vision technology, is an important branch of the artificial intelligence family. In recent years, with the development of deep learning technology, the accuracy of face recognition by artificial intelligence programs has exceeded the average level of human beings.

Facial recognition can not only be a security guard but also on the phone to ensure the security of your transactions. Many mobile phone banks, when they need to verify the identity of a business agent, will turn on the front-facing camera of the phone and ask you to leave a real-time image of your face, while the smart face recognition program will do your identity comparison in the background. Ensure that mobile banking applications are not stolen by criminals.

In a broad sense, machine vision includes not only face recognition but also image and video object recognition, scene recognition, location recognition, and even semantic understanding. All of these smart algorithms can now be found in ordinary mobile applications.

For example, almost all of today's major photo management programs offer automatic photo sorting and retrieval. The most intelligent and powerful of these is Google Photos. With Google Photos, you can upload all your photos and videos—yes, all your photos and videos, whether it is a dinner photo from yesterday or a home video shot for your kids a dozen years ago—to the cloud. Without any manual sorting or tagging, Google Photos will automatically identify every person, animal, building, landscape, and location in the photos and will give you quick and accurate search results when you need them.

Using Google Photos, you can easily find every great moment you have had in the past few years, as well as browse through some of the most famous places you have visited in the past year. Or, simply type in the name of any animal, such as "seagull" to see if you have ever taken a photograph of a seagull before. In the summer of 2016, Prisma, a mobile drawing app, became popular among friends. Prisma does not create paintings out of thin air. Instead, it transforms a photograph into a particular style of painting based on a user-specified image.

Prisma uses advanced artificial intelligence algorithms to understand every color and edge on a cat in a photograph. Then, the computer learned from a large number of classic painting techniques, brush techniques, and dry and wet painting techniques applied to this real photo.

We can think of the whole process as a child learning to paint a picture of a cat in the creative training. The boy, Prisma, has received a rigorous art education, copying a large number of Chinese and Western classic paintings and can skillfully use a variety of oil paintings, watercolors, and even caricature techniques to create. Based on this cat photograph, Prisma has been able to use the artificial intelligence "brush" to create artistic "creations" in as many as twenty different styles of painting.

In many people's eyes, search engine is born in the 20th century as an Internet core technology. More than two decades have passed since Google's founders, Larry Page and Sergey Brin, introduced a Page Rank algorithm in 1996 that greatly improved the ranking of search engine results. Is there room for artificial intelligence here?

Google has long used ML to help search engines rank results. This idea is different from the traditional algorithm. In the direction of machine learning, the mathematical model of how to sort web pages and every parameter in that model is not fully defined by a person but by a computer based on big data automatically learned through a complex iterative process. How important each factor (in machine learning, each factor is also known as a "feature") is, or how it participates in the final ranking calculation, is largely determined by the AI algorithm's self-learning. Since 2011, with the revival of deep learning and the success of the Google Brain project, Google's search engine has relied more and more on deep learning for its web ranking algorithms. The relevance and accuracy of the results have also been greatly enhanced. It is no exaggeration to say that by the time took charge of Google's search team, Google search was a new generation of search engine powered largely by artificial intelligence.

The resulting rankings are just the tip of the iceberg in the use of artificial intelligence in search engines. Turn on Google or similar mainstream search engines, and the magic of AI is everywhere. Today, we can ask the search engine questions directly at Google, and the search engine will intelligently answer many intellectual questions.

In recent years, with the use of artificial intelligence technology in speech recognition, natural language understanding, Knowledge Atlas, personalized recommendation, web ranking, and other areas of great progress, mainstream search engines such as Google and Baidu are transforming from simple web search and web navigation tools into the world's largest knowledge engine and personal assistant. No doubt artificial intelligence technology makes search engines smarter.

It is a great dream that human beings have been pursuing since ancient times to break the language boundary and use automatic translation tools to help human beings communicate across nations, languages, and cultures. The 1799's discovery of the Rosetta Stone has pushed this kind of communication even further across time and space. With the wisdom of the Rosetta Stone and linguists, it is amazing that we can read ancient

Egyptian writing thousands of years ago and understand what the ancient Egyptians did, thought, and said.

Today, though not perfect, AI-based machine translation tools are helping people communicate and communicate around the world. Of all the popular translation tools, Google Translate has the most languages supported and the best results.

There is no doubt that autopilot is one of the most intriguing areas of artificial intelligence for the average person. The cars, planes, and spaceships that are automatically driven by computer algorithms used to be the most important elements of the future in most science fiction. Everyone will be thrilled to think that, one day, we will be able to get around without a driver's license and just give a direct order to a car.

But what many people do not seem to realize is that the self-driving car itself, or at least the technology behind it, is already working around us and creating tremendous commercial value.

Compared with Google's conservatism, Tesla has been more aggressive in promoting self-driving technology. As early as late 2014, Tesla began selling electric cars alongside an optional driver assistance program called autopilot. The computer can automatically adjust the speed of the vehicle and control the power of the motor, the braking system, and the steering system by the real-time information of the road surface acquired by the on-board sensors and the experience model acquired by the machine learning in advance.

The basic technology of helping cars avoid collisions from the front and the side and preventing them from skidding off the road is similar to Google's autopilot.

Beyond the consumer market, self-driving technology may soon find its way into certain industries. In the rental industry, leaders like Uber and Didi are actively positioning themselves for the use of autonomous driving technology in a shared economy. Uber's driverless cabs are already being tested on U.S. roads. In the logistics industry, self-driving trucks are likely to be on the road before general-purpose self-driving cars. Some R & D teams have even dreamed of fast, safe motoring on motorways with self-driving vans in formation. Small start-ups like Utrend have come up with the idea of self-driving cars being the first to take on the tasks of commuting in a small community on a more independent community road.

Robots are another area of artificial intelligence that is often thought of as technology. It has been many years since industrial robots began to play a role in manufacturing. In mainstream car production lines, and even in Foxconn's mobile phone production lines, not using industrial robots is the news.

In 2012, Amazon acquired a company called Kiva for the sole purpose of acquiring the ability to design and build warehouse robots. Based on Kiva, Amazon has mass-produced a small orange robot that can automatically carry goods to a designated location by moving them quickly through Amazon's large storage centers.

In addition to drones that can land directly in your own backyard, a number of start-ups are also working hard on unmanned delivery vehicles in the form of intelligent robots. Domino's, a pizza chain, is experimenting with car-shaped robots to deliver pizzas. Starship Technologies, a start-up, has designed a car-shaped robot that can carry up to 20 pounds of cargo, including safety locks, intelligent driving, precise positioning, and intelligent communication. It can run for up to a mile, serving not only as a courier but also as a way to pick up things on your way home from shopping.

Another hot area in recent years is educational and home robotics. But it is important to note that today's home robots are nowhere near as human-like as you might expect. From an investor's point of view, the more you pursue a robot project that looks like a person and tries to talk and do things like a person, the less commercial it will be. The more human-like a robot is, the easier it is for humans to compare it to a real person. At this point, the lack of technology will be exposed, in the "shortcomings of the magnifying glass"; the robot will only appear very stupid and clumsy.

What really impresses home users are smart appliances like the Amazon Echo, which are relatively simple, more appliance-like than robot-like, and are geared toward one or two limited but specific use scenarios. In other words, most users would prefer a small appliance with a certain amount of communication skills, which is cute and even "cuter" rather than a full-featured android with flaws everywhere.

Educational robots do the same. Start-up Wonder Workshop, for example, has created a pair of tiny robots called Dash and Dot to help children over the age of five learn to code and develop their hands-on skills and imagination; however, they don't look like real people but rather a few cute geometric combinations.

Future of Artificial Intelligence

As machine learning heats up, artificial intelligence—words that seem to dominate the world's attention—has taken off, with self-driving robots coming to life and intelligent robots becoming the norm. Artificial intelligence has quietly come to our side, and everything in life has an inseparable connection.

Computational Advertising

Advertising is one of the most important modes for Internet commerce to realize. Digital advertising is the most important cash flow for most internet giants. According to Alphabet,

Google's parent company, in the first quarter of 2017, advertising revenue was $21.411 billion, or 86.5% of total revenue. Facebook's share of ad revenue is even higher at a staggering 98%, making it a veritable advertising company. In addition, Alibaba and TenCent's advertising departments are also the core departments of the companies.

The history of digital advertising dates back to 1995. At that time, Yahoo was the representative of the web portal as an online magazine for sale and in accordance with the agreed form of delivery. At the time, digital advertising was very similar to the way traditional media sold ads but moved content from offline to online. Since 1998, search engines such as Google have been leading the way. Unlike portals, commercial monetization of search engines takes the form of paid search combined with search services, where ads are targeted to users' immediate interests (search terms). This kind of advertisement is sold by competitive bidding; the advertiser can optimize the effect of the advertisement according to the real-time interest of the user, so the effect of the advertisement is more accurate than the portal. Since 2005, the online video business has been growing in traffic, representing sites such as YouTube and Hulu, which have been cannibalizing the market for traditional TV ads because their advertising models are similar to traditional TV ads.

The Internet advertisement pattern obtains each big advertiser's favor, has the following several reasons. First, as users spend more and more time on the Internet, advertisers must spend more on the Internet advertising in order to reach the younger generation of users. Second, the threshold for online advertising is very low. Ads can be placed after Google opens a self-service account for $100; meanwhile, ads can be easily personalized and quantified and optimized by AB testing. With the rapid development of the Internet advertising, more and more attention has been paid to the algorithm model behind it. In 2008, at the 19th ACM-SIAM symposium, Andrei Broder, senior researcher at Yahoo Research Institute, presented the concept of computational advertising. He believes that computational advertising is a new branch of science that includes information science, statistics, computer science, and microeconomics. Its research goal is to achieve the best match of context, advertisement, and audience.

The most important form of auction advertising is search advertising. The target of a search ad is a keyword, and each search ad can bid for a specific keyword. The user enters a query that matches the keywords used in the ad auction, retrieves all the ads that match the criteria, and selects one or more of the ads to display with the search results, usually at the top of the page. Search ads are generally paid by click; after users click on the keyword in accordance with the advertiser's bid fee, so click is not charged. That is why click rate estimation algorithm is crucial to the optimization of competitive advertising.

Procedural transaction advertising allows advertisers to more flexible choice of their audience and exposure time. At the time of each display opportunity, the ad trading platform will send the relevant traffic information and bidding request to the demand side platform (DSP), which will bid on behalf of the advertiser according to the actual traffic situation. The highest bidder gets this exposure. Procedural transaction advertisements are usually settled by CPA (cost per action), so it is necessary to consider the click rate, conversion rate, and other factors.

Different types of ads differ in the design of advertising systems. For example, contract ads generally do not need to consider the actual effect of ads, so there is no CTR module; procedural transactional ads need to interface with third-party information such as ad trading platforms, so more data docking modules are needed. But overall, the overall architecture of the advertising system is generic. The system consists of a distributed computing platform, a streaming computing platform, and an advertising machine.

The distributed computing is responsible for performing batch calculations based on the huge volume of posting logs, and getting the results of algorithm analysis and modeling, such as user profiling, CTR modeling, and so on, all run on the distributed computing and will get the user labels, model features and parameters, and other data updated to the database. The stream computing platform is responsible for collecting and calculating the data such as user labels, features, and click feedback and synchronizing them into the database in real time. When a request comes, the advertiser searches, sorts, and selects the ads based on the user, context, and the current state of the database. After an ad is placed, the relevant records are captured and processed by the streaming computing platform in a timely manner, and they are also collected in the placement log for later use by the distributed computing.

Each algorithm module of the advertising system is not only related to Spark, HDFS, Kafka, and other big data tools but also involves a lot of machine learning knowledge. If you want to become an advertising algorithm engineer, in addition to lay a solid foundation for the algorithm and also the commercial model of advertising, the business function of each module has a deeper understanding. Here's a breakdown of the algorithms and machine learning involved in each module of the advertising system.

- **User Portraits**

    The user profile is one of the core components of computational advertising, which is widely used in contract advertising, search advertising, procedural transaction advertising, and other product forms. In the contract advertisement, the advertiser can specify the suitable orientation condition according to the audience of his own brand in order to save the cost; search ads and procedural transaction ads can be based on the user's portrait of the user of each ad click rate and conversion rate for a more accurate estimate, thus optimizing the overall delivery effect.

Supervised learning and unsupervised learning are widely used in the user profile. For example, the gender prediction problem is a typical supervised learning problem. We can get the gender of some users based on the gender information they fill in, and for others, we can't get their exact gender, but there are ads that ask for specific gender-specific branding. For example, an advertiser who specializes in men's clothing may need to target ads to men. To meet the similar needs of advertisers, we need to model and predict the gender of users based on past behavior and other established characteristics, such as the historical behavior of a user who regularly watches football, boxing, etc.

The probability of predicting that he is a man is higher and similar to other hashtags. As long as we have enough annotation samples, we can use supervised learning to model and predict user tags.

The supervised learning model can use logistic regression, support vector machine, decision tree, random forest, gradient lifting decision tree, feed-forward neural network, and so on. In search engines, for example, it is possible to predict a user's gender based on their search and browsing history, leading to more accurate search advertising. Experiments were conducted using historical access data from a large web site. The features entered were historical web page text that the user had searched and browsed, with each word as a separate one-dimensional feature. The final classifier learns more significant text features.

It was found that children, food, family, and so on were more important traits in predicting women; for men, sports, cars, the Internet, and so on were more significant. Therefore, the results of feature learning are more intuitive.

Another major class of user profiling method is the use of unsupervised learning. The purpose of unsupervised learning is to discover the rule of data itself, and it does not need to use labeled data.

We can group users into specific categories based on their past behavior and existing characteristics. For each type of user, although it is difficult to describe their exact label, it is known that they have a high degree of similarity and are expected to have some similar interest in advertising.

In this way, through the application of clustering technology and the clustering results used for click-through rate estimation, advertising ranking and selection usually can bring significant improvement. The commonly used clustering methods are k-means, Gaussian mixture model, subject model, and so on, which all belong to the category of unsupervised learning.

- **Click-Through Rate Estimates**

Click-through rate estimation is one of the most important algorithms in effect advertising. In order to optimize the advertising effect, first of all, we must have an accurate judgment of the effect after the advertising display (i. e. click rate, conversion rate, etc.). In search advertising, the results are usually evaluated and settled by the number of clicks on the ad, so the accuracy of click rate estimation plays a key role in the effect optimization. If the end result is a conversion, then you also need to estimate the conversion rate after the click. In many scenarios, the actual conversion data is very rare. It is difficult to directly use the conversion data to train the model, so it is often reduced to the next step, the second jump, add to the shopping cart, and other behavior modeling. The modeling principle of conversion, second jump and adding to the shopping cart, is very similar to the click rate prediction, so we only introduce the algorithm flow and common models with the click rate prediction as an example.

Click-through rate estimation can be abstracted as a dichotomous problem. The problem it solves is that given a request and the ads that match the request, the probability of getting a click after the ad is displayed is predicted. Tagging can be obtained from actual drop data, and in historical drop results, the record of hits is labeled 1, and the rest is labeled 0. Click-through rate estimation is mainly divided into sampling, feature extraction and combination, model training, model evaluation, and other steps.

- **Advertising Search**

The task of the advertising retrieval stage is to retrieve all the advertisements which meet the conditions of putting in according to the query, the audience, and other directional conditions. For example, depending on the query's ambiguity, advertisements that are semantically similar to the query text should be recalled as much as possible for the next stage of the ad sorting and selection algorithm. This phase is mainly based on the recall rate as the evaluation index because the missed ads in the future will not have the opportunity to be displayed. The classic solution to the pattern matching problem is query expansion. In layman's terms, a set of semantically related queries is found for the current query, and ads retrieved by at least one of the queries can be added to the alternate set. The essence of query expansion is to calculate the text similarity between two queries or to find the probability of generating another query for a given query. The former can be realized based on the topic model and Word2Vec algorithm, while the latter can be modeled by deep neural network and other methods.

- **AD Sorting/Selection**

Different advertising business scenarios have different decision-making styles in this step. For contract ads, our goal is to meet the daily exposure requirement (the penalty for under-exposure) as stipulated in the contract and does not involve CTR estimation. Therefore, the problem of advertising ranking and selection can be modeled as a constrained optimization problem. So the choice of advertisement can be expressed as a bipartite graph matching problem; the goal of optimization is to maximize the total revenue.

Machine Translation

Machine translation, a branch of computational linguistics and an important application of artificial intelligence, dates back to the 1950s. With the rapid development of the Internet, people's demand for language translation is increasing day by day. According to Wikipedia, there are hundreds of different languages on the Internet and English accounts for about half of all the Internet content. English-speaking Internet users make up only a quarter of all Internet users. The cross-domain language barrier having access to more content on the Internet is a growing demand.

Machine translation, that is, the translation of text from one language into another language by computer, has become one of the important methods to solve the language barrier. As early as 2013, Google Translate was offering translations a billion times a day, the equivalent of a year's worth of human translations worldwide and the equivalent of one million books.

The research of machine translation has experienced three stages: rule-based method, statistics-based method, and neural network-based method. In the early days of machine translation, rule-based methods were mainly used. Machine translation system is a mechanical process, which is based on the translation rules written by language experts. Rule-based methods are limited by the quality and quantity of manually written rules, which are time-consuming and laborious to write, and translation rules cannot be used between different language pairs. At the same time, the increasing number of rules and the increasing number of conflicting rules make it difficult to cover the whole situation of human language, which is also the bottleneck of the machine translation system.

In the 1990s, statistical-based machine translation (ST) method was proposed, and then quickly became the mainstream method in MT Research. Statistical Machine Translation (SMT) uses a bilingual parallel corpus (a corpus contains both the source language and the target language text with which it is translated) as training data. The well-known Rosetta Stone can be thought of as an ancient parallel corpus with identical texts written in the sacred script, secular script, and ancient Greek script. It was the discovery of the Rosetta Stone that gave linguists the key to deciphering the script.

Statistical machine translation models mine the alignment relationships between words in different languages from parallel corpora and automatically extract translation rules based on the alignment relationships. A classical statistical machine translation model usually consists of three parts: translation model, reordering model, and language model. The translation model is used to estimate the probability of words and phrases being translated into each other, and the reordering model is used to model the sequence of language fragments after translation. The statistical translation model reduces hum an participation, and the model itself is independent of the training process, which greatly improves the performance and application range of machine translation.

In recent years, with the introduction of neural network-based methods into the field of machine translation, the performance of machine translation has been greatly improved. According to information released by Google's machine translation team, Google Translate launched its China UK neural network model in September 2016 and has supported 41 pairs of bilingual translation modules as of May 2017. More than 50% of translation traffic is already provided by neural network models.

At present, the effect of machine translation is still difficult to reach the level of human translation, but with the improvement of machine translation performance, its application scenario is more and more diverse. Google Translate launched in 2006, is more than a decade old and now supports hundreds of different languages, with web pages, mobile clients, app APIs, and more.

In May 2017, Google Translate was providing translations to 500 million people a day. Microsoft, Baidu, NetEase, and other domestic and foreign companies are also constantly optimizing their machine translation services for the public to use. Although various types of machine translation services cannot be directly used for written translation, the barriers to understanding other languages have been greatly reduced, and machine translation has played a very good auxiliary role in many scenarios.

When traveling abroad, the language barrier is a big pain point for many people. A variety of mobile phone app photo translation allows people to easily and quickly understand foreign landmarks or menus.

The field of machine translation has attracted more and more attention, but it also faces great challenges. How to overcome the existing shortcomings (such as the poor interpretability of the neural network model) to achieve further improvement of translation performance is still a problem to be solved. At present, the application of machine translation is still in the simple understanding of other languages, auxiliary translation, and so on.

But with all the attention and talent coming in, machine translation will continue to flourish, and the Tower of Babel in the human world will be rebuilt.

Human-computer interaction is also the direction of artificial intelligence integration. In the process of human-computer interaction, speech and image recognition enable machines to understand human input signals, and prediction models and reinforcement learning models help machines make effective and rational judgments and acquire the ability of learning.

Intelligent control methods allow machines to perform human-specified actions or provide effective feedback. It can be said that human-computer interaction contains all aspects of artificial intelligence; the rapid development of human-computer interaction means the overall progress of artificial intelligence level.

In the past few decades, the field of human-computer interaction has made great progress, which has experienced three important leaps. First, in the early 1970s, the concept of the human-computer interface was formally proposed, the First International Conference on the man-machine system was held, the first relevant professional journal (IJMMS) was launched, and many research institutions and companies established human-machine Interaction Research Center one after another. Second, in the early 1980s, the discipline of human-computer interaction gradually developed its own theoretical and practical framework, placing greater emphasis on the theoretical guidance of cognitive psychology as well as behavioral and sociological humanities In the practical framework, more emphasis is placed on the feedback interaction between computers and human beings, and the term human-computer interface/interface has been replaced by human-computer interaction. With the rapid development and popularization of high-speed processing chip, multimedia technology, and Internet web technology, the research of human-computer interaction focuses on human-computer interaction, multi-modal (multi-channel) and multimedia interaction, virtual interaction, and intelligent interaction.

How to Excel Yourself in Artificial Intelligence Era

In the age of artificial intelligence, the stylized, repetitive skills that can be learned by memory and practice alone will be the least valuable skills that can almost certainly be accomplished by machines; conversely, the skills that best embody a person's overall qualities. For example, people's comprehensive analysis of complex systems, decision-making ability, aesthetic ability and creative thinking of art and culture, intuition and common sense generated by life experience and cultural edification, the ability to interact with others based on one's own emotions (love, hate, passion, indifference, etc.)—these are the most valuable, most worth cultivating and learning skills of the AI era.

If I had to sum it up, I would say that the most central and effective ways to learn in the age of artificial intelligence are:

- **Take the initiative to challenge the limit.** Take the initiative to accept all challenges, in the challenge to improve themselves. If humans do not improve by challenging themselves, it may indeed be possible to fall completely behind intelligent machines.

- **Learning by doing.** Facing practical problems and comprehensive and complex problems, combining basic learning with applied practice, instead of learning first and then practicing. While to some, like modern professional sports players to match for training, on the personal quality of higher requirements, the effect is better with learning while practicing the method.

- **Focus on heuristic education to foster creativity and independent problem solving.** Passive command-oriented work can be replaced for the most part by machines. The value of people will be reflected in more creative work. Heuristic education is very important here. Rote memorization and rules will only "block" the source of students' inspiration and creativity.

- **Although face-to-face classes will still exist, interactive online learning will become more and more important.** Only by taking full advantage of online learning can educational resources be fully shared, and the quality and fairness of education can be guaranteed. Innovation works ventures such as VIPKid and Boxfish are examples of companies that are investing in educational innovation using online and machine assisted education to help children learn.

- **Active machine learning.** In the future of human-computer collaboration, what people are good at and what machines are good at will be very different. Humans can learn from machines and draw from the results of AI calculations models, ideas, and even basic logic that can help improve the way humans think. In fact, Go pros are already modestly learning better patterns and moves from AlphaGo.

- **Learning human-human cooperation and human-computer cooperation.** The future communication ability will not only be limited to human-human communication. Human-computer communication will become an important learning method and learning goal. From the first day of study, students discuss with face-to-face or remote classmates (either human or machine), design solutions, and progress together.

- **Learning is about following your interests.** In general, your interests are those that are deep, so if you follow your interests, you are more likely to find a job that will not be easily replaced by a machine. For beauty's sake, for curiosity's sake, and for the sake of interest for other reasons, these interests are likely to reach a higher level where human beings can create value that machines cannot replace.

Conclusion

Thank you for making it through to the end of *Machine Learning for Beginners: Machine Learning Basics for Absolute Beginners*. Let's hope it was informative and able to provide you with all of the tools you need to achieve your goals whatever they may be.

The next step is to learn more about machine learning algorithms in detail with the help of academic journals and textbooks. We have discussed machine learning in detail with abundant examples linked with real life and had got a thorough understanding of the artificial intelligence era that will lead the world soon.

This book has given a lot of information about machine learning and deep learning algorithms along with real-world examples that are interlinked with our daily life. To know more about machine learning, if you are interested, please look at the IBM Watson website where you can perform various face recognition exercises for free. Watson is famous for its complex experiments. To have a better overview of machine learning, start looking for it everywhere. Strangely, it is not so difficult because you can find it in many real-life applications. When you know how machine learning is implemented with your real-life examples, you can better understand the complexity of artificial intelligence and its technologies.

We have also discussed deep learning in detail with examples of facial recognition that can enrich humanity. Machine learning is a great boon for our world with its infinite applications that can change our world into a strange new place which is a lot better than what we are in now.

This module covers machine learning in detail, and if you are interested in computer networking, which the backbone of the Internet, and in much detail about artificial intelligence, you can look at our other books in the module.

Finally, if you found this book useful in any way, a review on Amazon is always appreciated!

Artificial Intelligence and Machine Learning for Business

How modern companies approach AI and ML in their business and how AI and ML are changing their business strategy

Scott Chesterton

Introduction

Many people still relate Artificial Intelligence (AI) with science fiction dystopias, but that tendency is slowly declining as AI expands and becomes commonplace in our daily lives.

Today, artificial intelligence is a common phrase that is used everywhere.

While acceptance of AI in the mainstream, society is a new spectacle, it is not a new idea. The new field of AI came into existence in 1956, but it took several years of work to establish substantial progress toward building an AI system and making it a reality.

When it comes to business, artificial intelligence has a wide range of application. In fact, many of us interact with artificial intelligence in one way or another daily. From the mundane to the breathtaking, AI is already changing every business process in all industries. As artificial intelligence technologies continue to develop, they are becoming necessary for a business that wants to sustain a competitive advantage.

This book will shed light on how artificial intelligence and machine learning are transforming the business sector. We shall start by exploring the basics of AI and machine learning before diving deep on the applications of AI and Machine learning. You will also learn how to implement AI in your enterprise. Keep reading to learn more.

Chapter 1: Getting Started

Ten years ago, if you said the phrase "artificial intelligence" in a boardroom, there's a high possibility you would have been laughed at. For many people, it would make them remember sci-fi machines and sentiment.

Today it is one of the most popular phrases in business and industry. AI technology is a critical lynchpin of much of the digital changes happening today as companies position themselves to take advantage of the ever-growing large size of data being produced and collected.

Well, how does this change happen? Partly is because of the Big Data revolution itself. The nature of data has resulted in extensive research into methods it can be processed, analyzed, and implemented. Machines being more suitable than humans to this work, the focus lies on training machines to perform this smartly.

This raises the interest in research in the academia-industry and other open source community which resides in the middle. It has led to various success and developments that are demonstrating their ability to generate huge change.

What is Artificial intelligence?

The idea of what describes AI has changed over time, but in the center, there has always been the concept of designing machines which can think like humans.

Human beings have shown that they can interpret the world around us and use the information we collect to implement change. If we want to create machines to assist us in doing this efficiently, then it is sensible to use ourselves as a blueprint.

AI then can be seen as awakening the potential for abstract, and creative thinking plus the ability to learn.

Research and development work in Artificial Intelligence is divided between two branches. One is called "applied AI" which applies the principles of activating human thought to implement one specific task. The other is labelled "generalized AI"-which tries to implement machine intelligence that can convert their hands to any responsibility, much like a human being.

Research conducted in applied, specialized AI is already providing success in fields of study from quantum physics where it is used to model and predict the behavior of systems.

In industry, it is applied in the financial world for uses that extend from fraud detection to enhancing customer service by predicting the services that customers may need. In manufacturing, it is used to control workforces, and production operations plus predicting faults before they happen, thus allowing predictive maintenance.

In the consumer sector, most of the technology we are applying in our daily lives is being driven by AI from smartphone assistants like Google's Google Assistant, and Apple's Siri Assistant to autonomous vehicles which many people think will come to surpass the manually driven cars within our lifetimes.

Generalized is AI far off to achieve a complete human brain activation since it would require a comprehensive understanding of the organ than we currently have, and more computing power than is now available to researchers. However, that may not last for long given the speed at which technology is changing. A new computer chip technology is known as "neuromorphic processors" is being developed to help run the brain-simulator code efficiently.

Key Developments in AI

All these developments have been realized because of the focus on imitating human thought processes. The field of research has been most successful in recent times is "machine learning." You will briefly learn about this. This field has become essential to contemporary AI that the phrases "artificial intelligence" and "machine learning" are sometimes used interchangeably.

But this an imprecise application of the language and the correct way to think of it is that machine learning demonstrates the current nature-of-the-art in the broader field of AI. The middle ground of machine learning is that instead of being taught to implement every step by step, machines if they can be instructed to think like us, can learn to work by classifying, observing, and learning from its mistakes, the same way we do.

Machine Learning Defined

One thing that both Google's self-driving car and Netflix's recommendation share is that they use machine learning to a certain level to execute repeatable decisions, implement particular tasks and independently adapt with minimal human interaction.

Machine learning can be defined as the science of making machines learn and behave similarly like humans while autonomously learning from real-world interactions and sets of training data that we feed them.

Machine learning isn't a new technology. The algorithm behind pattern recognition and machine learning application have been in existence for quite some time. But it is only now that machine learning models are beginning to connect with more complex data sets and learn from previous computations and predictions to generate important decisions and results. Develop a correct model, and you have an excellent opportunity to avoid unknown risks and select profitable opportunities across your business.

Machine Learning Tools in the Business Sector

Google, Microsoft, and Apple are some of the tech companies leading in the application of machine learning. Apple has already produced its Core ML API, which is meant to increase the speed of artificial intelligence on the iPhone. Microsoft has the Azure cloud services that include an Emotion API that can detect human emotions like anger, surprise, sadness, and disgust.

One thing that these tools share is that they are dynamic and can adapt to new rules, newly acquired information, and new environments. Right from recommendation engines to facial recognition, machine learning is the primary tool for companies that handle big data and make big decisions. In a situation where the business has to be ahead of the current threats, human error, and competition, this technology allows organizations to become agile and reactive than before.

Additionally, incorporating machine learning to improve processes and make data-driven decisions, companies should be able to control the security of their data more effectively and in ways that don't slow employees down. The solution is adequate data protection.

Machine learning supports the analysis of large data quantities. While it provides faster, and more accurate results to select profitable opportunities, it may also demand extra time and resources to train it well. Integrating machine learning with AI and cognitive technologies can make it more effective in executing large volumes of information.

Chapter 2: Why Use Machine Learning

Artificial Intelligence will transform our future more potent than any other type of innovation. The frequency of acceleration of AI is already surprising. Nowadays, there is a rapidly growing volume and variety of available data, computational processing that is cheaper and more affordable storage of data.

Machine learning and Artificial Intelligence have been around since the middle of the twentieth century but only started to become popular in the last few years. Why is that so, and why is machine learning meaningful.

As previously defined, machine learning is a field of computer science that provides the computer with the potential to learn. The main focus of machine learning is to generate algorithms that can be trained to execute a task.

It is closely connected to the field of computational statistics and mathematical optimization. It has numerous methods such as Semi-Supervised Learning, Supervised Learning, and Unsupervised Learning and Reinforcement Learning, which each contains there on algorithms and use cases.

Why Machine Learning Matters

Artificial intelligence is critical in the future. Anyone who doesn't understand it will soon be left behind. They will be surrounded by technology to the point where they may start to think it is magic.

The speed of acceleration is already shocking. In 2015, Google successfully trained a conversational agent that besides interacting with humans as a tech support helpdesk, but it could still discuss morality, respond to general fact-based questions, and express opinions.

In the same year, DeepMind builds an agent that outplayed human beings at 49 Atari games, receiving game score and pixels as inputs. In the following year, DeepMind obsoleted their success by generating a new state-of-the-art gameplay method known as A3C.

At the same time, AlphaGo defeated the best human players at Go-an outstanding achievement in a game led by humans for two decades after machines defeated chess. Many masters could not understand how it is possible for a tool to master the complete nuance and complexity of this ancient Chinese war game strategy.

To better understand machine learning uses, consider some of the situations where machine learning is applied. Some of these areas include cyber fraud detection, self-driving Google car, and online recommendation engines such as Facebook, Netflix displaying movies and shows you may like, and "more items to consider," and "identify something for yourself" on Amazon.

All these examples describe the vital role machine learning has started to perform in the current data-rich world. Machines can support filtering of critical information that can assist in significant developments. We are currently seeing how the following technology is presently being used in different industries.

With the constant change in the field, there has been a continuous rise in the application, the role of machine learning, and demands. Big data has become quite popular in the last few years, that is because of the rise in complexity of machine learning, which assists in analyzing big loads of data. Machine learning has further changed how data extraction happens, and the interpretation happens by applying automatic sets of generic methods that have substituted traditional techniques.

Chapter 3: Supervised Learning

How much money will we generate by spending more dollars on digital advertising? What may happen to the stock market tomorrow?

When it comes to problems in supervised learning, we begin with a data set that has training examples with marked labels. For instance, when you learn to categorize handwritten digits, a supervised learning algorithm will accept thousands of pictures of handwritten digits plus names holding the correct number each image represents. The algorithm will then learn the link between images and related figures, and use the learned relationship to categorize new photos that the machine hasn't seen before. This is how you can deposit a check by taking a picture using your phone.

To demonstrate how supervised learning works, let us review the challenge of predicting a yearly income based on the years of education a person has completed. Expressed formally, we would like to create a model that estimates the link f between the number of years of higher education X and related annual income Y.

$$Y = f(X) + \epsilon$$

Still, you can define a complex model by adding a few rules that explain the degree type, school tiers, and years of experience.

However, sometimes, this rule-based programming may fail to work correctly with complex data.

Supervised machine learning overcomes this challenge by letting the computer complete the work. By selecting the patterns in the data, the machine can create heuristics. The critical difference between this and human learning is that machine learning can operate on computer hardware and is best learned through statistics and computer science.

For supervised learning, the machine tries to learn the connections between income and education from square zero by executing labeled training data via a learning algorithm. This learned function can be used to approximate the income of people whose income Y is unknown, provided you have years of education X as the inputs. This means you can apply the model to the unlabeled test data to approximate Y.

The focus of supervised learning is to make accurate predictions of Y when supplied with new examples of X.

Two Functions of Supervised Learning: Classification and Regression

The regression will predict a continuous target variable Y. It will allow a person to approximate a value, such as human lifespan depending on the input data X.

In this case, the **target variable** describes the unknown variable we focus on predicting, and **continuous** means there are no gaps in the value that Y can take on. The weight and height of a person are constant values. On the other hand, discrete variables can only assume a finite number of benefits. For instance, the number of kids a person has is a separate variable.

Income prediction is a classic example of regression. The input data X is made up of all relevant information about persons in the data set that can be used to predict an income like years of education, years, job title, years of work experience, and many more. These properties are described as features, which can be numerical or categorical.

You may need a lot of training observations as possible connected to these features to the target output Y so that your model can learn the connection f between X and Y.

Data consists of test data and training data. The training data contains labels, but the test data doesn't come with tags. This means you cannot tell the value you are trying to predict. It is critical that your model can generalize to instances it hasn't come across before so that it can do well on the test data.

So how are models created that make accurate, and essential predictions in the real world? Well, this is achieved through supervised learning algorithms.

Now let us move to the exciting part: learning more about algorithms.

We will learn some of the methods to implement regression and classification, and demonstrate significant machine learning concepts throughout.

Linear Regression in Machine Learning

This is a simple model for regression problems where the target variable is a real value.

For example:

Let us begin with an example. Assume we have a dataset holding information about the location of the house and the price. Our task is to create a machine learning model which can predict the price. Here is a look of our dataset:

Area (sq.ft)	Price (1k$s)
3456	600
2089	395
1416	232

When we plot our data, we may create something that resembles this:

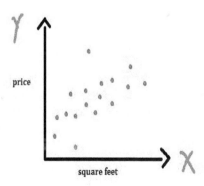

Let us dive deep into linear regression to comprehend this:

Linear regression belongs to the linear model. The model determines a relationship between input variables and the single output variable (y). They can be computed from the right mix of input variables (X).

If a single input variable is present, then it is called simple linear regression. However, multiple linear regression occurs when numerous variables are present.

Simple Linear Regression

This defines a link between the target variable, and the input variable using a regression line. Overall, a range is represented using this equation y = m * X + b. In this case, y is the dependent variable, X is the independent variable, m is the gradient, while b is the intercept.

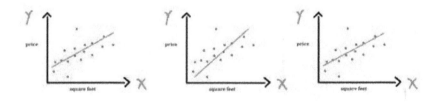

Multiple Linear Regression

The multiple linear regression equation can be applied when there is one input variable. But often you will handle datasets that have multiple input variables. A situation where there is more than one feature is called multiple linear regression, or linear regression. The previous simple linear regression can be summarized to multiple linear regression:

$$y(x) = w_0 + w_1 x_1 + w_2 x_2 + \ldots + w_n x_n$$

In the case of multiple linear regression, the prediction is a hyperplane in n-dimensional space. For instance, in the case of 3D, the plot will appear this way:

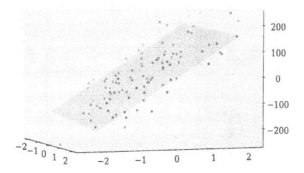

The cost functions

Different weight values provide different lines, and the task is to identify weights for which we attain the best fit. One thing that you want to find an answer is how you can determine the best line for your data. Or provided with two lines, how can you learn the best. For this, you need to create a cost function which measures, provided a value for the w's, how close is the y's to the corresponding true's. In this case, how does a specific set of weights predict the target value?

The mean squared error cost function is applied in linear regression. This is the mean over the different data points (xi, yi) of the squared error between the predicted value y(x) and the target value actual.

$$J(w) = \frac{1}{n} \sum_{i=1}^{n} (y(x^i) - y_{true}^i)^2$$

Residuals

The cost function describes a cost based on the distance between the exact target and predicted target, known as the residual. The residuals are defined as follows:

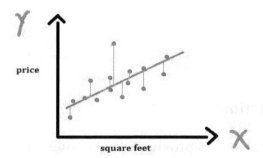

If a specific line is further from all the points, the residuals will be higher, and hence the cost function. In case a range is too close to the ends, the residuals will decrease, and thus the cost function.

Supervised Learning Use Cases in Data Science for Business

In recent years, machine learning (ML) has changed the way we run our business. A disruptive achievement that distinguishes machine learning from other techniques to automation is just a step from the rules-based programming. ML algorithms support engineers to leverage data without programming machines to adhere to a set of paths of problem-solving. But machines generate the correct answers depending on the data they receive. This ability makes business executives to reconsider the methods they use data to make decisions.

In layman language, machine learning is used to forecast on incoming data by applying historical data as a training example. For example, you may want to predict the lifetime value of a customer in an e-commerce store by determining the net profit of the future relationship with a customer. If you have historical data on various customer interactions with your website and net gains linked with these customers, you want to apply machine learning. It will support early detection of those customers who are likely to generate the net profit allowing you to concentrate more effort on them.

Although there are many learning techniques, the most common technique is supervised learning. In this section, you will learn about this field of data science and why it is low-hanging fruit for a business that plans to focus on the ML program, plus explaining the most popular use cases.

How Does the Supervised Machine Learning Operate?

Supervised machine learning requires that the expected solution to a problem is unknown for the incoming data but already is selected in a historical dataset. This means historical data have correct answers, and the role of the algorithm is to identify them in the new data.

For example, in a public dataset collected by a specific Portuguese banking institution during a 2012 marketing program, the bank focused on supporting its customers to subscribe to terms of deposits by making calls and pitching the service.

Typically, datasets are kept in tables that contain data items arranged in rows with variables in columns. The labeled data sets also include target variables, the values that need to be predicted in future data. In the following dataset, the target variable describes whether a customer has subscribed for terms of deposit after a call or not.

Unsupervised learning is used to identify defects in data that humans cannot assume themselves. It is more practical compared to reinforcement learning.

Use Cases of Supervised Learning

In 2016, Tech Emergence released results of a small survey among professional of Artificial Intelligence to describe low-hanging fruit applications in machine learning for small and large companies. Although 26 respondents could vote numerous times, they acknowledged that was evident already.

Interestingly is that groups used by Tech Emergence offered only a vague understanding of the distribution of use cases among various machine learning tasks. For instance, one can apply Big Data to any of the described groups because the algorithm can process massive and poorly structured datasets, no matter the industry and field of operation the data comes from. Additionally, sales tasks always intersect marketing ones when it comes to analytics.

age	job	marital	education	default	balance	housing	loan	contact	day	month	duration	campaign	pdays	previous	poutcome	target
30	unemployed	married	primary	no	1787	no	no	cellular	19	oct	79	1	-1	0	unknown	no
33	services	married	secondary	no	4789	yes	yes	cellular	11	may	220	1	339	4	failure	no
35	management	single	tertiary	no	1350	yes	no	cellular	16	apr	185	1	330	1	failure	no
30	management	married	tertiary	no	1476	yes	no	unknown	3	jun	199	4	-1	0	unknown	no
59	blue-collar	married	secondary	no	0	yes	no	unknown	5	may	226	1	-1	0	unknown	no
35	management	single	tertiary	no	747	no	no	cellular	23	feb	141	2	176	3	failure	no
36	self-employed	married	tertiary	no	307	yes	no	cellular	14	may	341	1	330	2	other	no
39	technician	married	secondary	no	147	yes	no	cellular	6	may	151	2	-1	0	unknown	no
41	entrepreneur	married	tertiary	no	221	yes	no	unknown	14	may	57	2	-1	0	unknown	no
43	services	married	primary	no	-88	yes	yes	cellular	17	apr	313	1	147	2	failure	no
39	services	married	secondary	no	9374	yes	no	unknown	20	may	273	1	-1	0	unknown	no
43	admin.	married	secondary	no	264	yes	no	cellular	17	apr	113	2	-1	0	unknown	no
36	technician	married	tertiary	no	1109	no	no	cellular	13	aug	328	2	-1	0	unknown	no
20	student	single	secondary	no	502	no	no	cellular	30	apr	261	1	-1	0	unknown	yes
31	blue-collar	married	secondary	no	360	yes	yes	cellular	29	jan	89	1	241	1	failure	no
40	management	married	tertiary	no	194	no	yes	cellular	29	aug	189	2	-1	0	unknown	no
56	technician	married	secondary	no	4073	no	no	cellular	27	aug	239	5	-1	0	unknown	no
37	admin.	single	tertiary	no	2317	yes	no	cellular	20	apr	114	1	152	2	failure	no
25	blue-collar	single	primary	no	-221	yes	no	unknown	23	may	250	1	-1	0	unknown	no
31	services	married	secondary	no	132	no	no	cellular	7	jul	148	1	152	1	other	no
38	management	divorced	unknown	no	0	yes	no	cellular	18	nov	96	2	-1	0	unknown	no
42	management	divorced	tertiary	no	16	no	no	cellular	19	nov	140	3	-1	0	unknown	no
44	services	single	secondary	no	106	no	no	unknown	12	jun	109	2	-1	0	unknown	no
44	entrepreneur	married	secondary	no	93	no	no	cellular	7	jul	125	2	-1	0	unknown	no
26	housemaid	married	tertiary	no	543	no	no	cellular	30	jan	169	3	-1	0	unknown	no
41	management	married	tertiary	no	5883	no	no	cellular	20	nov	182	2	-1	0	unknown	no
55	blue-collar	married	primary	no	627	yes	no	unknown	5	may	247	1	-1	0	unknown	no
67	retired	married	unknown	no	696	no	no	telephone	17	aug	119	1	105	2	failure	no
56	self-employed	married	secondary	no	784	no	yes	cellular	30	jul	149	2	-1	0	unknown	no

Using ML to this dataset will assist determine the chances of other bank clients subscribing to terms deposit.

Training an ML algorithm means entering the above data into a machine using one of the mathematical approaches. The process supports the creation of a model that can define the target variable in future data. In this case, the role of an algorithm would be to categorize data items into two forms (yes/no). In general, supervised learning works with three major tasks:

Binary classification: The instance of binary classification is demonstrated above. The algorithm divides data into two sections.

Multiple classifications: In this approach, the algorithm selects between more than two types of responses for a target variable.

Regression: Regression models predict a constant value, while classification models focus on categorical ones. For example, predicting a net profit as a determinant of a customer lifetime value is a standard regression problem.

Challenges That Should Be Highlighted for Supervised Learning

Data Collection

Data is the central aspect of ML. The more data records you have, the better chance you have to create accurate models. You will learn more about data collection later on.

Labeling Data

In the previous example, labeling data doesn't appear like a hard task. If the data collection was carried out well, the labels were defined after the marketing call or after the campaign was over. But, typically, things are much complex than that.

Let us say you want to separate rotten apples from good ones automatically. And if you use image recognition methods, you will need to create a broad set of images comprising of rotten and good ones. Then you will need to place labels to them manually. Since image recognition can only work when you have thousands of examples, labeling may consume a lot of time.

In 2006, Google decided to crowdsource their image labeling by recommending to users a game-like experience that allowed them to label images hence contribute to the company's AI-development. Amazon also crowdsourced their labeling tasks through the development of a mechanical Turk platform where people can make money by allocating data labels.

Marketing and Sales

Digital marketing and online-driven sales are the major application fields that you may consider when you think of adopting machine learning. People interact with the web and leave a specific footprint to be reviewed. While there are substantive results in unsupervised learning techniques for marketing and sales, the most significant value impact falls in the supervised learning field.

Human Resource Allocation

The historical data from HR software, holidays, and vacations can be used to make expansive predictions concerning the workforce. Several automotive companies are learning from the patterns of unscheduled absences to predict the period when people may spend a day off and retain more workforce.

Time-series market prediction

This is an essential branch of machine learning, and statistics describe the time-dependent events. These can be cyclic changes in any market figures. Overall, time-series prediction takes into consideration time-dependent changes as seasons or holidays.

Today, time-series data can be applied both internal to ensure better planning features and for customer-facing applications. For example, eCommerce websites may be interested in monitoring time-series data linked to Black Friday to create discount campaigns better and make more sales.

Security

Most of the cyber-security methods revolve around unsupervised learning, especially the techniques that focus on anomaly detection. Discovering data items that may cause a threat. But there are different use cases where supervised learning is applied.

Filtering of spams: In 2017, 56.87 percent of all emails were spam. The abundance of spam examples supports both textual and metadata to filter this form of correspondence.

Malicious emails and connections: To detect malicious attacks is essential for all IT offices in organizations. Nowadays, different types of public datasets offer labeled records of malware that can be directly applied to create classifying models to secure your organization.

Asset Management and IoT

Digitalization goes past internal IT infrastructure. As corporate assets continue to become smart using the Internet-of-Things, different smart sensors can collect and stream asset data directly to public clouds where it can be centralized and further applied in resource management and supply chain enhancement.

Logistics: Finding solutions to logistics cases is a dynamic task because managers need to account for the delivery time, whether focus, budget, and driver's features, and other changing data. Since supply chain management is a big challenge for many businesses that have real datasets and assets, then creating AI-backed recommendation systems is a great opportunity that can be adapted easily.

Prediction of outage: Another great opportunity is to make use of the history of machinery outages to predict early failures. Complicated ML algorithms can predict based on apparent factors that humans may not know. This makes it possible to support the maintenance of lower cost. And this method suits industries where asset management has been highly controlled.

Entertainment

Another use case field for machine learning is entertainment. In this field, users interact with algorithms directly. These can drive the gamut from face recognition and various visual alterations. This sector belongs to AI startups that plan acquisition and software shipping that can be embedded in different market products.

Jumpstarting machine Learning involves data

The most approachable industry for supervised learning is those that produce the most data, which can be organized and centralized inside a company. In case the data sets have been already labeled, this makes it easy to adopt.

As the business continues to become digital, the data they gather may become more ML-friendly. This means paper ledgers and spreadsheets used in offices disappear for good, while CRM and different tracking systems reach the plateau of standard practice.

So the first thing to jumpstart the machine learning program is to examine the data and consider a classification plan and terms of regression to describe the type of responses you can acquire.

Chapter 4: Unsupervised learning

Unlike supervised learning, when it comes to unsupervised learning, the dataset doesn't have a label. What you will perhaps learn, when there are no labels, is how to reconstruct the input data using a representation. Given the low percent of labeled data around the world, the notion that supervised learning cannot be used in most data, and the fact that models can learn best when more data is trained, the opportunity for unsupervised learning on datasets without labels is massive. The future of AI, in large part, relies on unsupervised learning become better and better.

The properties acquired by deep neural networks can be applied in clustering, regression, and classification. Neural nets are typically universal approximators applying non-linearities. They generate "good" properties by learning to compile data via pretraining. In the latter case, neural nets get into arbitrary loss functions to integrate inputs to outputs.

The properties learned by neural networks can be directed into other types of algorithms, including traditional machine-learning algorithms that combine input, logistic regression that classifies it, or simple regression that predicts a value.

So, you can consider neural networks as an aspect that regularly combines into other functions. For instance, you can create a convolutional neural network to learn the image properties on

ImageNet using supervised training, and then you could pick the features learned through a neural network and transfer them into a second algorithm that would learn to group images.

Here are properties of use cases build using neural networks

K-means Clustering

This algorithm is used to automatically label stimulations depending on their raw distances from other input in a vector space. There is no loss or target function; k-means has centroids. It builds centroids using repeated averaging of all the data points. K-means defines new data by proximity to a certain centroid. Each centroid is connected to a label. This is an excellent example of unsupervised learning.

The primary function of clustering is to generate data points groups.

Steps of K-Means Clustering

1. Definition of the k centroids. These will be initialized at random. They are also better algorithms for initializing the centroids that create more convenience.

2. Find the nearest centroid and update the cluster assignments. Allocate each data point to every k clusters. Every data point is allocated to the closest centroid's group. In this case, the measure of "nearness" is a hyperparameter.

3. Transfer the centroids to the center of their clusters. The new position of every centroid is computed as the average position of all data points within the group.

Continue repeating steps 2 and three until when the centroid stop is moving at every iteration.

That is a brief description of how k-means clustering operates.

A real-life application of k-means clustering is defining handwritten digits.

Hierarchical Clustering

Hierarchical clustering resembles regular clustering, except that you focus on creating a hierarchy of clusters. This can be important when you need flexibility in the number of groups you want. For example, think of arranging items on an online marketplace like Amazon. On the homepage, you may need specific broad categories of items for easy navigation, but as you get specific, you will want to increase the levels of granularity.

In the case of outputs from an algorithm, the cluster assignments also create a great tree that notifies you about the hierarchies between the clusters. Next, you can select the number of groups you require from this tree.

Steps for hierarchical clustering

1. Begin with N clusters, one belonging to each data point.

2. Integrate two clusters close to each other. Now you will have N-1 groups.

3. Recalculate the distances between the clusters. There are different ways to achieve this. One of them is the average linkage clustering. In this approach, you need to consider the distance between two clusters as the average distance between all the respective numbers.

4. Repeat steps 2 and three until you find a single cluster of N data points. You see a tree as the dendrogram.

5. Select different clusters and draw a horizontal line inside the dendrogram. In this example, if you want k=2 groups, you need to bring a horizontal line around a certain distance.

The curious pupil in unsupervised learning

For several decades, machine learning has attained massive progress in different sectors. These successes have highly been achieved through deep neural networks. Both approaches require a training signal to be developed by a human and transferred to the computer. Therefore, the limits of learning are regulated by human trainers.

While some scientists think comprehensive training is enough to give rise to general intelligence, some believe that real knowledge will demand more independent learning approaches.

Take, for instance, how a toddler learns, her grandmother may sit with her and show her cars, or reward her with a gift for completing a puzzle. However, most of the toddler's time is spent exploring the world, trying to understand her surrounding, play, and make observations.

Unsupervised learning is an approach developed to build autonomous intelligence by gifting agents with rewards for learning something about the data they observe without a specific task in mind. This means the agent learns for learning.

An excellent motivation for unsupervised learning is that, although the data transferred to the learning algorithms are rich in internal structure, the targets and rewards applied in training are generally sparse. This means that a massive percentage of what is learned by an algorithm must include understanding the data itself instead of using the knowledge to a specific task.

Learning by Creating

Probably, the most straightforward goal for unsupervised learning is to train an algorithm to produce its own data instance. These are referred to as generative models, not only reproduce the data prepared, but create a model of the class from which the data was extracted. The guiding rule of generative models can create a convincing data example.

For images, the best generative model has been the Generative Adversarial Network (GAN) where two networks-a generators and discriminator take part in a contest of discernment.

The generator releases images to challenge the discriminator to believe they are real. Meanwhile, the discriminator receives a reward for detecting the fakes.

The reproduced images, random and messy, are enhanced over numerous iterations, and the ongoing dynamic between the network results to ever-more realistic images that are, in most cases, indistinguishable from real photographs. Generative adversarial networks can also produce details of landscapes determined by rough sketches of users.

Developing by Predicting

It is a notable family inside unsupervised learning. Here data is divided into a sequence of tiny parts, each of which is anticipated in turn. These models can be used to produce data successively by guessing what will arrive next, entering the guess as input and making a guess. Language models where every word is predicted from words before it is the best-known example. These models run the text predictions that appear on some messaging apps and email. A recent development in language modeling has allowed the production of plausible passages.

An exciting inconsistency within the text is that unicorns are considered as "four-horned," it is essential to probe the problems of the network's understanding.

By regulating the input sequence used to control the predictions, autoregressive models can be used to change one course into another.

Autoregressive models learn about data by trying to predict each piece of it in a specific order. A general class of unsupervised learning algorithms can be created by predicting any section of the data. This may involve excluding a word from a sequence, and trying to predict it from the remainder.

By learning how to create localized predictions, the system is forced to learn the whole data. A significant worry about generative models is the ability for misuse. Altering video and photo evidence has been achievable for a long time; generative models could make it easier to edit media with malicious reasons.

Re-imagining intelligence

Generative models are essential in their ways. Waiting for an agent with the potential to produce data is a means of imagination, and thus the possibility to plan and reason about the future. Even without explicit generation, the studies indicate that learning to predict various features of the environment enhances the agent's world model, and thus raises the ability to find solutions to problems.

These results synchronize with our intuitions about the human mind. The potential to learn about the world without explicit guidance is the reason for what we refer to as intelligence.

Implementing supervised and unsupervised learning in your business

Machine learning can be an excellent tool for creating actionable business insights from big data. However, machine learning algorithms differ in the way they apply data to learn, with critical implications for business applications. Learning how supervised and unsupervised techniques work and the differences between them is important to automate your business.

Supervised learning

Supervised machine learning expects data scientists to train the algorithm to generate the correct result for a particular input dataset. Typically, this requires feeding the algorithm with massive data, along with the conclusions that the machine needs to extract from the data.

With sufficient training data, the machine learning algorithm should develop the correct conclusions when transformed to lose on new data.

This is a unique algorithm when it comes to business with the bandwidth to train the algorithm because it can be used to complete tasks from error-correcting financial audits to automate unstructured data entry.

Supervised machine learning algorithms can be applied as cognitive automation to support image recognition and draw information from unstructured data.

The drawback to supervised learning is that it extracts data. Most importantly, that data should be manually curated by human beings before training the algorithm.

Data has to be labeled based on a defined set of input variables and classified into a limited set of output possibilities. While more training data will result in an accurate algorithm, this process demands additional labor and depends heavily on having a stockpile of historical data.

Unsupervised learning

Unsupervised learning is much more complicated than supervised learning, but it creates doors for a particular set of applications. Unsupervised learning doesn't have a training phase. However, the algorithm is provided with a dataset and uses the variables inside the data to select and separate natural clusters.

The benefit of the following algorithm is that it doesn't need the same labor-intensive data curation that supervised learning demands. Secondly, unsupervised learning can detect patterns that cannot be seen by humans because of the human biases during analysis.

A significant application of unsupervised learning is customer segmentation. In this example, the algorithm is naturally blind to underlying biases in the way the company may focus on its customer demographics. The result is that unsupervised learning can generate a particular set of customer segments, with inferences for marketing practices.

In conclusion

Data scientists use different types of machine learning algorithms to identify patterns in big data that result in actionable insights.

Supervised machine learning is popularly used between the two. It includes algorithms like linear and logistic regression, and enable vector machines. Supervised learning is named so because of data scientist performs the role of a guide to train the algorithm what conclusions it should develop.

Supervised learning requires that the expected output of the algorithm is known plus the data used to list the correct answers.

For instance, a classification algorithm will identify pictures of cars once it is fed with a dataset of images that have been labeled with the names of vehicles and some features of identification.

On the flipside, unsupervised machine learning is focused on artificial intelligence. The concept that a computer can learn to detect complex processes and patterns without a human to guide.

While unsupervised learning is complicated for specific business use cases, it sets the path to solve challenges that humans would want to handle. Examples of unsupervised machine learning algorithm include k-means clustering.

Although a supervised classification algorithm depends on entered labeled images, the unsupervised algorithm will determine inherent similarities between the models and separate the groups accordingly.

Chapter 5: Building Machines to be More Like Us

The function of Artificial Intelligence in business has changed from initial sci-fi notions of movie robots and talking doors. In a world where human-machine interface technologies change at a terrific speed and one where talking doors are a more of a reality, the more imperfect and almost human the next developments of AI can be, the more "perfect" it becomes.

Now we can apply AI tools to decide whether social media outputs-Flickr images, tweets, Instagram posts are being produced by software bots programmed by malicious hackers or whether they were created by genuine humans. The critical thing here is that computers are still slightly too perfect when they complete any task that emulates human behavior.

Even when programmed to include common misspellings and the phrases of the local language, AI is still flawless. Humans are more interactive, more context-aware, more relaxed, and altogether imperfectly entertaining. Programming in sarcasm and traits of human personality are always a significant risk. It appears like medical developments like robots taking over risky tasks and automation of difficult tasks are some of the significant benefits that AI can bring to people of all types.

Martin Moran-director at InsideSales, a company that focuses on self-learning engine for sales acceleration highlights engineering, customer service, and administration as the areas set for AI growth.

"Essentially, it is the admin-heavy departments that stand to benefit most from AI today. We have taken AI out of the movies and reached the tangible 2.0 generation of cognitive intelligence," he says.

Moran believes that the next step of AI will emulate humans more closely and be developed on the ground of massive processing power, access to large amounts of data and highly complex algorithmic logic, similar to our brains. Similarly, the right and lasting effect on business will only occur if this AI intelligence is deeply rooted in the workflow process itself.

The state at which we can interplay the nuances of natural language understanding with human behavior trends in their right contextual environment pushes us to a higher level of AI machine control. The ability to develop AI using idiomatic peculiarities of actual people could make it possible to apply AI in real business workshops, offices, and factories. Well, how can we build machines to be more like us?

Operational Intelligence company Splunk says the right way to entirely change AI exists in the machines, and not in any study of humans in the first instance.

The foundation of machine learning lies in the insights that can be generated through analysis of humans using machines by the data left on those machines.

Every human interaction with a machine leaves a trace of machine data. Extracting this data provides us with an accurate record of our exact human behavior, from our activity on an online store to who we communicate with or where we travel through the geolocation setting on a device.

The majority of this type of data is only partially retained by most organizations, and some of it isn't traced at all. When we begin to digitize and locate the world around us to a more granular level, then we can start to develop more human-like AI that has a closer reflection of our behavior.

The central aspect that AI requires to focus on is where it fits more naturally into what we may refer to as the narrative of human interactions. AI intelligence has to be intrinsically embedded in the fabric of the way firms operate. Only then can the AI brain begin to learn about the imperfect world surrounding us. Humans require to adapt to a future where we need to interact with and work alongside computer brains every day.

A new report released by the Project Literacy campaign, overseen and convened by learning services company Pearson, predicts that the present speed of advancement in technology driven by AI technology will come to defeat the illiteracy level of more than one in twenty British adults in the next 8years.

Machine reading isn't mastering the complete nuances of the human language. But progress in technology means that it is likely machines will attain illiteracy potential surpassing those of 16 percent British people in the next decade. This is according to professor Brendan O'Connor of the University of Massachusetts Amherst.

What will happen next with AI is emotional? This means AI will manage to understand, categorize, and then act upon human emotions. Typically, this work has been straightforward. A picture of a person smiling and showing their teeth is probably happy. An individual with furrowed eyebrows may be angry or frustrated and so forth. Of late, we have begun to include additional contextual details about what the user may be doing, or where they may be situated, then a correct picture of mood and emotions is developed.

The natural language interaction company Artificial Solutions believes it is working on the next generation of AI cognizance. By building a world full of computer "conversations" that are a world from what we may consider being textbook English.

Artificial Solutions is working hard to develop AI that recognizes bad human habits and can acknowledge our unpredictable colloquial distinctions. AI today is at the point of becoming emotionally sensitive, believably naturalistic, and humanly imperfect. So be kind to your computer. It is about to get closer to you.

Chatbots Can Learn What You Want

The next change in customer service is powered by artificial intelligence so companies can start to focus on consumers with products based on their taste.

There was a time when it looked ridiculous to think artificial intelligence could be used to create a more human-like customer experience. Well, but that is what AI is being used today. AI examines a large amount of emotional and behavioral data in a move to communicate with us and generate brand experiences that are predictive and personalized.

When Unilever decides to incorporate AI in its operation in a move to increase the sale of Lipton tea, then you know times are changing.

AI is providing retailers with new strategies to ensure shopping is straightforward. The modern cognitive technology can understand, learn, reason, and interact the same way human beings do. This is a rapidly changing field.

IBM Watson, the company's cognitive computing service, was conducted by North Face-an outdoor clothing brand to drive their virtual shopping assistant. Artificial Intelligence supports shoppers to complete their online shopping by picking the correct jacks depending on their responses to questions linked to where they will use it, and when they will use it.

US department store chain Macy developed a shopping smartphone app driven by machine learning. This app allows customers to shop and ask questions like where a brand is found, and whether an item is out of stock.

AI will continue to be used to solve problems for customers instead of selling products. Advertisers can now spend effectively on their ads. Retailers can consider past behavior patterns, and personalize offers correctly.

We are living in times where cognitive technologies can be trained by the most experienced employees and this knowledge transferred to all staff and customers directly.

Various trends have powered recent developments. First, there has been a dramatic rise in the size of data associated with consumer behaviour. Secondly, computational power to support AI is more affordable. Thirdly, there is a big development in key AI techniques and machine learning algorithms.

When it comes to the organizational side, AI has caused a massive change in the way companies to look at the role of AI in building customer experiences. Although corporations thought that AI conflicted with the human design of experiences, they now acknowledge that it improves efforts.

Although many companies felt like AI interfered with human design experiences, now they see that it improves the experiences.

AI is doing well for subscription companies which sell and curate beauty products and clothes. Most e-commerce stores have applied AI to act as virtual personal shoppers to fill the gap left by shoppers who don't have time to shop.

There is no argument that AI has allowed companies to build a personalized experience that can predict what will embrace customers across the world.

For example, look-alike modelling where companies automatically detect the features of current customers and create an online platform for a lookalike collection of new prospects.

Application of similarity metrics makes it possible to micro-segment customers by detecting subtle patterns in behaviour that bind them.

AI has created a new playing field when it comes to the development of customer experience. If you have a powerful data and you can execute it with intelligence, smaller and savvy online customers can improve the grade too.

According to AI board level stuff Mr Singh, the current world is in an arms race and weapons n are adapting algorithms. The algorithms, transparency, and application will shape the competitive landscape.

The next phase of AI is concerned with personalization, where brands want to merchandise products depending on personal preference.

Retailers have been discussing personalization for years, but it has been an inspiration. So far, anyone with the potential to execute AI at scale, it is possible. Paradoxically, AI can customize experiences without the need to know personal information at all, but just by looking at online behavioural trends.

Computers conversing with humans

The chief strategy officer of Artificial Solutions Andy Peart says that through the application of Teneo Analytics Suite, computer brains are being trained to create sentences together to understand and successfully follow human conversation interaction.

Nowadays, computers have become smarter. What is important now based on the way computers react with us, complete speech, and display features of artificial intelligence is not simple as machines having the ability to "hear" us or react to our commands.

Now we want computers to understand us and create a degree of contextual awareness associated to what we are talking about. It is like we need to have "conversations" with other devices.

Why is computer speech recognition a bit thin in the first place?

Human languages are filled with colloquial terms, changeable dialects and a different accent. Then there is the problem with homonyms-words said the same way but with different meanings, so it is hard for a machine to differentiate between site, cite and sight. For example, cricket is an insect, and also a game.

Why does it seem hard to give computers a conversational power?

As smart as it is, plain old automated speech identification technology has begun to be commoditized and, in some cases, made free. What is happening is breaking sentences up into blocks and offering contextual conversation memory. For instance, a virtual assistant can send a single request to the user's previous comment or question.

When computers started speaking to us, it was based on a simple children's language. Some of the voices were designed for children. My Speak & Spell was a box with a handle and a small green screen that tested skills in a grating tone.

But for adults, the clunky computerized voices of the 1980s, '90s, and early laughs were from real. When the train's voice said that the next stop was Port Chester using two phrases instead of Dorchester, then you knew that was a machine. It could not tell that New Yorkers pronounced the word as one instead of two. Put simply, a voice that sounded like a human was a person, and a voice that sounded like a machine was a machine.

This was okay when all we wanted were basic announcements with short phrases. However, if a fire erupts in a train, we all want to hear a human voice addressing us-and not just it would relax our nerves. It is because automated voices are very hard for us to understand for anything longer than a shorter sentence. We have adapted to interpret nonverbal voice cues while we listen to our fellow humans, and we get lost when they are missing.

If we want to replace assistants with Google Assistant, or we want an actual conversation with Alexa for the future, it has to speak like a human. Responding to verbal cues and sticking to the rhythm, music, and freewheeling flow of human conversation. To be truly important to us, we require computers to behave like humans. And that is really difficult.

What makes it hard? Prosody. That is the tone, intonation, stress, and rhythm that provides our voices with their special stamp. It is not the words we speak-it is the way we say the words. The great secret to the human voice is the melodies. Beyond the actual words we use, there is a lot that is going on that is difficult to teach a computer all of it.

What we hear currently are enhanced human voices, selected for us by the people who created them.

Intonation is a mix of four qualities: tone, intensity, speech, and loudness. A person can perform multiple combinations of these qualities while speaking, but Siri cannot.

There is always a limitation to what a machine can do. For instance, it can only speak what was fed, and each of us is special in different ways. When you are feeling happy, you have different means to reveal your happiness in your voice. The drawback is that we cannot feed that into a computer. This is a tough problem for engineers: algorithms have a limitation, but the human voice is not limited.

Some tech companies have solved this problem by picking a human voice with many personalities to include in their A.I-which then combines them to create speech.

So what you hear now and in the coming years are transformed human voices, selected for us by the people who build them.

As the voices improve, it is vital for the system not to trick you. You require a signal to the listener that it's a robot.

We are still in that period before fake voices start to compete with the real voice. Even with the various complications that exist, experts believe that we are left with a few advancements and computers will converse with humans. Reaching that point will solve various technological problems but will generate as many legal and ethical ones.

So, can artificial solutions make computer conversations more human-like?

It is not just a matter of them being human-like, although we have to build a new level of informal realism that is tangible and can even be chatty if you want.

Interactions like human memory power, and one that features "meta-level" awareness of the entire world, as long as the awareness is extracted from the internet. The free-format unstructured content in most of the human conversations makes it difficult for computers to establish the true intent of a user.

Chapter 6: Visualizing the Predictive Model's Analytical Results

Typically, you need to display the results of your predictive analytics to those who are essential. Below are some methods to apply visualization techniques to present the results of your models to the stakeholders.

Visualizing Hidden Groupings Within Your Data

Data clustering refers to the process of unearthing hidden groups of connected items inside your data. Most of the time, a cluster is made up of data objects of the same type as social network users, emails, and text documents. One way you can view the results of a data-clustering model is demonstrated in the graph. The graph represents clusters that were found in data gathered from social network users.

The data linked to customers were gathered in a tabular format, and then a clustering algorithm was applied to the data, and the three clusters were found: wandering customers, loyal customers, and discount customers. Imagine that the X and Y axis represent two principal components produced from the original data. Principal component analysis refers to a data reduction technique.

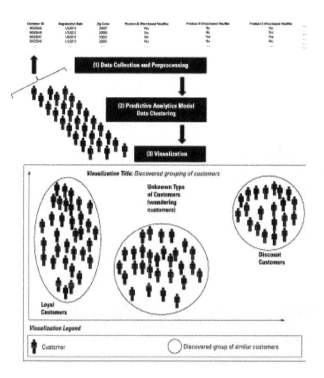

In this case, the connections between the three groups already describe where improved and targeted marketing efforts may perform most of the good.

Visualizing Data Classification Results

A classification model often assigns the specific class to a new data point it examines. The individual courses can include groups developed from clustering work.

Once you apply a clustering algorithm and identify groups in a customer data, you enter into a moment of reality: you get a new customer, and you want the model to describe the type of customer he or she will be.

The picture displays information on how a new customer detail is fed into the predictive analytics model, which then predicts the group of customers the new customer belongs to.

Customers A, B, and C are about to be assigned clusters based on the classification model. The application of a classification model results in a prediction where Customer A would belong to loyal customers, Customer B would be a wanderer, and Customer C would show up for the discount.

Determining Whether Your Machine Learning Model Has the Correct Performance

Once you create a machine learning model for your predictive modeling problem, how can you tell whether the performance of the model is good?

This is a commonly asked question beginners face.

Beginners always search for a solution to this question. You want someone to tell you whether the accuracy of x% or an error score of x is good or not.

In this section, you will learn the answer to this question and know whether your model is good or not.

Model skill is relative

Your predictive modeling task is special.

This consists of individual data, the tools you are applying, and the skill you will attain.

Your predictive modeling challenge hasn't been solved before. In other words, you cannot tell how a good model appears, or the kind of skill it may have.

You may have clues of what a skillful model appears as depending on the knowledge of the domain, but you aren't sure where the skill scores are attainable.

The best thing you can do is to compare the operation of machine learning models on your data to other models trained on the same data.

The baseline model skill

Since the performance of machine learning is relative, it is important to build a strong baseline. A baseline is straightforward and easy to follow the procedure for generating a prediction on the predictive modeling task. The skill of this particular model presents the foundation for the least acceptable performance of a machine learning model on your dataset.

The results generated from a baseline model displays the point from which the skill of all other models trained on the data can be achieved.

Examples of baseline models include:

- Predict the mean outcome result for a regression challenge.

- Predict the mode result value for a classification task.

- Predict the input as the output.

The baseline performance on your task can be used as the yardstick by which other models can be evaluated.

If a model attains a result below the baseline, something is wrong, or the model is not right for your problem.

What is the best score?

If you are dealing with a classification problem, the best score is always 100% accuracy.

But if you are dealing with a regression problem, the correct score is 0.0 error.

These scores are hard to achieve. All predictive modeling tasks have a prediction error. The error originates from various sources like:

- Noise in the data

- the incompleteness of the data sample

- Stochastic property of the modeling algorithm

You cannot attain the best score, but it is important to understand the best possible performance depends on your selected measure. You understand that actual model results will include a range between the baseline and the best possible outcome.

However, you need to look at the space of potential models on your dataset and identify what good and bad scores appear.

Identify the Limits of Model Skill

Once you select the baseline, you can decide to look at the extent of model performance on a predictive model challenge.

To identify a model that you can showcase works well in determining predictions on your specific dataset.

There are many approaches to this challenge. Two ways that you may want to try out include:

- Start High: Pick a machine learning method that is complex and known to work well on different predictive model problems like gradient boosting. Review the model on your problem and apply the result as a benchmark, look for the simplest model that realizes the same performance.

- Exhaustive Search: Review all the machine learning approaches that you imagine on the problem, and choose the method that attains the correct performance about the baseline.

The "Start High" approach is fast and can allow you to choose the boundaries of the model skill to expect on the challenge and identify a simple model that can attain the same results. It can still allow you to determine whether the problem is predictable fast, which is important because not all tasks are predictable.

The "Exhaustive Search" is slow and meant for long-running projects where a model skill is critical than any other concern.

Both methods will generate a population model performance score that you can compare to the baseline.

Why should you be sensitive when applying a predictive model to score new datasets?

The creation of a predictive model is a complex procedure, which involves different assumptions, challenges, and acknowledging the truth of what is being modeled. Models are not just created because a person is motivated to build one. A model is created from a well-defined theoretical conceptualization of the truth that is being modeled. Keeping that in mind, the modeler searches for the required datasets, which he knows can be used to create a model to predict results that are likely to attain whatever result that is being predicted.

Therefore, it is practically repetitive and irrelevant always to create models to predict the same results using "good" historical data of the reality that is being modeled. Once a model is created, it can be applied on new data tables with the same historical data and context used to create the model with knowledge of what is being predicted and what the historical nature of the new data appears like.

For instance, an auto insurance company creates a predictive model to address new customers who may want to enroll in their auto insurance policy, but need to score new customers to know the risks of using a range of variables. The insurance company requires to identify a score for every customer, which could be applied in the computation of their insurance cost and premium plus the risk that could be predicted and the associated liability.

A predictive model that is already created can be subjected to these new customers to calculate their predictive scores, which represent the level of risk. In determining the new dataset, it is critical that every variable applied in the model development is demonstrated in the new data table that is scored. Once the model is used on the new data table, a predictive score of the risks is calculated, and the score can be used by their system to determine the cost of insurance per year. The higher the score, the more unlikely you will generate a substantial effect to the insurance company in turns of the number of claims in a certain year. The lower your score, the more likely you will submit a claim. The scores can be arranged into decile.

That said, there could be a lot of things wrong with this technique. The assumptions applied both theoretically and in the application itself could result in negative results.

It is vital that you learn the historical context of the data that you want to model, or what you want to apply a model on.

A retail company may choose to build a predictive model to examine the type of catalog campaign features a higher performance. The historical nature of every campaign has to be understood clearly. As a result, building a model using historical circulation data of a certain catalog campaign and applying that model to score other campaigns may generate positive and negative results.

Predictive Modeling Techniques
Definition of predictive analytics

It is the use of statistical algorithms, and machine –learning techniques to compute the probability of future results depending on the historical data.

The focus is to go beyond descriptive statistics and demonstrate what has happened.

Predictive models have a known result and can be applied in building prediction results for new data. The results of modeling reflect the probability of the target variable.

A lot of companies are using predictive analytics to boost their operations and generate a competitive advantage using predictive analytics.

And the reason is that:

- It is faster and requires cheaper computers.

- Increasing volume and data type plus a lot of interest to generate important information.

- Harder economic status and a need for competitive differentiation.

Since the software has become more interactive and easy to use, predictive analytics isn't just a field of statisticians and mathematicians. Business professionals are also using these technologies.

Predictive modeling techniques have become the best tool in a marketing expert for enhancing the effect of campaigns and illustrate the return on investment.

With creative methods to improve data appears a focused, driven method to applying the correct content in front of the audience, at the right time. As long as teams access clean, and quality data, the ability to create campaigns to connect a target audience is better than ever.

This section will review some of the common predictive modeling approaches, with a major focus on three different types:

- Propensity models

- Intelligent recommendations

- Segmentation models

Within each category, you will identify five predictive modeling approaches your business can begin to implement immediately you have the tools in place to make it happen.

Segmentation models

The idea of customer segmentation has a long history in the marketing sector. What was once thought as an educated guess, has become a strategic approach fueled and assisted by hard data?

Below are predictive modeling approaches that help you to improve customer data to develop a refined audience for your campaigns.

1. Behavioral clustering

While leads convert customers, the path that directs them to conversion becomes valuable for a marketer concerned on leveraging predictive analytics.

That information, referred to as behavioral data, means fairly little alone. When integrated with demographic data, it inspires marketing teams to select commonalities and trends that build new target segments.

By pushing future leads that resemble the demographic background of that new target segment with the same series of behavioral actions, marketers can enhance conversions and correctly predict the effect of their campaigns.

2. Share of wallet estimation

This technique describes the percentage of a customer's budget that has been assigned toward your solution. The higher the percentage, the less likely that growth may occur through upselling or cross-sell opportunities.

When this technique is joined with product-based clustering, a correct share of wallet estimation indicates the amount of customer's budget is with competitors as well as the services or products you can sell to the customer to boost your wallet share percentage.

3. The likelihood of churn

Most marketers use predictive analytics purely for lead generation; this is wrong because the defensive abilities of strong predictive modeling are an exciting use cases.

Since it can be more expensive to get a new customer versus maintain a current customer, securing your current client-base should be the most important aspect across all industries.

You are determining a customer's ability to generate leverages of the same methodology created to classify possible leads by behavior. If you can correctly predict the chances of a lead converting a new customer, you can accurately determine the probability of the customer leaving.

Predictive modeling depends on quality data

None of this can take place without the presence of clean, quality data assisted by the best data management system. Quality data is the bedrock from which accurate predictive analytics depends on.

Chapter 7: Neural Networks and Deep Learning

What is Deep Learning?

Both deep learning and machine learning fall under artificial intelligence, but deep learning represents the next transformation of machine learning.

When it comes to machine learning, algorithms developed by human programmers are responsible for learning from data. They make decisions depending on what they have learned from data. Deep learning achieves that using an artificial neural network that acts similar to the human brain and enables the machine to analyze data in a format same as humans.

Deep learning machines don't need a human programmer to show them what to do with the available data.

Real World Examples of Deep Learning Models & AI

For many of us, concepts such as deep learning and AI are still unique. Most people who come across these terms for the first time respond with mixed feelings. How is it possible to make machines learn and implement job meant for humans? What defines a whole industry build upon making devices act like humans?

Although these questions are critical and demand discussion, it is easy to do away with a lot of skepticism. That means if we are ready to consider some real-world applications of deep learning and AI. This chapter will explore ways AI and deep learning are transforming industries.

Where Does Deep Learning Originate?

Both machine learning and deep learning are branches of AI. Deep learning is the advanced stage of ML. When it comes to ML, human programmers build algorithms that learn from data and perform analyses.

Deep learning differs from machine learning because it works on an artificial neural network which closely represents the brain of a human being. The same network enables machines to analyze data in the same way humans do. These machines with deep learning abilities do not need to implement the commands of human programmers.

Deep learning is realized through the vast amounts of data that we generate and use daily. Every deep learning model takes advantage of the data to support data processing.

Deep Learning Simplified

Artificial Intelligence is the most severe progress in human development. If you are reading this, probably you know concepts such as ML and deep learning.

So continue reading if you want to know more about how deep learning operates, and what is its position in AI and ML.

Deep learning is related to the emulation of human beings using the software.

Now that you know a lot about ML and AI. You may be asking these questions:

1. What is the function of deep learning in AI and machine learning?

2. How does deep learning operate?

1. What is the function of deep learning in AI and ML?

Both ML and deep learning belong to the same category of AI. Now, AI is a broad term. It is not something absolute.

In general, everything that we can do with machines and software that can emulate human intelligence is part of AI. It is found in certain technologies being used today.

Thus, in the following context, deep learning and machine learning are probably two methods, two methods to realize the condition of AI. But deep learning and machine learning are not independent of each other.

In other words, deep learning can include specific properties of machine learning, but the terms and application of machine learning do not require any properties.

Machine learning can be defined as a branch of AI where software programs can change their algorithms without the need for human involvement. Although traditional algorithms depend on input from engineers for changes in their functions, machine learning algorithms can manage to do so depending on the data used to train them.

Well, where does deep learning stands when compared with machine learning?

As said before, ML algorithms can change their algorithm to generate the right result. But an ML program has to be manually altered by an expert in case its predictions are inaccurate. However, the dataset used to train the ML algorithms have to be labeled and organized in a certain which allows the program to learn.

For instance, if you would like an ML program to learn to distinguish between images of dogs and cats, you need to feed the algorithm with different cat and dog images. However, it would only start to learn if you specifically label and organize the data in a means which supports the ML algorithm to master the differences between those animals' images.

Now you understand the challenges of ML, and the way an algorithm can alter its algorithm depending on the data fed isn't sufficient to activate human intelligence.

And this the point where deep learning comes in. Although ML attempts to activate human intelligence by mastering datasets and changing algorithms, deep learning strives to emulate the roles of the human brain itself.

Describing Deep Learning

Deep learning is a branch of ML. The link between deep learning and ML occurs because both have a role in AI. Additionally, both concepts work on the same principle. And that is changing algorithms without human involvement to generate the right result.

But unlike machine learning programming, deep learning network doesn't have to master the predicted outcome, but they can utilize unlabeled and unstructured raw data to generate the best results.

Alternatively, deep learning networks don't depend on a single layer of algorithms to generate results; these apply multiple layers of AI to process data and generate output.

What are artificial neural networks?

Artificial neural networks try to emulate the function of natural neural networks of the human brain. Therefore, to understand the way ANN operates, let us quickly learn how the neural networks inside our brains work.

Say, if I instruct you to choose a picture of a certain breed of dog among 10 different dog pictures, then you will need to look at each of the 10 pictures and ask yourself several questions to determine the breed of dog, and whether the breed is the one you are searching for.

In the process, there would be separate questions based on the query processed inside your brain's neural network. For example, what is the color of the dog? How large has it grown? Is the fur thick? The neural networks would analyze these questions in your brain in a split second.

In the same way, an artificial neural network(ANN) would have to analyze this case and accept the data through separate layers of a neural network. Each of the above layers would attempt to solve the challenge using its own set of concepts and queries. The final result would be the compilation of all the patterns that this neural network can identify within the data it was fed with.

Well, this is the way an artificial neural network operates in layman terms.

The next question to address is how does ANN fit in the definition of deep learning. Is ANN and deep learning the same thing?

Of course no, an ANN is not deep learning. However, we apply the term deep learning when pointing to a large number of ANNs.

For that reason, deep learning can still be considered as deep neural networks in certain cases. But no matter how you name it, there is no denying the fact that it plays a vital role in the AI implementation such as autonomous driving, and many others.

The best example of the abilities of the following neural networks was recently revealed to the world by NVIDIA with their study on a generative adversarial network, a form of ANN. These neural networks managed to define new and sensible faces by identifying patterns and learning through images send to the network.

Well, now you understand what deep learning is, but how can you use it in business.

For sure, these layman descriptions only serve to help with the basics of these concepts. Diving deeper into it would make it relevant to apply technical terms, which in general is irrelevant to those who are looking for business opportunities.

So here is what you need to know about using deep learning and neural network.

1. More power

Deep learning networks demand high computational resources, and most of its operations are GPU intensive.

2. Large amounts of data

Deep learning networks become what it is not just because of the development of its layers and algorithms, but mostly because of the way it learns. Data is the cornerstone of the above networks, the better the quality of data, the higher the information quality you draw out of these.

3. Highly effective machine learning development companies and software development teams

Not all companies require to invest in building deep learning algorithms by themselves. In fact, involving the best IT companies across the globe and having them as a partner is the most sought method for striking a competitive advantage through the application of technology.

Deep Learning Vs. Machine Learning

ML and deep learning have grabbed a lot of attention over the past two years. If you want to understand both of these terms in the most basic way, this section will help you.

So if you can stick with this part for some time, you will understand the real difference between deep learning and machine learning, and how you can leverage the two into exciting business opportunities.

So far, you are familiar with the basic description of the above terms.

This is a collection of cats and dogs' images. What do you think may happen when ML and deep learning networks may require to make some sense out of it?

Take a look at the above images. What you are seeing is a collection of cat and dogs' pictures. Now, say you want to select the images of dogs and cats separately using ML algorithms and deep learning networks.

Basics of deep learning and machine learning: When this task is solved using machine learning:

To help ML classify the images in the collection based on the two groups of dogs and cats, you will require to present it with the above images collectively. But how can the algorithm differentiate?

The answer to this question lies in the definition of ML, relying on structured data. What you will do is label the pictures of dogs and cats in a manner that will define certain properties of animals. This data will be sufficient for the machine learning algorithm to learn, and then it will continue to work based on the labels it learned, and categorize millions of other pictures of both animals it learned via the said labels.

When the Problem is Solved Using Deep Learning

Deep learning networks will use a different method to solve this same problem. The primary advantage of deep learning networks is that they do not really require structured data of the pictures to categorize the two animals. The ANN network using deep learning transfer input via different layers of the network, with each network hierarchically defining certain properties of images.]

In a way, this resembles how the human brain works to solve problems by sending queries through different hierarchies of ideas and related questions to identify the answer.

Once the data is processed through layers in deep neural networks, the system identifies the correct identifiers for categorizing animals from their images.

Note:

This was just an example to help you learn the difference in the way machine learning basics and deep learning networks operate. However, both deep learning and machine learning are not simultaneously suitable to most cases, including this example. The reason for this will be explained later.

Therefore, in this example, you have seen that machine learning algorithm demands structured data to learn the differences between images of dogs and cats, understand the classification and generate output.

On the flipside, a deep learning network was able to group images of both animals using data processed inside the network layers. It did not require labeled data, because it depended on the different outputs processed by every layer which compiled to create a unified means of classifying images.

Key points

1. The main difference between deep learning and ML emerges from the data presentation system. ML algorithms almost always need structured data, while deep learning networks depend on layers of the ANN.

2. Machine learning algorithms have been designed to learn to do things by relying on labeled data, then use it to generate other outputs with additional data sets. However, it requires to be protected from human intervention when the actual output isn't the one expected.

3. Deep learning networks don't demand human intervention because the nested layers in the neural networks subject data through hierarchies of separate concepts, which finally learns through their errors.

4. Data is the primary resource. The quality of the data determines the quality of the result.

What is not seen in the example, but is still essential to underline.

1. Because machine learning algorithms require structured data, they are not the best for solving complex tasks which involve a large amount of data.

2. While this example revealed the application of deep learning networks to solve a small task, the real application of deep neural networks is on a larger scale. In fact, going by the number of hierarchies, and concepts these network process, they are only suitable to compute advanced computations instead of simple ones.

3. Both of these branches of AI require data for it to generate any form of "intelligence." But what should be understood is that deep learning demands a lot of data than a traditional machine learning algorithm. The reason for this is that it can only highlight differences within layers of neural networks when exposed to million data points. On the other hand, ML algorithms can learn through pre-programmed defined criteria.

So with the above example and various explanation of deep learning and machine learning, you should now be able to tell the difference between deep learning and ML. Since these are layman descriptions, they do not involve a lot of technical terms which are most challenging to understand to those looking to using AI and ML for their businesses.

Below are nine applications of deep learning in different industries.

1. Computer vision

High-end gamers use deep learning modules frequently. Deep neural networks drive bleeding –edge object detection, image segmentation, and image restoration. So much so, they even drive the detection of handwritten digits on a computer system. Deep learning is running on a powerful neural network to support machines to repeat the mechanism of the human visual agency.

2. Sentiment-based news aggregation

News aggregators use deep learning modules to eliminate negative news and display only the positive things happening.

3. Automated translations

Automated translations did exist before the introduction of deep learning. But deep learning allows machines to perform better translations with the guaranteed accuracy that was missing in the past. Plus, deep learning is vital in translation extracted from images-something new that could not have been possible using traditional text-based interpretation.

4. Customer experience

Most businesses already apply machine learning to work to enhance the customer experience. Great examples include online-self-service networks. Also, many companies now rely on deep learning to build a reliable workflow. Many of us are already familiar with the application of chatbots by organizations. As the use of deep learning continues to grow, we can expect to witness changes in this sector.

5. Coloring illustrations

At a certain point, including colors to black and white videos used to consume a lot of time in media production. But deep learning models and AI introduced color to b/w photos and videos making the process simple. As you read, hundreds of black and white illustrations are being recreated in colored style.

6. Autonomous vehicles

The next time you are fortunate to see to an autonomous vehicle driving down, know that there are different models of AI working simultaneously. Although certain models highlight pedestrians, others are familiar at street signs. A single car can be trained by millions of AI models while moving down the road. Many have considered AI-driven cars as safer than human.

7. Language selection

This attempts to determine whether deep learning can distinguish dialects. For instance, machine learning will decide whether a person is speaking in English. It will then determine the difference as per the dialect. Once the dialect has been chosen, additional processing will be dealt with by a separate AI that focuses on a specific language. Not forgetting to say that there is no human invention in any of these steps.

8. Generation of text

Computers now can produce new text from scratch. They can learn the style of a text and highlight useful news pieces. AI focused text generation is fully equipped to deal with the complexity of opinion pieces on matters related to you and me. At the moment, text generation has made it possible to generate entries on just everything from scholarly topics to children rhymes.

9. Image analysis and generation of the caption

One of the best things about deep learning is the ability to detect images and produce intelligent captions. Also, the image caption done by AI is so accurate that most online publications are ready to take advantage of these techniques to save cost and time.

Chapter 8: Operationalizing AI and ML Projects by Companies

With a powerful technology that creates massive changes as ML, it can be hard to ignore the hyperbole. Sure, billions of dollars in investment are being invested in ML projects. Machine learning is the foundation of digital transformation methods. And to be sure, machine learning is what people talk about when they mention the general term "AI." So, it is essential to take time to review real-world ML capabilities being developed and used across different companies around the world.

Typically, the abilities of AI allow the computer to examine massive datasets to attain a "reasoned" conclusion regarding the subject being addressed, activating the human decision procedure, always with better decisions being generated.

Although it is simple to define AI and ML, the problem has been the application of AI daily. One field that has attained success is the content matching and suggestions for streaming media, radically changing the on-demand viewer experience. Instead of trying to limit the "expert" human work required to categorize, curate, and segment content into consumable forms, machine learning has become a critical tool in personalized content delivery. By reviewing user behavior, preferences, and most streaming services can accurately personalize recommendations and push the targeted content with a higher ability for monetization and interaction.

Overall, every industry should consider applying AI into their business models. You don't need to be a big company to use AI to get better services to your customers. AI can assist both small and mid-sized businesses, and complete customer product needs faster, transform the inventory systems by applying Just in Time processes, limit shipping, and stocking mistakes as well as facilitate the payment and collection procedure.

Business domains where AI is transforming the landscape

Life Sciences and Pharmaceuticals

Wherever you get into a death disruption argument, we can all acknowledge that aging is a challenging experience. Even if you don't look forward to immortality, you probably recognize that increased joint pain and susceptibility to illness and injury will destroy the quality of life a person.

However, deep learning can slow the aging process. Scientists now use technology to detect biomarkers associated with aging. Soon, a simple blood test could be sufficient to show the parts of your body displaying wear and tear, and your doctor could assist you to eliminate, and probably reverse the effects through lifestyle changes and medication.

Food

About 40 percent of a grocer's revenue is from sales of fresh produce. So, to assume that maintaining product quality is critical is like an understatement. But it is easy to say so than doing it. Grocers are at the whims of their supply chains and consumer uncertainty. Maintaining their shelves stocked and products fresh can be a dangerous balancing act.

However, growers have discovered that machine learning is the solution to smarter fresh food. They can feed ML programs with historical datasets and enter data about promotions and store hours as well, and apply the analysis to measure how much of every product to order and display. ML systems can as well gather information about public holidays, weather forecasts, and other contextual information. Then they release a recommended order after 24 hours so that the grocer has the right products in the correct measure in stock.

Businesses that apply machine learning in their workflows limit the out-of-stock rates by up to 80 percent, plus 9 percent in gross margin rise.

Media and Entertainment

Media companies can now make their content accessible thanks to machine learning. ML has made it possible for deaf Americans and those with hearing-impaired to watch and enjoy YouTube videos through the automatic captioning program.

Information Technology

Although machine learning generates multiple business insights, many organizations have failed to tap in AI technologies. But it has been predicted that there would be about 2.7 million data science jobs by 2020.

Law

Deep learning programs are critical in the legal industry. Legal phrasing can be hard to understand, but deep learning programs can analyze more than ten thousand documents.

There was a time when legal professionals tasked with the role to examine contract clauses that impact their client's business had to review stacks of documents manually. Now it is possible to feed them into a program that works faster and detect important terms for further review.

Insurance

Minimizing risk and underwriting is the goal of every individual, and that is why ML is an excellent tool in the insurance industry. Machine learning algorithms can use customer data and real-time data to determine the level of risk.

Also, the algorithms can customize rates based on the information, probably creating savings for insurance companies and consumers.

This process could be transformed using an in-depth analysis where ML programs gather unrelated social network data to create an accurate profile. The insurance industry can include artificial intelligence to define policyholders gainfully employed and who tend to be in good health.

Mostly, a person responsible for those parts of their lives will be a responsible driver too.

Education

Intelligent Tutoring Systems (ITS) has a massive ability in helping students learn. These AI programs work as virtual tutors and adapt their digital lessons depending on the strength of every child. Every time a student completes a quiz, an ML program analyzes the information to personalize future materials.

By "learning" the unique needs of a user and choosing the type of lessons most effective for them, the ITS ensures that student overcomes learning problems and retain a lot of knowledge. Research shows that students who apply intelligent tutoring systems do well on tests compared to peers who learn through group instruction.

Health care

Compared to other developed nations, the US spends a lot on health care per person than any other country. For example, the U.K spends less per person ($3,749) annually on health care than the United States. Despite the high spending, the United States doesn't have the best health outcomes.

The discovery of AI in decreasing the number of tests and making the right decisions on treatment promises to reduce the health care costs in the United States with more effective lifesaving results. As a result of the high expenses related to health care and the advantages generated by health care decisions, there is a likely chance of seeing exponential growth in the application of AI.

How AI and ML are Improving Customer Experience

What can machine learning and artificial intelligence do to enhance the customer experience?

AI and ML have already been intimately applied in online shopping. You cannot use Amazon or any other shopping service without receiving recommendations, which are typically personalized depending on the vendor's knowledge of your traits: browsing history, purchase history, and much more. Amazon and other online businesses would enjoy creating a digital version of the salesperson who knows you and your tastes and can guide you to products you will like.

Everything starts with quality data

To make this decision a reality, you need to begin with some heavy lifting on the back end. Who are your customers? Do you know them? All customers leave behind a data trace, but that data trace is a sequence of fragments, and it is challenging to associate those fragments to each other. If a customer has numerous accounts, can you detect?

If a customer has different accounts for business and personal use, can you connect them? And if a company uses various names, can you identify the single organization responsible for them? Customer experience begins with knowing exactly who your customers are and how they are connected. Removing your customer lists to avoid duplicates is referred to as entity resolution. It used to be the field of large organizations that could manage substantial data teams. Right now, we see the democratization of entity resolution. There are no startups that offer entity resolution software and services that are right for small to medium organizations.

Once you establish who your customers are, you need to find out how well you know them. Having a holistic view of customer's activities is key to mastering their needs. What data you have concerning them, and how do you apply it? ML and AI are being implemented as tools in the data collection process. When it comes to computing data streams that originate form apps, sponsors, and other sources, data collection can be intrusive and ethically questionable. As you continue to develop your customer knowledge, ensure you have their consent and that you aren't affecting their privacy.

ML isn't different from any other type of computing: the principle "garbage in, garbage out" still works. If you have low-quality training data, the results will be reduced. As the number of data sources increases, the number of possible data fields and variables changes, plus the possibility for error: typographic errors, transcription errors, and so forth. Traditionally, it could be possible to manually correct and repair data, but fixing data manually is an error-prone and tedious thing that disturbs most data scientists. For entity solution, data quality and data repair have been the topic of research, and a new set of machine learning tools for automating data cleaning are starting to appear.

When it comes to applications of ML and AI to customer experience, the standard field is in recommendation systems and personalization systems.

In recent years, hybrid recommender systems-applications that integrate multiple recommender strategies have become a lot common. Most hybrid recommenders depend on many numerous sources, and massive amounts of data and deep learning models belong to these systems. Although it is famous for recommendations to feature models that are only retrained periodically, advanced recommendation and personalization technologies will require to be in real time. Applying reinforcement learning, bandit algorithms, and online learning are starting to develop recommendation systems that frequently train models against live data.

Machine learning and AI are improving various enterprise tasks and workflows, plus customer interactions. We have seen Chatbots that automate different customer service. Currently, chatbots are more annoying than helpful. However, if it is well-designed, bots can result in excellent customer acquisition rates. However, we are just at the early stages of natural language processing and understanding, and in the last year, there have been different breakthroughs. As the ability to create complex language models changes, we will see Chatbots transform through various stages: from delivering notifications to controlling simple question and answer cases.

As chatbots change, we expect them to form an integral organ of customer service, not just an annoyance that you have to work through to get a human. And for chatbots to attain this performance level, they will require to include real-time recommendation and personalization. They will need to know customers as well as human.

Fraud detection is also another field that is incorporating machine learning. Fraud detection is trapped in a constant battle between the right people and criminals, and the stakes are rapidly increasing. Fraud artists are beginning sophisticated techniques for online crime. Fraud is no longer person-to-person: it is automated just like the bot that buys all tickets to events so that they can be resold by scalpers. As seen in recent elections, it is easy for hackers to gain entry to social media by building a bot that floods conversations with automated responses. It is difficult to identify those bots and block them in real time. That can only be done using machine learning, and still, it is a difficult task that can only be solved partially. However, solving it is an important part of re-building an online world where people feel safe and respected.

Development in speech technologies and emotion detection will reduce friction in automated customer interactions even more. Multi-modal models that integrate separate types of inputs will make it easier to respond to customers correctly. Customers may be able to reveal what they want or send a live video of a challenge they are experiencing.

Although interactions between robots and humans constantly place users in a creepy "uncanny valley," it is okay that future customers will be more comfortable with robots than we are now.

However, if we are going to look for customers using the uncanny valley, then we need to respect what they value. Al and Ml applications that impact customers will have to respect privacy; they will have to be secure and be fair and unbiased. None of these are simple, but technology will not increase customer experience in case customers end up feeling abused. The result could be more efficient, but that is a bad tradeoff.

What can machine learning and artificial intelligence perform for customer experience? It has already achieved a lot. But still there is a lot that it can make, and it has to implement in creating a frictionless customer experience of the future.

Chapter 9: Step-by-step Method to Develop AI and ML Projects For Business

The technology sector is in love with AI. Many different applications have been developed, ranging from automated customer service to high-end data science; this technology is famous across the businesses.

Artificial Intelligence is a prominent driving force in the technology sector. AI is the leading topic of discussion at conferences and revealing the possibility across different industries, including manufacturing and retail. New products are getting connected with virtual assistants, while Chatbots are responding to customer questions on everything.

At the same time, big corporate companies like Microsoft, Google, and Salesforce are embedding AI as an intelligence layer across their tech systems. Sure, AI is having its moment.

It is not AI that pop culture has made us expect; it is not the Skynet, or sentient robots, or even Tony Stark's Jarvis assistant. The AI plateau is taking place below the surface, making our current tech smarter and opening the power of all the data that enterprises gather. This means a broad development in machine learning, deep learning, and natural learning. These have simplified the process of incorporating an algorithm into a cloud platform.

For businesses, practical uses of AI can show up in different ways based on your organizational needs and the business intelligence insights extracted from the data you gather. Enterprises can incorporate AI from obtaining data to generating engagement in customer relationship management to maximizing logistics and efficiency in monitoring and maintaining assets.

ML is playing a huge function in the development of AI. Currently, AI is being powered by the recent changes in ML. There is no single success you can refer to, but the business value that we can mine from ML now is off the charts.

From the enterprise perspective, what is taking place now may affect some important business processes around control and coordination, as well as scheduling resources and reporting.

This section will describe tips from experts on the actions to take to include AI in the organization and to ensure that the implementation is successful.

1. Familiarize with AI

Find time to understand what modern AI can deliver. You can use TechCode Accelerator wide array of resources through its coordination with organizations like the University of Stanford. Still, you can turn to online resources and learn more about AI. There are remote courses offered by platforms such as audacity, and code academy. These can kick start your journey.

More online resources you can use to get started include:

- Microsoft's open-source Cognitive Toolkit

- Stanford University's online lectures.

- Google open-source software library.

- The link for the development of Artificial Intelligence.

2. Select the problems you need AI to solve

Once you are familiar with the basics, the next thing is to start exploring unique ideas. Think of how you can include AI capabilities to your current products and services. The most important thing is that your company should have in mind specific examples of AI applications to solve business challenges.

When working with a company, it is important, to begin with, a brief description of its major tech programs and challenges. You want to demonstrate how natural language processing, ML, and image recognition suit those products. The specifics change depending on the type of industry. For instance, if the company performs video surveillance, it can retain a lot of value by including ML to that procedure.

3. Prioritize important value

In this step, you analyze the financial cost of the business across different AI applications you have chosen. To prioritize well, you have to review the dimensions of feasibility. It should offer you a chance to prioritize and establish the value for the business. This step will also demand ownership and acknowledgment from top-level executives.

4. Accept the internal capability Gap

There is a difference between what you want to achieve and what a company can achieve in a specific time frame. That is why it is critical for a business to be aware of the limits from a tech perspective before diving into AI.

Sometimes, this can demand more time; however, by concentrating on your potential internal gap implies that you know what you want to achieve.

Depending on the available business, numerous projects or teams can help you to do this organically.

5. Look for professionals and prepare a pilot project

Once your business is good to go, next, you need to think of integrating AI. The secret with this step is to start small, set project goals, and keep in mind what you know and what you don't know about AI. This is the perfect moment to invite external experts.

For a first project, don't set a lot of time, even 2-3 months could be enough for a pilot project. Once the pilot project is over, you should figure out what the longer-term project will be and whether the value proposition is necessary for your business as well as people who are skilled in AI.

6. Start a team for integrating data

The first you need to do before you can apply ML into your business is to clean the available data. Corporate data is found in different data silos and could be in the hands of business groups with a different objective. For that reason, the correct step to ensure that you acquire useful data is to set up a team that will clean the data and removes any inconsistencies that may be present.

7. Implement small

When it comes to the implementation phase, you will require to do it in little bits instead of going big. Make small implementations, and try to read the feedback. From the feedback, you can improve slowly.

8. Have storage plans in your AI program

Once you shift from a small size of data, you will require to factor in the storage requirements to involve AI solution. Enhancing algorithms is a vital step towards attaining great results. However, without a large volume of data to assist develop accurate models, AI technologies cannot offer much to ensure you attain your computing needs.

Besides that, you need to improve AI storage for data workflow and modeling. Setting aside time to analyze your options can have a significant positive effect on how the system works once it is online.

9. Involve AI as part of your daily plans

AI provides addition automation and insight, and this is an excellent tool for workers to make AI become part of their daily routine instead of something that replaces it.

Corporate organizations should be open on the way tech operates to solves problems in a workflow. This will provide employees with a unique experience so that they can visualize the way AI optimizes their role.

10. Incorporate some balance

While creating an AI system, it demands you fulfill the needs of the tech and research project. The main thing you need to factor in before you begin to design an AI system is creating balance within the system. This may look obvious, but in most cases, AI technologies are built around specific features of how the team considers realizing its research goals, without mastering the requirements and limitations of the hardware and software that would augment the research.

For companies to realize this balance, they should ensure that they have enough bandwidth for storage, networking, and graphics processing.

Alternatively, you require to balance the way the general budget is used to fulfill research with the desire to safeguard against power failure and other means via redundancies.

How to Develop an AI Startup?

Right now, AI is a big thing. Everyone has a say, and this can be difficult to avoid the hype, and dive into practical down to Earth questions.

In this section, you will learn what AI is at a basic level, without getting confused by the extensive knowledge. Next, you will learn the four general steps you need to follow when you want to launch an AI business.

It is also important to note that the hype around AI can make you feel like if you are not using AI, you are going to be left behind. But in many forms, AI is still in the infant stage, and it is not always clear when it's the right time for you, and when it is over complicating matters.

That doesn't mean that you should avoid using AI if you are about to launch a new company. Many severe problems need to be solved, and AI technology as it is now can help.

AI at the Conceptual Level

You would be forgiven for failing to know how to perceive AI. Can it be a robot walking in your house or an app in your smartphone? Maybe it's the entire phone. Much of what has been documented about AI makes it difficult to fail to know what AI is. Plus, there are debates about AI vs. ML. In this section, we shall gloss over the differences, and focus on the broader topics, and how they apply to the problems entrepreneurs face.

Put, AI is a software piece that, like much other software, can accept input, and turn it into output.

The only significant difference from many other software types is that the program doesn't give it a step by step commands on how to perform a transformation, and may not even be aware what those steps are.]

Just like any other software, AI can be packaged in different ways; it could be incorporated within an app, a voice managed the device or a website.

To keep things simple, when we talk about AI, we will be referring to the software bit that accepts input and generates output. The critical thing is that it can shift from input to output in moments where it is difficult to write down explicit commands on how to get from input to output.

These are tasks that humans are traditionally good at and computers are historically bad at, at least individually. But in most cases, humans are worst at everything.

Common examples consist of identifying a photo, highlighting emotion from a sentence, and scanning medical test results by searching for subtitles but high deviations from the expected data.

Classifying AIs

You can divide AI into two types: one that performs common tasks in many different forms like converting spoken speech into written words, and one that deals with varying tasks like choosing whether a set of heartbeat data reflects on a heart problem. The difference is critical because the common challenges are already solved, and you can use an existing AI instead of building your own.

Existing AIs

There are several problems where AI is good at evaluating. For instance, face detection in photos or even speech recognition. Since these are common problems, most of the work has gone into developing AIs to solve them. This means you don't need to complete the hard part of these AIs; you can benefit from the work a person has already completed.

The big cloud offers various developed AI products for different tasks, which you can apply on a "pay as you use" model.

Alternatively, since these services are AI based, it is irrelevant if you are using them. All you need to care is that it provides you with the correct answers.

Before you can move forward to develop your own AI, determine if there is one already developed and packed in a manner that you can use.

Custom or Bespoke AIs

The next type of AI is custom built. This is the most interesting part. If you are attempting to complete a task that isn't common enough for current solutions to be readily present, you need to build your own.

At the abstract level, this is simple, but like other things, it gets difficult to dive into the detail.

A Brief Look into AI Details

There are several technical approaches, but the one that receives the highest focus is neural networks. A neural network refers to a complete collection of simulated neurons that are joined together. A signal is transferred to the first neurons that may or may not signal other neurons, and so forth. At the other end of the network, an output signal is generated. For instance, the output signal may comprise a list where the faces are located in a photo.

There are two methods of creating a neural network: building the web and training it. To build the net, you have to select the number of neurons there are and the type of connections between them.

Once you have developed a neural network, you need to train it. Training a system means configuring every node using a mathematical function that notifies it when to transfer a signal it gets, and when not to. Luckily, you cannot do this by hand; it is incredibly impractical.

To train a neural network, you use a training framework to supply your system with a large percent of training data. The training framework builds the math functions for each neuron.

The integration of size and connection of neurons, plus these functions is referred to as a model.

Once you have a model, there are several containers that you can load it in, and the standards exist that let you load your model in a web-based platform.

From an individual attempting to build AI to apply in a business context, the biggest challenge you will encounter is the type of data you need and where you can get it.

Recommendation for a person creating an AI-based startup

There are four important steps:

Determine your problem-solution fit

As with any startup, if you are not solving a problem that customers are ready to pay for, then you don't have a startup.

Before you make big steps, it is crucial to test and be sure that there are people ready to pay for what you want to create, and that is possible to establish what you have in mind.

You can test to see whether people are ready to cash in for your solution by implementing different solutions like a traditional lean technique. The most exciting thing about AI is that it is easy to build a simple version of your solution by involving real humans with a mix of various components.

In most cases, a mix of AI services, existing non-AI services and different humans completing major activities can develop a prototype that simulates your expected solution, allowing you to execute product solution tests before you commit to creating a complete AI.

This triggers the question; do you need to develop AI? Just because it is a solution to a problem, it may not be the only method to do so. Each case is unique, but at this point, when you are applying real humans to test your problem, stop and ask yourself this question: "What is it about my problem that means an AI is the best or even only solution?"

It is difficult, but still necessary to determine whether the AI you are going to depend on can be developed. Not every problem requires to build AI. This is something challenging to do on your own, but you can look for someone who can assist you in running tests with your data to determine whether it is possible.

A building game

If you have attained a level where you know your customers exist and you are confident your AI can be developed, it is time to move forward, establishing the first generation of your AI. As said before, you need to collect some data, curate it, and ensure it is important, next design a model and train it.

Practically, you need to be aware that in most cases, the task of searching for data, curating, and controlling the data is the most significant and hardest part of the problem. Training a model usually consumes most of the computer time, but it is collecting and understanding the data that still require human intelligence, and that is the point where you need to expect to spend most of your time.

Create your product

At this stage, you have a working AI, but it is not easy for your users to get tasks done. By now, you are probably okay with talking about trained models, but it is unlikely your users are.

Probably, they want to pick their phone and launch their app, or even access a website or talk to their voice-activated the home assistant.

This means you will need to package your AI into a product. Something that contains a user interface, and probably performs several things beyond just what AI does.

Keep in mind that a great product is one that creates solutions to a real-world problem. It is not good to have an AI program that can only look at a photo and tell you where the faces are. If your real-world problem is allowing people to learn names from a collection of photographs, you'd need to do a bit more.

For instance, you would want to package that AI in a product that discloses your user's original photo, with boxes near the faces, and maybe ask them to write out the name of each face in a text field. That way it can disclose to them a sequence of flash cards to recall the names of everyone they are going to encounter when they attend that wedding, their new data just requested them to meet them.

Develop ways for enhancing your AI

Training your AI with quality data makes it better. Once your startup is running, you will discover that you have a lot of data to work with. You will find that you are receiving a massive amount of data. You will have data that you initially didn't have when you began to train your AI.

As you collect a lot of data, you will want to retain your data for training purposes. So the things you need to factor in are how you will test the data in case the new generation is better than the old one.

In summary, this chapter was to give you a primer on AI so that you feel motivated to move forward with the idea you are thinking about. Moving forward may imply to begin testing out and building your own AI, or it may mean requesting whether you need to go down the AI pathway. If so, that is an excellent question to ask.

Whichever way, your next step is to have a conversation with your technical team. If you are yet to set up a professional team, you can get in touch with someone to get more information, and answers to your questions.

Having experience in creating projects, knowledge about data sets, and working with AI, you will be in an excellent position to help you with your questions.

Chapter 10: Relationship Between Big Data and Machine Learning

Since 2010, "Big Data" has become the universal term to refer to all the data generated by people from their mobile phones, social media, web history, and purchasing tendencies, plus any other information that organizations hold about them.

Why is big data unique from any other form of data? In one way, there is no difference; it is just zeros and ones at the end of the day. But the phrase "Big Data" is used to refer to a massive collection of different data which are volatile, and where an individual will struggle to categorize using traditional computer hardware and software.

It is also the fact that big data typically incorporates specific types of data that were not widely applied for customer analysis until relatively recently. In particular, big data involves:

Text. What people say and write can be processed to determine what they are talking about. If a product is being discussed positively or negatively, this is likely to indicate whether someone will buy the product or not.

Images: This deals with videos, photos, and medical imaging. One use of machine learning is to apply features in scans and x-rays to compute the chances that someone is suffering from a particular disease.

Social network data. This contains data about people's relationship and who they know. Network data includes the number and type of connections that people hold plus the data about connected individuals. If all members in your group are sci-fi geeks, that is probably a great indicator that you may be one too.

Biometrics: Data related to blood pressure, heartbeat, and so forth, gathered from smart watches, and so on.

The product generated: Everyday equipment from coffee makers to televisions are being developed to share information between themselves and over the internet. Nowadays, your washing machine, kettle, and so on can be controlled through your smartphone. The IoT concept is continuously being developed, but it will finally present lots of data that can be applied to refer to people's behavior using machine learning.

Back in the 1990s, there were no smart devices. Few people owned a mobile phone, and the internet was still in its developing stage. There was little electronic data about people. Supermarkets didn't have an idea of what individual customer purchased every week, insurance companies were not aware of how people drove, and the health services stored patient records in paper files.

The life of data science during these years was pretty simple because all the electronic data was stored up in a clean format of rows and columns. The data was also relatively static.

In the present world of big data, data is continuously being updated more frequently in real time. Additionally, most of it is "free form" unstructured data like speech, tweets, blogs, e-mails, and so on.

Another factor is that most of this data is often produced independently by the organization that wants to use itself, then they can control the way the information is formatted and apply checks and controls in place to make sure that the data is accurate and complete. However, if data is produced from external sources, there is no assurance that the information is correct.

Externally sourced data is always "messy." It demands a considerable amount of work to enhance it and get it to a useable format. Besides, there are a lot of concerns over the stability and on-going availability of the data, which generates a business risk in case it is an organization significant decision-making potential.

This means that traditional computer architectures that organizations use for things like processing sales transactions, managing customer account records, billing, and debt collection, are not best for storing and analyzing all of the new and different data types that are available. Similarly, over the last few years, an entire host of new and exciting hardware and software solutions have been created to deal with these new data types.

Notably, modern big data computer systems are excellent at:

Maintaining large data sets. Traditional databases have limits to the size of data they can hold at a reasonable cost. New methods of storing data have made it possible to store unlimited data.

Data cleaning and formatting. Different data needs to be transformed into a standard means before it can be applied for machine learning, report management, and other data related tasks.

It is processing data fast. Big data isn't just about the presence of more data. It has to be processed and analyzed quickly for it to be useful.

The problem with traditional computer systems is that practically they were too slow, cumbersome, and expensive.

New data processing and storage techniques like MapReduce/Hadoop have allowed tasks which would have consumed weeks or even months to process in just a few hours and at a fraction of the cost of more traditional data processing methods. The way Hadoop implements this is by letting data and data processing to spread across networks of cheap desktop PCS. Theoretically, thousands of PCs can be connected to generate massive computational potentials that are comparable to the largest supercomputers in existence.

Whether data is big or small, it doesn't have any intrinsic value. And one of the greatest mistakes that companies make is to assume that if they invest in big storage, and collect every data they can, then that will add value. Value can only be achieved if the data is processed and something useful is made from it.

ML is the primary tool that is used in data analysis and generating a predictive model about the behavior of people.

The best way to look at the link between ML and big data is that data is a raw material that is entered into a machine learning process. The tangible advantage to a business is determined from the predictive model that is generated at the end of the process, and not the data used to create it.

As a result, machine learning and big data are always discussed in the same breath, but there is no balanced relationship. You require machine learning to make the best out of big data, but you don't need big data to use machine learning effectively. If you have only a few items of information, then that is sufficient to start building predictive models and perform essential predictions.

How to Empower AI and Machine Learning through Big Data?

In the internet era, the amount of data is increasing across the world. This massive amount of information is processed via "Big Data Analysis." Alongside Big Data, the other two technologies that bring change to the IT world include AI and ML.

Nowadays, AI and ML are the forms of technologies that support computer systems and other connected devices in this way:

- Through recursive experiments
- Through a continuous update to data banks
- Through human interventions.

Machine learning and Artificial Intelligence are intertwined and peripherals motivated by the above technologies can be programmed in a manner that they can learn new things on their own using algorithms and programs. The machines can extract relevant and important information using big data analysis.

For instance, if a person has a leather garment company and wants to determine the market requirement of a country for a given season, then he can achieve this using Big Data Analytics. The information can be examined and accessed fast via reports that are produced using Big Data tools.

How Big Data Can Be Used to Extend AI and ML Workforce

As a result of AI, it is assumed that the complete workforce will be limited to a large extent in the coming years, and most of the tasks will be completed by AI-based computers. Still, big data can change this prediction. For Big Data analysis, human intelligence and sentiments are often required and applied, while machines don't have this human sentiments and emotions.

For this, let us consider the example of a Pharmaceutical Company that employs prominent data professionals to examine the data of the South-East Asian market. In this case, experts can rapidly since the pharmaceutical prescription of that place along with local reservations. Here, computer-focused big data analysis can never generate sensitive and contextual results.

In other words, the merging of Big Data, ML, and AI will only yield results for experts and capable data scientists. It will allow them to multiply in the market. Additionally, this merging will rise in the future by integrating three technologies.

How Can Big Data Benefit from AI and ML Service Providers?

At the moment, the international market of AI and ML solutions is incomplete. When Big Data is compiled with AI and ML machines, the devices become smarter, and their potential to implement complicated analysis increases. For that reason, complex AI solutions will cause the market and demand for these machines to increase.

In Latin America, big-data focused schools implement AI solutions for a long time. They are applying AI-based academic solutions and supporting a lot of educational institutes to implement AI into their educational systems. Thus, the educational market sector may experience significant growth because of this technological progress.

Big data assists in global diversification of AI and ML

With the rise of most innovative and advantageous technologies, the price of AI-based solutions and ML fall significantly. As a result, these AI-based techniques can be used by different religious, cultural, political affiliations, and spiritual inclinations. Additionally, AI and ML-based systems require to be trained based on local ethics.

Big Data analysis for different regions assists in designing the AI and ML-focused solutions depending on demographic requirements of that particular place without concentrating on their emotions. These solutions will be successful and famous for customers.

Business Areas Where Big Data, AI and ML Can Contribute

At the start, we said Big Data, AI, and ML can change business processes. Here are some of the familiar places that can be enhanced using these technologies.

- Improve the application of Social media data for business feed
- Enhance predictive models safer business using ML and AI support.
- Increase online Sale using chat bot analysis.

Overall, AI Big Data analytics, and ML can transform the business data so that it is accurate and straightforward. By extracting real-time business insights, decision-makers can implement strategic and better decisions. Volume and velocity aspects are the main factors that make Big Data powerful. In this case, we can say that both AI and Big Data complement each other. Business can receive real-world insights through the integration of Big Data and AI. But a lot of activity and companies are generating benefits from ML, AI, and Big Data integration.

In summary, ML, Big Data, and AI are the future of business across the world. If you want to assist your business to grow, then think about using these technologies. Where AI and ML deliver smarter and intelligent devices, Big Data may help in making decisions with more insights.

Chapter 11: How Machine Learning Can Enhance the Competitiveness of Any Business

Companies that are yet to make plans to invest and innovate will soon be eclipsed by the new economy driven by machine learning.

Machine learning is already transforming the whole world. As a major branch of AI, it allows computers to run and learn on their own, without any prior programming, by making use of data and experience instead of being explicitly programmed.

Netflix recommendations, YouTube recommendations, and virtual personal assistants like Alexa and Siri are some of the most popular AI applications. These features are not just for eCommerce and entertainment websites. Machine learning is now relevant to any organization and any size, for processes ranging from routine to revolutionary.

To stay competitive in the current market demands a working knowledge of artificial intelligence and machine learning skills.

Turning Data Overload into a Critical Mother Lode

Nowadays it is common that the more information you have, the better. This is especially true for business. The more information you have in your belt about your niche, products, customers, and marketplace, the higher your competitive advantage.

By 2017, 90 percent of data in the whole world has been generated in the last two years alone, at a rate of 2.5 quintillion bytes of data per day. Everything from mobile phones, web browsers, and sensors on devices provide an endless and exponentially growing stream of information. That is Big Data. However, not all that data is useful. The biggest hurdle for business lies in predicting which data is important, accurate, and actionable.

In The Evolution of Analytics by Patrick Hall, he says that organizations are now pushed to perform an advanced search in their data to identify new and innovative methods to increase efficiency and competitiveness.

The problem is that analyzing, gathering, and making use of all this data has grown past what is humanly possible, even applying traditional data analytics. This means companies are nearing a breaking point with the amount of data they can process, analyze, and implement.

Forrester Research approximates that about 60-73 percent of the data collected is never successfully used for strategic reasons.

The answer to transforming this massive data into something fit for construction lies in applying machine learning to automate the development of data analysis models. In general, humans can build 1-2 models per week, but machine learning can generate tens of thousands of models per week.

Machine learning not only deals with massive raw datasets, but it also craves for this data. The more you supply it with data, the smarter it becomes. Machine learning algorithms can define patterns, clusters, and associations among data, and then forecast results and recommend actions.

With the potential of machine learning and other applications of AI, your business can later make your data useful to business and your customers. In case data is not running your organization, it has to be.

Much of the information that companies have about their customers is self-reported data. In other words, this is data that is captured in lead forms from newsletter subscriptions, downloads, product registrations, customer service feedback, and surveys. The rest of the data is automatically monitored via website visits, search engine data, and cookies. Still, anonymous visitor data can be important. Social media is another data source, in particular reviews, engagements, and click-through. Data related to your competitors can be resourceful if you know how to mine it.

Most of the data generated by human beings are in text form. As a result, web crawling is a great way to mine information about what customers think. This then gives you an added advantage to stay ahead of competitors.

With a lot of the human-generated data being text. Web crawling is an important process for acquiring information about what customers are thinking for a competitive edge, maintaining brand reputation, and evaluating community awareness of organizational initiatives.

Transactional data is the most current, accurate, and used data. Some predict that by 2020, business transactions through the internet will hit 450 billion per day. Include the constant flow of data generated automatically via IoT like health monitors and appliances.

The size of data that we generate and copy annually will double each year and by 2020 is forecast to hit 44 zettabytes. Collecting and maintaining this data has grown past the potential of traditional storage. But Hadoop –an open source Java application has free modules that anyone can use. This application is mainly designed for extensive data sets. It has made it possible for the processing of large-scale data and is an important tool for competitive advantage.

Those who can successfully mine historical data can attain a significant advantage in the future. Alternatively, the cloud provides the opportunity for virtually unlimited storage at the lowest price point, and cloud leaders such as Microsoft Azure, Google Cloud, and Amazon Web Services are contributing unique and better computing services.

Those that push their IT architecture to the cloud have a better chance of staying ahead of the competition and building a system of interference that sets the stage of market leadership.

To optimize machine learning, diverse data is kept in a repository known as a "data lake." A data lake is different from traditional data warehouses because it stores the data in its raw, natural form, whether it is structured, unstructured, or semi-structured.

Although this makes the data easier to identify things, its level of inflexibility makes it hard to carry out innovative analyses.

A structured data makes it possible for you to respond to specific questions, but the structure may fail to accommodate issues that emerge at some point in the future.

The data lake idea permits unstructured data, and more flexibility to respond to new questions. Performing these analyses and responding entirely to further problems are accurate what machine learning performs, and hence provides the raw material for achieving a competitive advantage.

Now, you have the data with you, what next?

Ready with a large volume of data, machine learning algorithms can be "trained" depending on experience, then exposed to new data and released to hunt for patterns, learn from what they discover and create predictive models on their own.

We need to create programs that analyze not only a large volume of data to identify historical patterns but also intelligent enough to adapt to new data and upcoming patterns and examine the impact of a set of predictive frameworks.

The two widely adopted machine learning techniques for most businesses today require supervised learning and unsupervised learning.

1. When it comes to supervised learning, it depends on data that have labels like dates, names, and financial strings. Kept in relational databases, this data is common to businesses, but only makes 20 percent of all data. Structured data originates from human input, websites, or point of sale devices. Supervised learning algorithms are important when a specific output is known, or if you have a question you want to ask like determining new data points that match a certain target value. This is important for functions such as recommendation engines, predictive maintenance, and inventory control.

2. Unsupervised learning depends on data that is unstructured, has no historical labels, and doesn't fit well into a database. This kind of data includes customer transactions, document text, graphics, social media, and other content. Around 80-90 percent of the data in many organizations is unstructured. With unsupervised learning, the algorithm has to generate its inferences to identify what is searching for. It does this by looking for

clusters and hidden patterns. This kind of learning is important for market segmentation, hardware fault diagnostics, and fraud detection. The benefit of unsupervised learning is that it allows you to identify patterns in the data that you don't know.

Whether you apply supervised or unsupervised machine learning or a mix of the two, there are five ways that any business can take advantage of algorithms to establish a competitive advantage.

1. Automate business processes

Businesses can immediately incorporate machine learning to automate back-office processes. Most of these processes are high volume, rules-based functions that may operate on a "lights out" plan, freeing the time for employees to allow them to realize strategic company objectives.

Some of the simple functions consume 80 percent of total transactions being carried out by human workers. This increases the support costs adding no value to customers and the company itself.

Most companies are already outsourcing multiple mundane tasks to computers. By tracking the existing processes and learning to identify different instances, AI increases the number of invoices that can be automatically matched. This allows organizations to limit the amount of work delegated to service centers and allows the finance staff to concentrate on strategic tasks.

Lights-out-IT

In a survey conducted by Tata Consultancy Services in 2017, out of 835 companies surveyed, IT was the largest adopters of AI. It was not only used to monitor the moves of the hacker in the data center, but IT used AI to provide solutions to employees' tech support challenges, automate the task of putting new systems and ensure employees applied technology from certified vendors. About 34%-44% of companies surveyed were implementing AI in their IT departments.

Hands-off HR

Human resource and acquisition of skills are fields where AI can have a huge effect on limiting the workload, improving efficiency, and preventing bias. Chatbots plus other applications of machine learning can deal with repetitive HR tasks such as:

- Scheduling interviews, performing reviews, and other group meetings.

- Shortlisting job applicants from hundreds of resumes.

- Measuring and maintaining employee interactions.

- Respond to questions about company policies, office procedures, and basic conflict resolution.

- Polishing office workflows.

- Attracting and getting in touch with top talent.

A well-adopted machine learning technologies can save a lot of time through the application of predictive analysis to limit time wasting in hiring and making the process accurate and reliable.

Machine learning can still be used to enhance human productivity. For instance, auto-generating weekly reports and tracking hundreds of news items, social media mentions, and other information sources. These tools can be applied for monitoring data and predicting results, and helping corporate teams to prioritize product development and marketing efforts.

Ears-on analytics

Machine learning can extract data from brand new and massive sources of data that were never accessible via human means.

Other advanced uses of machine learning can make companies more competitive by building new products and changing the reliability of current ones.

The company IKEA-specialized in furniture development relies on a machine learning algorithm to review social media and find data to create new products that solve problems raised online.

Machine learning is also great at analyzing the huge volume of the historical sensor, failure data from devices, logistics, and machinery. The model's prediction may later recommend preventive maintenance, eliminate transportation, or even detect problems in real time that would show failure is imminent.

A lot of businesses have yet to discover the full potential of machine learning. The advantages extend far beyond faster supply chains and increased level of productivity.

2. Marketing

Even before the coming of the digital age, marketing professionals have been eager and early adopters of the rising technologies. Machine learning and AI are some of the popular tools for digital marketers. This evolution will take place and grow in the next few years as data grows, new models develop, and marketers build new strategies for getting the edge on their competition. AI offers the right answer to the ages-old advertising technique of finding the perfect message to the right individual at the correct time.

Machine learning can limit most of imprecise marketing nature. Applying behavioral data, marketers can focus their audiences in effective methods that highly enhance the chances of transforming shoppers to customers.

Here are some of the methods that companies apply in machine learning to improve their marketing and advertising, both offline and online.

- Customer churn risk modeling

- Demand prediction and sales projection.

- Targeted cross-sell and bundling.

- Dynamic and personalized product ranking.

- Augmented reality

- Polishing lead sourcing

- Micro-segmentation

- Optimized-message targeting

- Customer qualifying applying web data.

- Text-to-video creation.

Machine learning and other important technologies have created new methods for investing their market budget in smarter methods.

These technologies make it possible to check huge volumes of data in real time. Controlling big data and getting actionable insights are some of the most critical basics for any online business these days.

Smarter segmentation

List segmentation and personalization have been critical drivers since the time of direct mail. Most google natives enter a workforce where they pay-per-click, and the AI-marketing tools are ubiquitous to the point where they appear routine. This makes it difficult to differentiate from competitors. It demands expert knowledge of these skills and an open eye to new machine learning products and creative methods.

One thing that machine learning is important is the customer journey. Algorithms can tell what differentiates high-value customers from low-value ones, and so you know where to concentrate your sales efforts. Machine learning still identifies clusters of the best customers who share shocking properties. Your company may wish to review a section of customers that buy at the same time of the year and determine the factors that impact their purchasing behavior.

By mastering a certain cluster of customers, you can make decisions about the kind of products to suggest to customer groups via personalized offers and promotions.

Lead sourcing and scoring

For new leads, the traditional sourcing methods require purchasing lists or wasting hours looking for and scraping contract information from company sites.

Machines not only assist with the original data collection of lead generation, but AI can analyze unstructured data like phone calls, emails, and social posts to identify patterns and determine who is a right prospect.

The right marketing demands a deep understanding of customers and prospects. The more you thoroughly understand them, the more precisely you can concentrate on them. Not only machine learning automates this intelligence collection from familiar databases and sources, but the algorithms enter the external world to analyze, collect, predict and learn.

AI applications such as these are already present as products from third-party vendors; digital marketing experts don't need to be data scientists. But it is beneficial for marketers and executives to understand the key aspects of machine learning to master the potential and build strategies before making a massive investment in high-value resources. It is also important for marketers to learn the fields where humans do well and the things that are better left to computers.

Pay-per-click savings

If there is a field where machines do well, it is bidding. Bidding requires picking a human-defined strategy and changing bids based on the expected return on ad spend or cost per acquisition. Doing this manually or paying a third-party vendor to perform this can be expensive.

Since bidding depends on pattern recognition and statistics, this is one of the best application of machine learning. Machines can easily predict how a user may use an ad depending on previous behavior and the keyword stats.

Dynamic pricing

Another great application of AI for marketing lies in supporting elasticity in online pricing. Unlike human pricing models, AI-driven dynamic pricing can change at the time of shopping based on a broad range of real-time factors, including competitors pricing, shoppers level of interest, and prior interactions via previous marketing.

This demands a lot of data about how different customers are ready to pay for a great service change across different situations. But companies such as ride-share and airline services have successfully developed dynamic price optimization methods to improve revenue.

No matter how it is deployed in your marketing technology stack, machine learning eliminates waste-wasted budget, wasted labor, and so on. Machine learning can allow you to do more marketing with less capital. Search for opportunities where AI may assist you to generate more products with the same number of people you have today.

This is only the start of the bell curve for machine learning's role in marketing.

3. Transforming customer experience

One way that machine learning can assist any business strike a competitive advantage is via applications that analyze and enhance the overall customer experience.

In a connected economy, customers expect highly personalize and real-time interactions. Nowadays, nearly every company tries to remain competitive by enhancing their digital experiences with customers and tapping data and insights to make those experiences important and valuable.

Churn modeling

There are different methods that machine learning can set this difference to your customers. First is to help you understand them. Churn modeling is good not only for marketing but also for customer support and product enhancement.

Machine learning allows big data analysis at speeds that aren't humanly possible. Algorithms can be applied in determining these factors like customer purchasing behavior, marketing histories, and website. Next, they can determine the risk models that compare simulations based on preventive actions to find out how these interventions affect the odds of churning. Risk analysis from churn modeling can provide live customer support teams with the best problem resolution paths.

Customer support

In a 2017 study published in Chatbots Magazine highlighted that about 55% of UK consumers report that the most critical factor when it comes to the customer experience is finding a prompt and effective response to questions.

Companies require to generate faster customer service replies, and all the data associated with the customer journey, previous interactions, and other issues. Machine learning makes this a reality.

Thanks to the low-cost speech analytic tools and recording, tracking customer service interactions among themselves can also provide insights to contact centers.

Rather than just directing callers via prompts, speech analytics will assist classify them and review the responses based on what you say and how you say it.

Chatbots

Automated customer support via AI-driven Chatbots is already achieving acceptance and popularity. Since 75% of all consumers fall between 18-25, intelligent digital agents are the solution for providing customers with quick web chat service.

Additionally, because of the thousands of AI-based customer support, consumers can now comfortably interact with Chatbots.

Consumers are used to interacting with technology via voice commands smart assistants, smart devices, and automated call centers. Machine learning supports speech-enabled Chatbots to improve customer service inquiries if relevant.

According to a 2018 McKinsey Global Institute report, deep learning analysis of audio makes it possible for systems to review customer's emotional tone, in case the customer responds badly to the system, the call can be rerouted automatically to human managers and operators.

Social media monitoring

Optimizing the power of machine learning to track social media is a great move for companies to remain competitive. Including social media gossip when mixing it with data from other transactions and customer demographic enhances product marketing and can still boost individualist product recommendations.

According to the McKinsey report, "Next product to buy" recommendations that focus on individual customers can result in a twofold rise in the rate of sales conversions.

Social media monitoring still makes an important step in ensuring the presence of quality customer support.

With the development of global chatter on sites like Facebook and Twitter, it can be hard for even a big business to attain all this valuable feedback.

Machine learning integrated with linguistic algorithms improves the process of establishing what customers say about you almost anywhere.

Social media monitoring is a great way to apply AI to collect competitive advantage. The same way you can monitor the mention of your company, the same concept can be applied to gain market share from your competitors.

Customer loyalty is diminishing because of other options, especially when these alternative options poach someone.

Becoming one with the machines

Applying a "wait and see" approach using machine learning is not an option, specifically for companies in competitive sectors.

But turning a blind eye on competitors who have robots is not an issue for B3C. All companies face challenges in the technology curve.

Early evidence shows that there is a business case to be achieved, and that AI can generate value to companies ready to apply it across operations and within their core functions.

Also, early AI adopters that integrate strong digital capability with proactive plans attain a higher profit margin and expect the performance gap with other firms to increase in the next few years.

Besides that, the cold start challenge with AI is a big challenge for many companies, whether big or small. The rapid changes in technology have made a lot of companies to become clueless about what they need to concentrate.

Most businesses are already convinced of the business example for machine learning. Based on a 2017 report highlighted by Louis Columbus in Forbes, 84 percent of the executive's report that AI allowed them to stay ahead of their competitors.

If you are starting the strategy phase of integrating machine learning into your competitive toolkit, you have several options. Some experts consider machine learning to represent the next phase in the evolution of analytics. Consulting with professional data scientists is an important first step. But for certain companies that may not be an option.

Most companies are establishing links with universities to identify recent graduates from specialized advanced degree programs in data and analytics.

But to some level, most organizations must implement the talent they already have.

Upgrading your staff in AI and machine learning technologies is a smart move.

For new companies in AI, beginning from inside is a safer investment. A common mistake is hiring several machine learning professionals who are too expensive before getting the data infrastructure and data accessibility in their organizations in order.

That is something that is usually a big problem, and what finally happens is a low return on investment, which results in bad engineering.

A certain report published by Gartner says that by 2022-one in five workers doing nonroutine tasks will depend on AI to perform the job. Well, this is not bad news for workers.

Often, we have realized that automating fairly simple transactions and workflows may let employees and customers spend a lot of time elsewhere, leading to a lot of value at the end.

Organizations that concentrate only on automation will transform their competitive edge. The most successful will concentrate on skills that distinguish them, and that can't be duplicated by AI or ML.

Those skills can be summarized up in a single word: humanness.

Is applying ML worth the pains? Experts say yes because ML offers the tools for visibility into your organization, processes, products, customers and even competitors.

Instant access to on-demand insights provides business with the edge they require to survive in a competitive environment.

Chapter 12: The Future of AI

While organizations and people struggle to control a wide range of information and a growing range of devices, there are still a few new techniques to apply to make a quality decision based on AI and the IoT.

It's around 10 am on a Tuesday and Jane, a marketing specialist is working with her colleagues to compile a presentation for a new business pitch. The client is a big corporate company, and the pressure is on to get the account.

Networking with teams in other locations, Jane has data coming in by text, e-mail, WhatsApp and instant messaging and by phone. At the same time, she is looking online for important facts and data for her project.

The global population is expected to hit 7.6 billion in 2020 with the number of IoT connected devices expected to increase between 20-30 billion by the same year. How can Jane and hundreds of million others control these information sources, determine what is important, and make the correct decision?

Compute this growing number of people and devices, and you will begin to see an exponential rise of data and ubiquitous information that is already generating 'infoxication.'

Artificial intelligence seems to solve this issue by building a set of technologies that can assist control information, and look for reliable data sources, accept informed decisions and take advantage of improved cognition.

Workplace hub focuses on the office, and in particular, the workplace of the future. It integrates all of an organization's technology through a single centralized platform plus enhancing efficiency by decreasing the general costs of IT management and service provision.

It offers real-time, data-driven insights that transform business processes. By implementing AI and IoT systems, workplace hub will change in the next five years to become what the company refers to as a cognitive hub.

This new technology will use intelligent edge computing to AI and augment human intelligence to expand the network of human interfaces and improve collaboration between teams and individuals.

Cognitive Hub will become a great platform for a company's information flows within the digital sector and offer augmented intelligence-based on the kind of services that everyone can apply.

It will also connect future devices like augmented reality glasses, flexible screens, and smart-walls. Cognitive hub merges entire company wisdom using AI to collect and process data to make life simple for teams, individuals, and companies, enabling them to work efficiently.

Although some people think that cloud computing is going to diminish, the fact is that it won't die. Instead, it will diverge and transform into a cortex-like structure made of complex three-dimensional tree. In this modern age, cloud computing is the glue between intelligent automation, cognitive computing, and other fields related to AI.

There is still a lot of work to deliver in the cognitive hub, but workplace hub has already transformed the way we work by allowing us to control the rapid rise in devices, connections, and information.

The future of AI in 2020

Talking of Millenials and the next coming generation, what distinguishes us from our predecessors is the discoveries, humans have so far invented and developed almost everything that we can touch in virtual. The only common thing between us, predecessors and the coming generation is the brain that changes the way we communicate and how we view things. Artificial Intelligence had been predicted for years, but it was initially connected to robots only. But now AI is integrated into almost everything we use and consider smart. AI is a software that emulates humans or has human-like behavior.

It has always been predicted, seen and witnessed as something with excellent ability to make us sit at a comfortable place enjoying while some of the tasks are completed, saving our time and consuming minimum energies and efforts to get things done.

Programming

This brings us to a new world where you can complete different things you never thought you could complete. AI connects us and acts as a transition between discrete actions. In other words, it allows you to interact in multiple things at one time, like translating from one language to another instantly. Ever since computers were introduced, we have been relying on a set of rules for dealing with our actions and letting us customize from their setting page. Transferring the same technology into AI requires the absence of these rules and training the algorithm of the computer to link up with the actions.

Predictions 2019

Artificial intelligence provides us with variables to work with and allows us to process all the variables in a programmatic style, which is simpler and provides a transparent level of confidence. It emerges as a controversial, but predicting what is going to take place in the coming years is accurate if done within the scientific realm of statistics. From the start, computers were known for dealing with all the mathematical tasks. Computing statistical relevance which is the cornerstone of machine learning when it comes to diagnosing diseases, predicting weather patterns, and playing chess. Since we are always heading towards increased data volume, and processing power, that makes the computer suitable.

Decisions

These days, companies make decisions based on the data extracted from management information systems because that data directly emerges from operations of their company-making it crucial to break or make rules. Integrating AI and decision management technologies are sufficient to push decision-making to different levels. Proficiencies in AI also benefit decision management technologies when it comes to defining customer data into prognostic models of important trends. This new trend has already made other departments such as marketing and consumer to change their efforts based on the major demographic.

We can say it is a matured technology with digital banking, which is currently being used in different enterprise applications.

Interactions

AI generates new forms of the interface using the least effort. With the invention of mouse and keyboards in our lives, we are using computers every day and conveniently as time goes. For digital communications, we have learned how to program and code so we can realize better results. Now, as the codes can be converted into human sentences and interrupt input from sensors and cameras-this interaction can be conducted smoothly and naturally.

What you should expect with the future of AI technology

Different types of technological inventions are changing the way we live, how we interact and move on with our everyday lives, but AI may provide the most interesting changes. Although AI has been around for quite some time, the recent changes have made AI adaptable. Reviewing the future of AI, one can see a world where AI controls each aspect of our lives.

The most promising AI innovations

Overall, artificial intelligence will change every phase of our everyday life. Although we shall find for ways to incorporate it at home, AI will still be used by companies, businesses, and government.

Right now we have self-driving cars that have been introduced on the road. While the self-driving industry is expected to expand in the coming years, the U.S transport department is already creating policies and regulations to control AI-driven vehicles.

Currently, the self-driving vehicles are in the lowest category where the vehicles require a human driver. Despite this, the ultimate plan is to create a complete automated self-driving car, which is predicted to be effective and safe. The public transportation sector and firms are still concentrating on AI to develop self-driving bus and planes.

AI and Robotics will integrate

Cybernetics has already incorporated AI, and that is a progress that is bound to continue. By adding AI technology into robotics, soon we shall improve our bodies, providing us with endurance, longevity, and strength. Although cybernetics may make us improve our bodies, the use of this technology is focused on assisting the disabled. Individuals with permanent paralysis or amputated limbs can be provided with a better life.

AI will create complete functional robots

Besides allowing us to improve our bodies, AI technology is predicted to help us build artificial lifeforms. Science fiction has, for a long time, exploring the idea of human-like robots capable of performing complex interactions. As the field of robotics continues to change and include AI, robots will become important in different ways. For example, they can pick a dangerous task and do work that may be hazardous to our health.

Impact on humans

Based on some statistics released by Gartner, by 2012, AI will eradicate 1.8 million jobs and replace it with 2.3 million jobs. If you consider the journey of human beings from the past three industrial revolutions toward the present digital revolution, our lives and standard of workings have changed substantially, and they would be changed again. Consider the world where we talk about work-life balance by spending two days working. It is pretty much expected.

But with these synthetic substances, AI is a massive deal. At the moment, we are in reality because we know where things finish fast, with more exactness, and in light of better learning.

2020 will be a great year in AI business progression because automated reasoning will resort to positive employment spark.

With the arrival of 2020, AI-based jobs will hit two million net-new employments in 2025.

Different advancements in the past have been linked with a short-lived employment misfortune, monitored by recuperation, at that point, the business will change, and AI will probably take this course. AI will improve the profitability of multiple occupations, disposing of a large number of center and low-level positions.

The future of AI in the workplace

Smart devices aren't just transforming our homes, but they are finding their way into multiple industries and disrupting the workplace. AI can change productivity, efficiency, and accuracy across a company.

However, many people fear that the advancement of AI will cause machines and robots to replace human workers and look at this development in technology as a threat instead of a tool to change our lives.

With discussion of AI going on in 2019, businesses require to understand that self-learning and black-box potential are not the answer. Many organizations have started to experience the unlimited power of AI, using the benefits of AI to improve human intelligence and acquire real value from their data.

Since there is a lot of evidence that shows the advantages of intelligent systems, many decision-makers have started to grasp the potential of AI. Research done by EY shows that organizations incorporating AI at the enterprise level are improving operational efficiency and making informed decisions.

The first companies to implement AI achieves competitive advantage. That is because it can reduce the cost of operations, and other head counts. From a business perspective, this is a positive thing, but not for people working in jobs that can be taken over by machines. Of course, the introduction of AI will create some conflict between humans and machines.

As we continue to build innovative systems, AI will have a huge impact on our economy by creating jobs that demand a specific skill.

There is a probability that AI will come to replace certain jobs that involve repetitive tasks and eclipse the current human ability. AI technologies will decide the place of humans.

Automated decisions will be responsible for tasks such as loan approval, detecting corruption, and financial crime.

Organizations will experience a rise in production levels because of the progress in automation.

How to maximize AI

Since many jobs may be affected by the development of AI, it is good to look at some of the problems that AI may bring.

- The business should find a solution to the bias problem around AI by identifying an effective implementation.

- The government must make sure that the profits of AI are shared in the society between the ones affected and those not affected by the developments.

To effectively take advantage of AI, problems must be addressed at an educational level. Education systems can focus on empowering students in tasks linked to working with AI.

This demands a lot of emphases be applied to STEM subjects. Besides, subjects that improve creativity and emotional abilities should be encouraged. While artificial intelligence will be productive than human beings, humans will always do better than computers in jobs that require imagination and relationship building.

Artificial intelligence will transform the world both inside and outside the workplace. Instead of concentrating on the fear of around automation, businesses require to embrace technologies to make sure they implement the most effective AI systems to improve and complement human intelligence.

Ensuring that the machines don't take over

When Stephen Hawking cautioned about the possibility of a certain technology, then it makes sense to think about it.

Stephen Hawking said in 2014 that AI could lead to the end of the human race. There many possible benefits because everything provided by civilization is a product of human intelligence. It is hard to predict what we may attain when this intelligence is reflected by the tools AI may offer, but the elimination of disease and poverty cannot be undermined.

Humanity's potential death at the hands of machines is a long journey. In a PWC's March 2017 economic report, it predicts that by 2030 close to 30 percent of UK jobs could be taken over by machines. Workers in the storage, manufacturing, transportation, and retail sectors are the ones to be at risk.

Despite this chilling report by PWC, some people hold a different believe than this. For example, Accenture forecasts that AI technologies will generate an additional $814billion to the UK economy.

There have been a lot of fearful stories about AI, and several studies have concentrated heavily on the job displacement effect. However, some people think this as a simplistic view.

The traditional boosters of economic growth and labor no longer work to increase the GDP, but AI provides hope.

The argument is that AI, to the point that it can be a new form of virtual labor, can effectively become a new wave of production that can transform the general picture of growth.

AI will support both intelligent automation and augmentation. Intelligent automation is different from the automation we had seen some time ago. It involves the application of data to deliver services and intelligently implement tasks. There is still a large effect of augmentation. Taking the things, we already do and allowing us to perform them productively.

What has awakened AI in the business industry is the increasing cost of computer power and an increase in cloud availability. The cloud-based platform, which relies on AI to analyze the shape of the network of data in near-real time, is applied by companies and governments across the world.

You can store each bit of data you find and combine the data with these algorithms to create an opportunity where it did not exist before.

If you require a professor specialized in mathematics to help you out with interpretation of AI and ML algorithms, then you cannot persuade your senior executives to proceed.

Ayasdi has achieved this by developing applications that rely on the underlying technology but focused at certain business challenges like helping hospitals determine the best practice in healthcare from their data so that they can generate the best quality care at a lower price.

Providers of AI are already helping firms and organizations to become smarter and efficient. There is a huge economic potential from AI technologies, but how can you develop people and infrastructure so that we get the economic benefit.

Jobs might be different in the coming years-you could be working alongside a robot or teaching them. How can you educate people now so that they are fit to deal with that?

Things to note about the future of AI

1. **AI is growing faster than you think and expanding exponentially.**

2. **You use artificial intelligence every day**

Google Now, Cortana, and Siri are some of the common examples of AI, but AI is definitely around us. It can be found in cars, video games, vacuum cleaners, and lawnmowers. E-commerce software, international financial markets, and medical research are some of the many examples.

3. **Robots will take over part of your job**

You could be doing well in your job, but the task you do may already be automatable, or it will soon be automated. How soon? In the next 30 years, most jobs will be done by robots, that is according to professor Moshe Vardi of Rice University. That may look bad, but many researchers in the field believe that technological unemployment will create the door to a future where work is something where people do as pleasure, but not out of necessity.

4. Many intelligent people believe building AI to human level is a risky thing to do.

Once machines become smart like human beings, so many worrying things can take place. There is a minimal probability that development in AI will stop at this point.

5. If AI gets smarter than us, then we have little chance of learning it.

We will never understand the things a super intelligent device can do, even if it attempts to describe to us. It may attempt for years to train us the simplest things it knows, but the actions would useless.

6. There three methods that super intelligent AI could work

7. AI could be the reason why we have never met aliens

An Intelligent future

The high power of modern computing technology plus the rise of human-like robots would make you understand that intelligent machines are not far from taking over our jobs.

However, the reality is that AI programs are sometimes suitable than humans at certain tasks, like playing video games and pattern recognition. They are still far from realizing the type of general intelligence that humans possess.

The human brains took years to grow its complex and efficient functions, and despite the ability of computers, they are not likely to suit their abilities for decades.

There is still a lot that even simple animal brains can show us how information is processed. For example, animals like bees and octopus reveal a certain level of intelligence despite lacking a forebrain.

These animals can perform better than AI based on how fast they can master different tasks with little time. Essentially, deep learning network requires millions of samples before they can learn.

In summary, artificial intelligence has been buzzing in our ears by almost all professions. Take, for instance, 2018, A.I has grown more than ever anticipated. Today, people have started to acknowledge AI after discovering how much it is going to make their lives peaceful. The general advantage of A.I is that it generates choices and activities of humans minus the natural human insufficiencies, for a sensation and time limitation.

Chapter 13: Global Tech Companies Compete in AI

When people think of AI, some switch their minds to methods they can apply to save the human race from rogue machines; familiar story performed on Hollywood screens in the past decades.

Although machine intelligence is far from coming close to human consciousness, an AI conflict is taking place in real life, and this is not between robots and humans, but among businesses competing to take over a lucrative market.

The history of AI date back to 1950, a time when computer science pioneer Alan Turing wrote and published a paper mentioning that one-day machines will think like humans.

Between Turing's landmark paper published several years ago and today's wild market valuations, significant AI developments have either fallen in terms of research or involved machines defeating people at human games.

IBM won the pride when its Deep Blue computer overcame chess grandmaster Garry Kasparov. After 15 years, Watson defeated human beings on TV game show Jeopardy. Not long, Google captured the headlines with the 2015 victory of the AlphaGo program.

AI today

In the last couple of years, AI has made huge strides beyond research and televised fights between man and machine to become a technology loved and used by millions of people daily. Thanks to a trio of essential developments.

First, the ubiquitous application of online services, smart devices, and social media has made data to become available on a mass scale. Data is the power for building algorithms for deep learning, a form of AI that makes it possible for machines to learn and create software. The more data that the system receives, the better it becomes at completing tasks.

Hosting large amounts of data was previously an expensive initiative that would have continued to prevent AI development had it not been for the coming of affordable cloud storage from Google, Microsoft, and Amazon.

Completing this was the rise of powerful chipsets, boosting the process for training computers to behave and act like humans.

All this reflects the great promise of AI can finally be attained in industries extending from healthcare and energy to self-driving cars. The result is a competition among the most significant technology firms to cement their position as leaders in AI applications.

The AI market

The importance of the AI industry can now be experienced not only in the realms of enterprises starting to implement this technology but also in the market performance of companies that are already enjoying the demand.

American chip creator Nvidia, for instance, has seen its stock price increase in the past year after the graphics processing components became the favorite choice for companies training AI systems. This motivated rival Intel to spend around $15.3 billion to buy Mobileye, a chip creator for trucks and cars.

Some years ago, Nvidia committed itself as a company for investing in deep learning. Now that commitment is generating a lot of fruits, and we find ourselves in a state of leadership because this new computing model takes the world by storm.

Data dominance

Ownership of data is vital because tech giants cannot hold all of the world's AI talent, but they can own the data required to train AI. This has led to a big six of tech firms said to enhance AI because of the data-intensive nature of their primary businesses.

Google, Apple, Amazon, and Microsoft, for instance, have managed to take advantage of the data they have gathered from their other businesses to grab an early lead in the race for intelligent personal assistants. Facebook has relied on machine-learning to build a messenger chatbot, while IBM has been an early driver in the cognitive computing sector with Watson. All have made their AI technology open to allow any developer to create on their cloud infrastructure because they know data is the main difference.

If AI truly emulates human consciousness, the stuff of films in our lifetime will originate from one of those companies because they are the only ones with the data to train a model of that complexity.

AI will trigger a new data gold rush, defined by data-driven acquisitions. Companies that search data assets around a specific use-case will win. The final barrier to entry will be unimaginable.

This ability to lead in specific use-cases implies that non-tech firms have the chance to get a piece of their segment. Engineering giants are investing heavily in factory automation.

Similarly, there is a notion that AI startups and companies in other industries can gain from the democratization of AI via the big six's open source tools like Microsoft's CNTL.

Some consider this democratization as necessary in making sure AI can solve the broad level of business and societal challenges, and that restricting innovation to a small pool of companies will provide them with a lot of control and destroy AI's ability.

This has sent chills because Google's largest reservoir of data has some weak points. If Google and Amazon dictate the world of AI, then the resulting systems will be biased, even if they have the best objectives and intentions.

The more people take part in AI debates, the more industries will gain, and the earlier we shall see the effects across the business, government, and society.

However, some people think that the option to democratize AI is gone. Spreading innovation past the big six is unrealistic because of the absence of programming talent and high costs of acquiring it.

Even with the presence of free platforms, you still require to have an experienced, and specialized data scientist to develop efficient solutions that offer real value to users.

When an extensive AI programming skill is finally brought to the market, the big six companies don't have to worry. By making their AI technology open source, they have already sent a message to the rest of the world that software is no longer an advantage to them, but data is.

Despite AI being present in people's homes and many other big businesses, the most powerful applications are yet to be achieved. But when they do arrive, the big six companies have set the path to benefit the most, but still, they have each other to compete with. At the same time, the market will be sufficient enough for startups and enterprises to build a lead using special use-cases.

Chapter 14: Building an Enterprise AI Strategy

Overwhelmed by a decade-long run that has realized considerable gains in computer power and storage costs, businesses have the relevant requirements to ensure intelligence is a reality.

The question enterprises need to address today is not whether to become intelligent, but is a matter of how and how fast. Every business will become knowledgeable in the same manner every enterprise is a digital enterprise. If they don't evolve and embrace AI, then they will stop to exist.

To realize intelligence, enterprises require to adapt and develop an intelligent application approach while simultaneously preparing the organization to narrow that intelligence. A strategy created around smart applications enables enterprises to develop experience, express business value, and establish a framework for repeatability.

The focus, however, is to create intelligent applications. The ability to identify patterns in data without preconceived notions: this depends heavily on unsupervised machine-learning techniques.

An unsupervised technique automatically chooses algorithms and dramatically limits risks by removing bias. The ability to accurately predict relies on new data models trained on historical data. This is a standard measure for many ML algorithms but is always confused for the whole field.

Intelligent applications must learn to justify their assertions. Black-box models cannot complete mission-critical tasks if they cannot be interpreted to the business owner. Transparency and justification generate trust.

Unexplored intelligence must also be accompanied by action. This means intelligence must train other applications autonomously or fall in the subject matter experts' workflow.

Lastly, intelligent applications are built with the ability to detect and react as data changes. An intelligent system is one that continuously learns.

By developing intelligent applications that involve all these properties, enterprises have a place to start. To narrow that effort, it requires extra considerations involving technology strategy and organizational changes.

For instance, organizations will always conduct a small-scale experiment using a subset of the above components. This builds a false sense of security for most enterprises. Wins implemented against sterile data or in an operational vacuum are not likely to convert well when required to scale to real-world scenarios such as detecting cyber-criminals within billions of financial transactions, or monitoring and eliminating global health epidemics. Establishing real-world applications will prepare an enterprise for long-term success.

This commitment to deployable intelligence should not come at the cost of speed. Enterprises that set fast timelines tend to learn pretty faster.

Intelligent systems will transform how you conduct specific business processes. Understanding this fact, ahead of time will allow the enterprise to optimize on the knowledge and to consolidate the wins, thereby establishing momentum for the future applications of intelligence. At the center of a successful change lies a center of excellence. From here, best practices are developed, processes change is improved, and prioritization is established depending on operational readiness, business need, and other factors.

The next generation of leaders will emerge from this center of excellence. So you need to staff it adequately.

Each organization should customize its intelligence approach to specific business needs. In the future, every analytics company will change to become an AI company. These changes will make it hard to differentiate truth from fiction, but the features defined to identify, justify, predict, and learn should present a framework to examine the validity. That framework, integrated with an application-first approach, should allow organizations to overcome these transformational changes.

Artificial Intelligence has the ability to change every business in the same manner the internet has completely changed the way we conduct our business. From smarter services and products tailored for business processes, AI has the potential to change everything. Those businesses that don't take advantage on the transformative power of AI risk being left behind.

That is the reason why you need develop an AI strategy for your enterprise whether small or big. To get the most out of AI, it has to be related to your business strategy and your entire picture of strategic goals. So the first step in any AI strategy is analysis of your business strategy. After all, you don't want to miss this strategy and apply AI to an irrelevant business objective.

In this stage, you need to ask yourself whether your business strategy is right? Is your strategy still current in the world of smarter services and products?

Conclusion

AI is the driving force of new enterprises. The main assumption made is that human intelligence can be represented using symbolic structures and operations.

A huge debate exists on whether AI can be a mind, or imitate the human mind, but no need to wait for the results of this debate, nor the hypothetical computer that can model the whole human intelligence.

AI is poised to make a vast transformational change on business. Informational technology is no longer about the automation process and programming business logic, but insight is the new currency, and the rate at which it can scale that insight and the knowledge it generates is the foundation of value creation and the goal of competitive advantage.

The effects of AI will increase in the coming decade, as every industry will change its main processes and business models to take advantage of AI and ML. The problem now lies in business management, implementation, and imagination. For business leaders, it is crucial to devise a plan for incorporating AI work in the organization.

AI demands that you have the vision to fulfill. But your vision should not be a cookie cutter, and so your AI application should not be either. With the advice and discussion in this book, you can move forward to introduce advanced analytics into your company strategy and understand the pros and cons of different methods depending on your goals.

Fields such as manufacturing, sports, banking, and retail have already found applications for machine learning and AI.

Don't forget that the current machines can complete narrowly defined tasks with great accuracy, and that accuracy is only as good as the quantity of the data that powers the model. The current state of ML will, with the input of customized data, attain countless improvements to existing products, and finally, lead to the development of free-standing AI.

However, as machine learning gets complex, we will move towards a sophisticated AI. The complexity of AI is realized through neural networks. That said, we hope you have enjoyed reading this book, found it resourceful.

Networking for Beginners

Be Familiar with Computer Network Basics. Learn What a Computer Network is, Why It Matters and How Networking May Raise a Challenge to Machine Learning.

Scott Chesterton

Introduction

Congratulations on downloading *Networking for beginners* and thank you for doing so.

The following chapters will discuss the basics of computer networking and its protocols in a clear crystal detail in a way such that you will be able to understand them easily in very less time.

Computer networking is the greatest invention mankind has ever seen due to its vast opportunities and great technologies that had made human life luxurious and had paved a way for the greatest knowledge transfer we could ever think of.

This book deals with computer networking in layman terms in a way such that newbies can appreciate the complex process that deals with computer networking. TCP/IP a famous network protocol is also described in detail for better understanding of the various protocols that are essential for good network communication.

Machine learning is a phenomenon in the tech industry which is efficient and accurate. Networking for beginners explains how machine learning can be interlinked with computer networks for better network security and thus a better Internet away from malicious hackers.

There are plenty of books on this subject on the market, thanks again for choosing this one! Every effort was made to ensure it is full of as much useful information as possible, please enjoy!

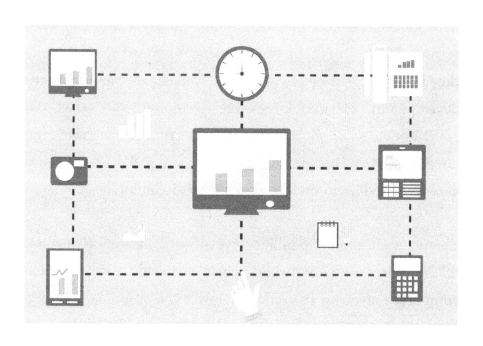

Chapter 1: Introducing Computer Networking

We know that some of the 21st century's important characteristics are digital, network, and information, these had made the world a better place to live. In order to realize information, we must rely on a perfect network, because the network can transmit information very quickly within a split of a second. Therefore, the network has now become the lifeline of the information society and an important basis for the development of the knowledge economy and even for government activities that go on in secret. The network has already had the inestimable influence on social life in many aspects as well as to social economic development.

There are three familiar types of networks namely telecommunications networks, cable television networks, and computer networks. In accordance with the original division of services, telecommunications networks provide users with telephone, telegraph and fax services. Cable television delivers a variety of TV shows to its users. Computer networks enable users to transfer data files between computers. These three kinds of networks all play a very important role in the information process, but among them, the fastest development and which plays a central role is the computer network.

With the development of technology, the telecommunication network and the cable television network have gradually integrated into the technology of the modern computer network for example as Skype and Netflix, expanding the original service range of they intended to be. But the computer network also can provide telephone communication, video communication as well as the transmission video program service to the user. In theory, the above three networks can be integrated into a network to provide all the above services but however, it is often not possible.

Since the 1990s, the computer network represented by the Internet has developed rapidly, from the free education and Scientific Research Network for Americans to the Commercial Network for global use as the largest computer network in the world. Computer networks have only been around for more than 50 years (the real computer networks began with the creation of ARPAnet by the Defense Advanced Research Projects Agency (ARPA) in 1969, which is described later in this book). In this short time of 50 years, the development and popularization of computer network technology in various fields really can be described as a phenomenal journey. It's really hard to imagine that the first-gigabit connection rates have grown to tens of gigabits in such a short period of time, increasing by thousands of times. With the development of computer network technology and its scope, the advantages and applications of the computer network are unimaginable. Before talking about applications of computer network let us discuss briefly the definition of a computer network.

The term information and Communication Society has become synonymous with the modern world. People can use mobile phones and other information terminals at any time to communicate anywhere, and this environment is dependent on the network to achieve.

However, with the development and popularization of the Internet, many new challenges have emerged. In order to transmit a large amount of data in an instant and efficiently, it is necessary to study how to construct a complex network. Even more, it is necessary to consider how to carry out strict routing control in such a complex network. In order to overcome these challenges, efforts are being made to improve the cost-effectiveness of network construction, to update network equipment according to market requirements, and to develop better maintenance tools for the stable operation of complex networks. At the same time, efforts are being made to train a group of capable network technicians as soon as possible.

The computer is having an inestimable influence on our society and life. Today, the computer has been used in a variety of fields, so that some people say "the greatest invention of the 20th century is the computer. ". Computers have been introduced not only into offices, factories, schools, educational institutions, and laboratories but also into personal computers at home. At the same time, the number of people who own portable devices such as laptops, tablets and mobile phone terminals (smartphones) is growing Even devices that look nothing like computers, such as home appliances, music players, office appliances, and cars, typically have a small chip built into them to give them the computer control they need. Inadvertently, our working life has been closely linked to the computer. And most of the computers we use and devices with built-in computers are networked.

In the beginning, computers were widely used in stand-alone mode. However, with the continuous development of computers, people are no longer confined to the single-computer model but will be connected to a computer network. By connecting multiple computers, information can be shared and information can be transferred between two machines located far away from each other. Initially, a network of computers is formed by administrators connecting specific computers together. For example, the connection of computers held by the same company or laboratory or the connection of computers between businesses doing business with one another. All in all, it's a private network. With the development of this kind of private network, people begin to try to connect several private networks to form a larger private network. This network gradually evolved into the Internet for public use.

When connected to the Internet, computer-to-computer communication is no longer confined to companies or departments but can communicate with any computer on the Internet. The Internet, as a new technology, greatly enriched the means of communication of telephone, post, and fax, and was gradually accepted by people.

Since then, people have been developing various Internet access technologies, enabling various kinds of communication terminals to connect to the Internet, making the Internet A world-class computer network to create the integrated communications environment we have today.

A computer network is like a person's nervous system. All the senses in a person's body are transmitted to the brain via nerves. Similarly, information from around the world is delivered to everyone's computer via the web. With the explosive development and popularization of the Internet, information networks have been everywhere. Community members, school students can be through the mail group (using e-mail Bulletin Board functions. All members who subscribe to the mail group can receive mail sent to the group.), The home page, BBS forum contact each other, it can even be accessed via a weblog (A text-centric home page or service. Users can update content as easy as keeping a diary.), Chat Rooms, instant messaging, and SNS (social networks). A network of individuals or groups on the Internet. Through SNS, people can publish their recent activities, life feelings and the latest works, so that members of the circle real-time personal dynamic.

Definition of Computer Network

A computer network is made up primarily of interconnecting common, programmable hardware. The hardware is designed for a specific purpose (for example, to transmit data or video signals). This programmable hardware can be used to transmit a variety of different types of data and can support a wide and growing range of applications.

According to this definition: (1) the hardware connected to a computer network is not limited to ordinary computers, but includes smartphones and other different types of devices like AR devices, smartwatches that are flooding the market every day (2) computer networks are not specifically designed to transmit data, but are capable of supporting a wide variety of applications (including those that may arise in the future).

We know that in the beginning, computer networks were really used to transmit data. But with the development of network technology, the application scope of a computer network is increasing, not only networks can transmit audio and video files, but also the application scope has far exceeded the general communication scope and can be perfectly used for many applications.

It is generally believed that computer network refers to the connection of multiple computers and network equipment with independent instruments in different geographical locations through communication lines (including transmission media and network equipment). A computer system for resource sharing and information transfer under the co-management and coordination of Network Operating System, network management software and network communication protocol. If you don't know what a computer network is, go home, or go to an Internet cafe, or go to your company and see for yourself. What you see is a network of pcs (personal computers) that appear to be independent and located in different places, connected by cables and boxes of devices (switches, routers).

Simply put, a computer network is a collection of computer systems, or groups of computer systems, that work independently and are connected to each other by communication lines, including connecting cables and network equipment. In this set of computer systems, resources can be shared among computers, access to each other can be carried out for a variety of computer network applications. The computers can be microcomputers, minicomputers, midsized computers, mainframes.

By sharing, I mean sharing resources. Resource sharing has many implications. It can be information sharing, software sharing, or hardware sharing. For example, there are many servers on the Internet (that is, a dedicated computer) that store a large number of valuable electronic documents (including audio and video files) that can be easily read or downloaded (for free or for a fee) by Internet users. Because of the network, these resources are as easy to use as if they were right next to the user.

A typical example of data resource sharing is database resource sharing, where each network user can centrally invoke relevant data information in a single database server. A variety of application servers are also examples of sharing data resources, such as receiving email through client-side programs like Fox Mail and Outlook, and the online games you and your friends play every day Or you and your Family Watch the same movie on the Internet every day on a different computer at home. There are many examples of sharing software resources, such as in the enterprise internal network we will provide all employees on the server to share some common tools, let users choose to install. If pushed to the Internet, it is more intuitive, we downloaded from the Internet are all examples of software resource sharing.

Now we will discuss different types of computer networks and how they are divided based on certain categories.

Categorized by the Scope of the Network
The Wide Area Network (Wan)
This is the core part of the Internet, and its mission is to transport data sent by hosts over long distances (across different

countries, for example) . The links connecting the switches of Wan nodes are usually high-speed links with large communication capacity.

Metropolitan Area Network (Man)

The scope of Metropolitan Area Network (MAN) is generally a city, can span several blocks or even the whole city, the distance of its function is about 5 ~ 50 km. A Metropolitan Area Network can be owned by one or more units, but it can also be a utility used to interconnect multiple LANs that is local area networks. At present, many metropolitan area networks (Man) are based on Ethernet technology.

Local Area Network (LAN) In the early days of Lan Development, a school or factory often had only one Lan, but now the LAN is widely used for different purposes. Most schools or businesses have many interconnected LANs (such networks are often called campus networks, or corporate networks).

Personal Area Network (Pan)

A Personal Area Network (Pan) is a Network that connects Personal electronic devices (such as portable computers) for Personal use wirelessly at a person's place of work or home. This is often referred to as a Wireless personal area network (WPAN), which has a small range of about 10m.

Categorized by the users of the network

Public network

This is a large network built at the expense of the Telecommunications Company (state or private) ."public" means that anyone willing to pay a fee under the Telco's rules can use the network. Therefore, the public network can also be called the public network.

Private Network

A private network is a network built by a department to meet the needs of a particular business unit. This network does not provide services to persons outside of the unit. For example, military, railway, banking, power, and other systems have their own private network.

Applications of Computer Network in the Real World

Before going to talk about a brief history of computer networks we will go through a few applications of computer network that has changed our world.

When it comes to computer networks, the first question you have to ask is what they are for, what we can do with them. If you go back more than ten years and ask about the use of computer networks, you might all agree that "resource sharing" is the answer. That was true of computer network applications at the time, and there were no obvious applications other than for resource sharing because there was neither the Internet nor any internal network applications within the LAN. Now, with the improvement and popularization of the computer network system, especially Internet technology, the application of computer network has seen unprecedented prosperity. Computer network Has penetrated into the ordinary people's Daily work, life and leisure, and other aspects.

While there are a lot of computer network applications out there, they fall into two broad categories one is business applications and the other is home / personal applications. Below section shows the detailed description and applications about day to day uses of computer networks.

Commercial Application

Business applications are the most important aspects of computer network applications, and later home / personal applications got developed on the basis of business applications. In the commercial application of computer network, the main network is the corporate Lan, and the internal Lan and Internet of the external users (such as subsidiaries, partners, suppliers, etc.) connected with the Corporate Lan. Business applications include resource sharing, data transmission, collaborative work, remote access and management, e-commerce, etc..

1)Resource sharing

One of the most basic and traditional applications in computer networks is Resource Sharing. The shared resources can be physical devices such as printers, scanners, fax machines, recorders, shared data files, software resources, and so on. The goal is to give everyone access to the devices, programs, files, and data that they allow. One of the simplest examples of resource sharing is when multiple users within a LAN share a printer over the network (some printers now support Internet-shared printing as well) to print there is no need for the company to provide each user with a separate printer, greatly saving equipment investment costs.

More important than physical device sharing in a corporate Lan is the sharing of programs, files, and data resources such as corporate internal public documents, database reports, or software installed by users and the company's database system. The advantage of a Lan is that we no longer have to copy data through removable media (floppy disks, USB sticks, removable hard drives, etc.), as we did in the absence of a computer network. This not only ensures the security of the shared data (because the sharing can also set different access rights for different users) but also greatly improves the efficiency of data sharing usage. Usually, there is a file server in the intranet to store these shared data resources.

There are more examples of resource sharing on the Internet, such as file uploading and downloading, audio and video sharing, file viewing, and viewing, etc..

(2) Network Communication
In the field of network communication, many functions are used in enterprises, such as remote network interconnection, remote

video conference, remote training, remote consultation and so on. The Remote Network Interconnection is currently between the Group Company and the Subsidiary Company or between the company and the partner, the supplier website through the special access way (at present mainly uses the VPN technology) to link each unit's network according to the application demand and the access permission. This can make communication between the network, user access more secure, convenient, but also more effective management of site data and e-commerce data.

Applications such as teleconferencing, remote training, and remote consultation are now common in large corporations and hospitals. On the other hand, the application of this function can save meeting and training cost (because it overcomes the time and space limitation of physical distance), on the other hand, it can make full use of all kinds of expert resources and solve some difficult problems in time.

(3) Data Transmission

Data transmission is most common in computer networks E-MAIL, FTP (File Transfer Protocol) file transfer, TFTP / RCP (simple File Transfer Protocol copy protocol) file upload and download, and so on. For example, we may send files to our friends through WhatsApp or MSN every day, many websites provide the function of downloading resources for users to choose to download the files in their Resource Library Now there are a number of dedicated resources for the upload and download site disk and so on. These processes of uploading and downloading are part of the data transfer application of the computer network.

(4) Working Together

Cooperative work is a typical application of computer network, which means to be in the same or different places through the network Even multiple systems in different countries share the way a particular network communication or network application task works. The most typical example is the load balance of server, switch cluster, many DNS servers in ISP, DC (domain controller) servers and so on can also realize the load balance to provide the corresponding service for the network user.

One of the current applications is the current Wikipedia, where content can be co-edited and refined by globally licensed particIPants. Also, a project can be completed by more than one person in the head office and branch office.

(5) Remote Access and Management

Remote access and management is the way that computer network users access and administrators manage clients and servers. Vpn solutions that support mobile Internet access, for example, allow company employees to connect to the company's network via a VPN at any time, anywhere, to view the files or data they need, and to upload or download the files they need. In addition, using "remote Web desktop" and "remote assistance" functions like those in Windows server systems, employees on business trips can access or even control a host or server on the company's internal network over the Internet. If they have an administrator account, they can also remotely manage and maintain the company's internal servers.

(6) Electronic Commerce

Now almost all the larger units have set up their own websites, one of the purposes is to promote their products to users around the world. In addition, the majority of enterprise users through their own web site to provide customers with online transactions, which is commonly referred to as "e-commerce. ". I'm sure most of you have had the experience of shopping on Amazon, where many businesses have set up shop to sell their wares, ranging from expensive jewelry and household appliances to groceries and books. Others, such as Alibaba, Flipkart and so on (there are so many, so many, so many of them) allow a variety of products to be sold on the site. These e-commerce sites are now commonly referred to as "e-commerce" to distinguish them from brick-and-mortar stores.

Home Applications

In the beginning, the computer network is basically all out of commercial applications, but with the Internet broadband access and the abundance of Internet applications, the computer network began to go into ordinary people's homes. Today, we can access the Internet from our home broadband connection and visit global websites from our home. We can make instant contact with friends and strangers from all over the world through instant messaging software such as Facebook and Twitter; we can also have our own local area networks, or personal websites, which people around the world can visit to learn about the products and services we offer, and the state of our work, school, and life.

Everything that you see in everyday lay comes under Home applications. From Netflix to Spotify to YouTube to WhatsApp. Everything you use in everyday life to communicate, educate yourselves, collaborate with people, plan a travel date or ordering a meal a comes under Home applications. Before moving on further take a paper and note down your best websites and just google how they work for a better understanding of your favorite websites or internet applications.

History of Computer Networking

The purpose of this section is to introduce the history of the development of computer and network. Computers became popular in the 1950s, and their usage patterns have changed a lot since then.

The development of the computer network has gone through several generations of changes. Not only has the connotation of the computer network changed tremendously, but Computer Network Technology and network applications are also no longer the same as a few decades ago, the first and second generation of computer networks can be compared. To understand the whole history of the development of computer network will help us to have a clear understanding of the development of computer network technology and application, and also help us to distinguish which are the mainstream application technologies at present What technologies are out of date that we don't have to learn. Of course, there must be computers before there can be computer networks, just as there must be people before there will be human society. Generally speaking, the development of the computer network can be summarized in the following stages.

(1) First Generation Computer Networks (Terminal-Oriented Computer Networks)

In 1946, the world's first digital computer came out. But there were very few computers and they were very expensive. Since most computers at that time used complex methods, the user computer would first print programs and data into paper tapes or cards, and then send them to the Computing Center for processing. In 1954, a terminal called a Transceiver was introduced, which was used for the first time to transmit data from punched cards over telephone lines to computers in remote computing centers. Since then, teletype has also been connected to a computer as a remote terminal, and users can enter their own programs on a remote teletypewriter and the results calculated by the computer in the computing center can also be sent to a teletypewriter far away and printed out. This simple transmission system was the basic prototype of the computer network. Of course, these are far from us, now we do not have to study these transceiver terminals and their data transmission princIPle.

In order to allow more people to use computers, Batch Processing systems have emerged. Batch processing refers to the way that the user programs and data are loaded into the tape or tape in advance and read by the computer in a certain order so that the programs and data executed by the user can be processed in batch. At that time, this kind of computer was too expensive and bulky to be used in an ordinary office. As a result, they are usually placed in computer centers that specialize in computer management and operations. The user has no choice but to load the program and data onto a cassette or tape in advance and send it to such a center.

At that time, the operation of the computer was very complicated, not all people can easily use. Therefore, in the actual operation of the program will usually be handed over to a special operator to deal with. Sometimes the program takes longer to process, and in the case of a larger number of users, the user program may not run immediately. At this point, the user can only leave the program to the operator and then come back to the computer center to get the results.

The first generation of computer networks was centered around computer hosts (in fact, what we now call "computer servers"), around which one or more terminals were distributed While the task of the computer host is batch processing, the user terminal does not have the ability of data storage and processing. In a sense, this is not a real computer network at all, because the terminal does not have the ability to work independently. So we now say that the birth of computer networks generally does not refer to the first generation of computer networks, but rather to the second generation of computer networks, which is described below. By "terminal", I mean a simple computer made up of a computer's perIPherals, somewhat similar to what we now call "thin clients", consisting only of CRT monitors, keyboards, and no CPU or hard disk So there's no data storage or processing power. The reason why the network is more computer terminal, because the computer is very expensive, in order to save costs, so the client is usually those with no key components of the computer terminal.

A typical application of the first generation of computer networks was the aircraft reservation system Sabre-i, which was developed jointly by American Airlines and IBM in the early 1950s and put into use in the 1960s. It consists of a computer and 2,000 terminals across the United States. The heavy load on the computer in the Computer Center makes the response to the terminal system slow and even brings the phenomenon of a server crash.

The reliability of a single host system is low, once the computer host is paralyzed, the whole computer network system will be paralyzed. Following batch systems, the 1960s saw the emergence of the TSS (Time Sharing System). It refers to a system in which multiple terminals (consisting of input and output devices such as a keyboard, a monitor, and, initially, a typewriter) are connected to the same computer, allowing multiple users to use the same computer at the same time. At that time the computer cost was very expensive, one person a proprietary computer cost for the average person is out of reach. However, the time-sharing system has realized the goal of "one person, one machine", which makes users feel as if "they are using a computer all by themselves". This also reflects the time-sharing system an important feature –Exclusivity.

Since the advent of time-sharing systems, the availability of computers has greatly improved Especially in interactive (interactive) operation (refers to the computer according to the instructions given by the user to complete processing and return the results to the user. This method of operation is extremely common in modern computers, but it was impossible before the advent of time-sharing systems.). Since then, the computer has become more human, gradually close to our lives.

The exclusive nature of the time-sharing system makes it easier than ever to equip a computer environment that users can operate directly. In a time-sharing system, each terminal is connected to a computer using a communication line to form a star-shaped (star-shaped (*) structure with a computer in the center and many terminals around it. It is from this period that the relationship between the network (communication) and the computer.

(2) Second Generation Computer Networks (Packet Switched Computer Networks)

In order to overcome the shortcomings of the first-generation computer network and improve its availability and reliability, experts began to study the method of interconnecting several computers. If there is a problem, solve it. This is the same way that all technologies are now improved. First, the concept of "store-and-forward" (which we will introduce as we learn about switch technology) was introduced in August 1964 by Baran in the Rand Corporation's research paper on distributed communications. Between 1962 and 1965, the Advanced Research Projects Agency (ARPA) in the United States and the National Physics Laboratory (NPL) in the United Kingdom studied the new technology. Later, in 1966, David Davis of the British NPL first introduced the concept of "packet". In December 1969, the world's first computer packet switching system based on packet technology ARPANET was produced. This is widely recognized as the originator of computer networks.

ARPANET was built by the Defense Advanced Research Projects Agency (DARPA) using telephone lines as the backbone of the network. It started with computer s connected to only four nodes -- UCLA, UC Santa Barbara, Stanford, and the University of Utah -- and grew to 15 nodes two years later. By the late 1970s, the network had more than 60 nodes and more than 100 hosts, spanning America and connecting many universities and research institutions in the Eastern and western United States It is also connected to computer networks in Hawaii and across Europe via the communications satellite.

The end-users in the second-generation computer network can share not only the line and equipment resources in the "communication subnet", but also the rich hardware and software resources of the "resource subnet". This "communication subnet" centered computer network became what we now call the second-generation computer network.

(3) Third Generation Computer Networks (Standardized Computer Networks)

By the 1970s, computer performance had soared, size had shrunk, and prices had fallen sharply. So, the computer is no longer limited to the use of research institutions, the general business gradually began to use the computer. That's because there's an increasing boom in the use of computers for day-to-day business. To improve work efficiency, people begin to study the technology of communication between computers.

Before the advent of computer-to-computer communication, it was cumbersome to transfer data from one computer to another.

At that time, data had to be saved to external storage media such as tape and floppy disks (pluggable devices for storing computer information. Originally just disks and floppy disks, now more commonly used electronic storage media such as CD / DVD and USB storage) These media are then sent to the destination computer for data dump. However, with the technology of communication between computers (which are connected by communication lines), it is easy to read data from another computer in real time, thus greatly reducing the time it takes to transmit data

Communication between computers significantly improves the availability of computers. People are no longer limited to using only one computer for processing, but gradually use more than one computer distributed processing, and finally get the results back together. This trend breaks down the situation where a company buys only one computer for business processing and enables the introduction of computers within each company on a departmental basis.

To process data from within the department. After each department has processed its data, it is sent to the computer at headquarters via a communication line and processed by the computer at headquarters to produce the final data results.

Since then, the development of the computer has entered a new historical stage. At this stage, the computer is more focused on meeting the needs of users, a more flexible architecture system, and a more user-friendly operation than before. In the early 1970s, people began to experiment with computer networks based on packet switching technology and began to study the technology of communication between computers of different manufacturers.

The "store-and-forward" mode is adopted in the transmission mode of the second-generation computer network, which greatly improves the utilization ratio of the expensive communication line resources. Because in this "store-and-forward" communication process, communication lines will not be exclusive communication between a certain node but can be shared for multi-channel communication. However, there are still many disadvantages in the second-generation computer network, such as the lack of unified network architecture and protocol standards. Moreover, although the second generation of computer networks has been divided into communication subnetworks and resource subnetworks, the network systems of different companies are only applicable to their own devices and cannot be connected. For example, in 1974, IBM introduced System Network Architecture (SNA) to provide users with a complete set of communications products that can be interconnected, and in 1975, Dec announced its own digital Network Architecture (DNA); In 1976 UNIVAC announced its Distributed Communication Architecture (DCA). These network technology standards are valid only within a single company, comply with certain standards, interconnect network communication products, only apply to equipment produced by the same company.

The network between different companies still can not interconnect. The computer network communication market is such a fragmented situation that users in the direction of investment at a loss, and is not conducive to fair competition between multiple manufacturers.

From the development of the first- and second-generation computer network technologies, we can see that they are driven by enterprises, that is, by companies developing related technologies and products according to their market and user needs Can Be said to be in the "hundred schools of thought" of the Times. Although "a hundred schools of thought" can fully demonstrate the advantages of each company, but after all, "no rules are difficult to square circle. As a result of the competition between these companies, the technologies and products developed by these different companies are not universal. As a result, no one is big or strong, and it is difficult for users to choose the development of the computer network is also very difficult to have substantive progress.

(4) Fourth Generation Computer Networks (International Computer Networks)

By the end of the 1980s, the technology of the local area network (Lan) was mature, and the technology of optical fiber and high-speed Ethernet appeared. With the birth of Osi / RM architecture in the third-generation computer network, it has greatly promoted the development of the Internet represented by the Internet, which is now the fourth generation computer network. The fourth generation of a computer network is defined as "a system that can realize resource sharing and data communication through the network software of communication devices and lines". In fact, the rudiment of the Internet is Darpa's ARPANET, and the protocol standard adopted is TCP / IP Protocol Specification.

The basic history of the Internet is as follows: In 1985, the National Science Foundation established NSFNET, a backbone network for scientific research and education, using the ARPANET protocol; in 1990 NSFnet replaced ARPANET as the backbone of the National Network And out of universities and research institutions into society, from this network of E-mail, file download and information transmission by people's welcome and widespread use; 1992, the establishment of the Internet Society; 1993, the National Center for Supercomputing at the University of Illinois succeeded in developing Mosaic, an online browsing tool that later became Netscape. That same year, Clinton announced the National Information Infrastructure Program Since then, the NSF has competed around the world for leadershIP and supremacy in an information society. At the same time, N SF stopped funding the Internet and fully commercialized it.

In the 1980s, a network capable of interconnecting multiple computers was born. It allows a wide variety of computers to be connected to each other, from large supercomputers or mainframes to small personal computers. A system that processes windows in the. The X Window System, commonly used on UNIX, as well as Microsoft's Windows and Apple's MAC OS X. These systems allow multiple programs to be distributed to run in multiple windows, and switching can be performed in sequence.) The invention of these systems has brought people closer to the web, making users more aware of the Web as a Convenient place. With a windowing system, users can not only execute multiple programs simultaneously but also freely switch jobs between them. For example, while creating a document on a workstation, you can log on to the host to execute other programs, you can download the necessary data from the database server, and you can contact friends via email. With the combination of the window system and network, we can surf the net freely on our own computer and enjoy the rich resources on the net

Into the 1990s, companies and universities focused on information processing had assigned a computer to each employee or researcher, creating a "one person, one machine" environment. However, this environment is not only expensive to build but in the use of the process will also encounter many new problems. That's why the term "downsizing" and "multi-vendor" (here refers to computer hardware or software vendors) was coined. The reason for the two slogans "connection" (a connection between heterogeneous computers) is that a network is built by combining the products of a variety of hardware and software vendors, rather than a single vendor (where both hardware and software are built using the same vendor's products). The goal is to create a lower-cost network environment by connecting computers from different vendors. The communication network technology connecting heterogeneous computers is the Internet technology we see today (in 1990, personal computers connected to local area networks usually used Novell NetWare system. However, when it comes to connecting to all types of computers, such as mainframes, minicomputers, UNIX workstations, and personal computers, TCP / IP is more of a concern

At the same time, ways of spreading information, such as E-mail (E-mail) and the World Wide Web (WWW), have mushroomed, allowing the Internet to spread from large companies to small families Faced with such a trend, manufacturers not only strive to ensure the interconnection of their products but also strive to keep their network technology and internet technology compatibility. These companies are no longer just looking at big businesses, but at every home or Soho (a small office or Home

Office as a place of business), and are rolling out specific web services and products

Now, like the Internet, E-mail, Web, home page and so on has become the most familiar terms. This also suffices to say that the information network, the Internet has penetrated into our lives. The personal computer, which started out as a mostly stand-alone device, is now more widely used for Internet access. And people around the world, no matter how far apart, can communicate and communicate in real time via their personal computers as long as they are connected to the Internet. The popularization and development of the Internet have had a great influence on the field of communication. Many web technologies with different paths are also moving closer to the Internet. For example, used to be used as a communication base.

By the Internet Protocol Network, which itself is the product of Internet technology. Through the IP network, people can not only realize. Now telephone communications, television broadcast, but also to achieve communication between computers, the establishment of the Internet. Also, devices that connect to the Internet. The Internet has allowed people from all over the world to connect freely across borders via computers. The Internet allows people to search for information, communicate, share information, view news reports, and control devices remotely. However, it's so convenient. The original purpose of a computer network was to connect individual computers to form a more powerful computing environment. In short, to increase productivity. From the age of batch processing to the age of computer networks, there is no doubt that this is the case. Now, however, there seems to be a subtle shift

One of the primary purposes of modern computer networks can be said to be to connect people. People around the world can connect, communicate and exchange ideas via the Internet. This, however, was not possible in the early days of computer networks. This human-to-human computer network has gradually brought about great changes in people's daily life, school education, Scientific Research, and company development. The vast majority of people know the Internet from the first contact with the application of the Internet. Now children can play games online, watch online videos, or chat with friends on Whatsapp. More adults are regularly searching and accessing information on the Internet. Now people often use the Internet to communicate with each other by e-mail (including the transmission of a variety of photos and video files), which makes the traditional postal mail business volume greatly reduced. Buying all kinds of goods on the internet is both convenient and economical, changing the way you have to shop. The purchase of air or train tickets on the Internet can save a lot of queuing time and greatly facilitate passengers. On the financial front, the use of the Internet for transactions such as money transfers or stock trading can save a lot of time.

(5) Next Generation Computer Network

Some people will ask, in what era are we now on the computer? It can be said that we are now in a transitional period between the fourth and fifth generations. But in the end, no one can say for sure what the next generation network will look like, at least not by a long shot. Generally speaking, it is generally believed that the next generation computer network (NGN, that is to say, the Fifth Generation Computer Network) is the convergence of Internet, Mobile Communication Network, fixed telephone communication network, IP network, an optical network. It is an integrated and open network framework that can provide various services including voice, data, and multimedia, and it is a service driven, service and call control separate, call and carry separate network; Is a unified protocol-based, packet-based network. In terms of function, Ngn is divided into four layers, namely access and transmission layer, media layer, control layer, and network service layer. We can see some of the main features of the next-generation computer network, including The current is the "three networks" (computer network, telecommunications network, television network) integration, the Internet of things, virtualization, cloud computing, HTML5, and other new revolutionary technologies.

Among these new technologies, "cloud computing" and "Internet of things" may be the two most important technologies that will revolutionize the current landscape and applications of computer networks in the future. "Cloud Computing" is really

352

similar to the IBM mainframe, is a centralized service, centralized management platform. Is for cloud computing operators to provide enterprise customers with a number of software, hardware platforms and a variety of required services and management, enterprise customers can enjoy the services and platforms they buy simply by connecting to the cloud computing platform of the operator located on the Internet through a relatively simple cloud computing client The investment of enterprise clients in computer network software and hardware platform (such as various server systems, enterprise switches, routers, firewalls, etc.) is greatly saved.

The Internet of things (IOT) is a new technology that continues to expand computer networks. It is simply the Internet of things. It uses radio frequency identification (RFID) technology, as well as infrared sensors, Global Positioning System, laser scanners and other information sensing devices, according to agreed protocols Connecting items (such as electric lights, electrical appliances, monitoring facilities, etc.) that are not currently connected to the computer network to the Internet for information exchange and communication between items, to achieve the intelligent identification, positioning, tracking, monitoring and management of items. Through the "Internet of things" we will be able to control the work at home lights, electrical equipment switches, monitoring home security monitoring facilities, truly ubiquitous internet applications.

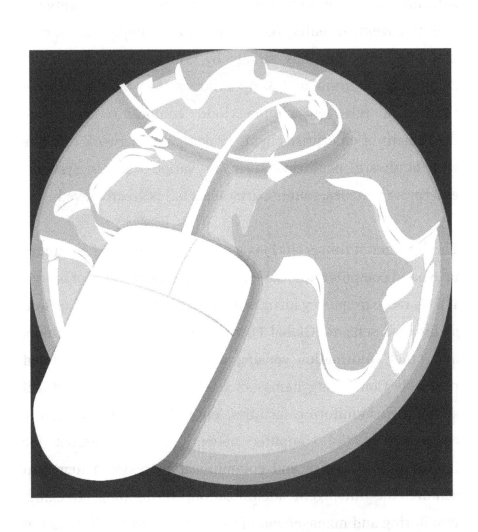

Chapter 2: Computer Networking Basics

Before discussing in detail about computer networks, we will first discuss Internet, the biggest network in the detail and few protocols in which it communicates with the end user for a better understanding of the Network architecture.

Why the Internet Has Become a Sensation?

The reason why the Internet can provide many services to users is that the Internet has two important basic characteristics, namely connectivity, and sharing.

Connectivity is when the Internet allows users to connect to each other, no matter how far apart they are (thousands of kilometers, for example) All kinds of information (data, as well as audio and video) can be exchanged very easily, very cheaply (and in many cases, free of charge), as if these user terminals were all connected directly to each other. This is quite different from using a traditional telecommunications network.

The Internet has become the largest computer network in the world, let's start with an overview of the Internet, including the main components of the Internet, so that we can have a preliminary understanding of the computer network.

The network connects many computers together, while the Internet connects many networks through routers. A computer connected to a network is often called a mainframe. The Internet has become the world's largest and fastest growing computer network, and no one can say exactly how big it is. The rapid development of the Internet began in the 1990s. The World Wide Web (WWW) developed by CERN, the European Organization for Nuclear Research, is widely used on the Internet, greatly facilitating the use of the Internet by non-network Professionals Has Been The main driver of this exponential growth of the Internet. The number of sites on the World Wide Web has also increased dramatically. Accurate traffic on the Internet is difficult to estimate, but the literature suggests that data traffic on the Internet is increasing by about 10 percent per month.

The part on the edge of the Internet is all the hosts that are connected to the Internet. These hosts are also called end systems, and "end" means "end" (the end of the Internet). End Systems can vary widely in function. A small end system can be an ordinary personal computer (including a laptop or tablet) and a smartphone with Internet access Even a small Webcam (which can monitor local weather or traffic and post it on the Internet in real time), and a large end-system can be a very expensive mainframe computer. The owner of an end system can be an individual, a unit (such as a school, an enterprise, a government agency, etc.), or an ISP (that is, an ISP can own some end systems as well as provide services to the end system). The edge uses the services provided by the core to enable multiple hosts to communicate with each other and exchange or share information.

Communication in the Internet

We need to define the following concepts. When we say "host a communicates with host B, " we actually mean that "a program running on host a communicates with another program running on host B. ". Since "process" is "running program", this means that "a process on host a communicates with another process on host B. ". This more rigorous approach is often referred to simply as "computer-to-computer communication. ". Communication between end systems at the edge of the network can usually be divided into two categories: client-server mode (C / s mode) and peer-to-peer mode (P2P mode). These two approaches are described below.

Client-Server Approach

This is the most common and traditional approach to the Internet. We use the client-server mode (sometimes written as client/server mode) when we go online to send e-mails or look up information on the web site. When we make a call, the ringing of the telephone alerts the called user that there is now a call. The object of computer communication is the application process in the application layer. Obviously, the application process cannot be notified by ringing. However, the client-server approach enables the two application processes to communicate.

Both client and server are the two application processes involved in communication. The client-server approach describes the relationship between the services and the serviced processes. Host A runs the client program and host B runs the server program. In this case, a is the client and B is the server. Client A makes a service request to server B, and Server B serves client A.

The main features here are:

The client is the service requester and the server is the service provider.
Both the service requester and the service provider use the services provided by the core part of the network. In practice, client and server programs typically also have some of the following main features.

Client Program:
(1) Running after being invoked by the user, initiating communication (requesting service) to the remote server during communication. Therefore, the client must know the address of the server program.
(2) no special hardware or complex operating system is required.

Server application:
(1) Is a program designed to provide a service that can handle requests from multiple remote or local customers simultaneously.

(2) the system is called automatically after starting up and is running continuously, passively waiting for and receiving communication requests from customers from all over the world. Therefore, the server program does not need to know the address of the client program.

(3) Strong hardware and advanced operating system support are generally required.

By the way, both the client and the server referred to above refer to computer processes (software). The person using the computer is the "user" of the computer, not the "client". But in many foreign pieces of literature, the machine that runs the client program is often called client (in this case client can also be translated as "client"), and the machine that runs the server program is called server. So, we should judge whether the client or server refers to software or hardware according to the context. In this book, we also use "client" (or "client") or "Server" (or server) to refer to a "machine that runs a client program" or "machine that runs a server program" when referring to a machine.

Peer to Peer Connections
Peer-to-peer, P2P. The number 2 is used here because the English word 2 is two, which is pronounced the same as to, so the English word to is often abbreviated to the number 2) refers to two hosts communicating without distinguishing between the service requester and the service provider. As long as both hosts

are running peer-to-peer (P2P) software, they can communicate on an equal, peer-to-peer basis. At this point, each party can download a shared document that the other party has stored on its hard drive. So, this way of working is also called P2P. The hosts C, D, E, and fall run P2P software, so the hosts can communicate peer-to-peer (such as C and D, E and F, and C and F). In fact, peer-to-peer connectivity is still essentially a client-server approach, except that each host in a peer-to-peer connection is both a client and a server. For example, host C, when c requests the services of D, C is the client and D is the server. But if C serves F at the same time, c serves as a server.

Peer-to-peer connections work in a way that allows a large number of peer users, such as one million, to work at the same time. BitTorrent is the best example for a peer to peer connections.

From typing a URL into a browser to displaying the contents of a web page on a screen, in a matter of seconds, many pieces of hardware and software work together in their respective roles. Each of the individual links is not complicated, as long as you read carefully will be able to understand. However, there is so much hardware and software involved in the journey that if you focus on each individual point from a micro perspective, you may lose sight of the whole and lose your way. So before we set out to explore, let's take a brief look at this journey. The following introduction also contains a road map for a journey of discovery, in case you get lost on the way.

The Complete Picture of the Web

Let's first take a look at the full picture of how a browser accesses a Web server. The process of accessing a Web server and displaying a Web page involves a series of interactions between the Browser and the Web server, primarily the following.

(1) Browser: "Please give me the web page data. "

(2) Web

(2) Web Server: "Ok will do it"

After this series of interactions is complete, the browser displays the data it receives from the Web server on the screen. While the process of displaying a web page is complex, the interaction between the browser and the server over the network is surprisingly simple. When we shop in an online mall, we type in the name of the product and the address of the goods we want to receive and send it to a Web server.

(1) Browser: "please process these order data. "

(2) Web

(2) Web Server: "okay, Order Data received.

While the actual processing of an order with the sales system after the Web server receives the order data is complex, the interaction between the Browser and the Web server is simple, as summarized below.

(1) the browser sends a request to the Web server.
(2) Web
(3) The Web server sends a response to the browser based on the request.

So at this level, where Web applications like browsers and Web servers interact, it should be relatively easy to understand how it works. The interaction at this level is very similar to the dialogue between humans and is easier to understand from this point 1.

To enable interaction between applications, we need a mechanism to pass requests and responses between the Browser and the Web server. The network is composed of many computers and other devices connected to each other, so in the process of communication, we need to determine the correct communication object and send the request and response to them. Requests and responses can be lost or corrupted during delivery, so these situations must also be considered. So we need a mechanism to send requests and responses to each other without fail, no matter what the situation. Since the request and response are both 0 and 1 pieces of digital information, it can be said that we need a mechanism to carry the digital information to the designated destination.

This mechanism is implemented by the network control software in the operating system, as well as the division of labor between switches, routers and other devices. Its basic idea is to divide the digital information into small pieces It is then shIPped in containers called "packs". The word "Bag" is a word that you may often come across when using a mobile phone, but here it is similar to the concept used in postal and courier services.

You can think of a package as a letter or package, and a switch or router as a sorting area for a post office or a delivery company. The header of the packet contains the destination information, which can be sorted according to the relay of many switches and routers, and then carried to the destination step by step. Whether it's a home and corporate LAN, or the Internet out there, they're just different in size, and the underlying mechanisms are the same.

Together with Web applications such as browsers and Web servers, these two parts of the Web make up the Web. That is to say, these two parts are put together, the whole picture of the network.

We'll start by exploring how the browser works. You can think of our exploration as starting with typing a URL into your browser. Of course, the browser is not personally responsible for the transfer of data. The mechanism that carries the digital information is responsible for sending the message, so the browser delegates the data to it. Specifically, the network control software in the operating system is delegated to send messages to the server.

One of the first to appear is the protocol stack (network control software called Protocol Stack). The software packages the messages it receives from the browser and adds control information such as the destination address. To use the post office analogy is to put the letter in an envelope and write the addressee's address on the envelope.

The software also has other functions, such as resending packets in the event of a communication error or adjusting the rate at which data is sent, perhaps we can think of it as a little secretary who helps us send letters.

Next, the stack hands the packet to the network card (the hardware responsible for Ethernet or wireless network communications). The Network Card then converts the packet into an electrical signal and sends it out over the wire. In this way, the packet enters the network.

What comes next will vary according to the form of Internet access. A client computer can access the Internet either through a home or corporate Lan or directly on its own. Unfortunately, our exploration does not cover all of these possibilities, so we have to assume, for example, that the client computer is connected to a home or Corporate Lan Then through ADSL and fiber to the home (FTTH) and other broadband lines to access the Internet.

In such a scenario, packets sent by a network card pass through a switch or other device to a router used to access the Internet. Behind the router is the Internet, and the network operator is responsible for delivering the package to the destination, just as the postman is responsible for delivering the letter to the recIPient after we drop it into the mailbox.

The data then travels from the router used to access the Internet to the inside of the Internet. The gateway to the Internet is called the access network. In general, we can use telephone lines, Isdn, Adsl, cable television, light, private lines, and other communication lines to access the Internet, these communication lines collectively known as an access network. An access network connects to a contracted network operator and to a device called a Point of Presence (PoP).

The entity of the access point is a router designed for the operator, which we can think of as the nearest post office to your home. Letters collected from various mailboxes are sorted at post offices and then sent around the country or even around the world, as is the case with the Internet, where packets are first sent through an access network to an access point and then sent from here to the rest of the country and the world. Behind the access point is the backbone of the Internet.

There are many operators and a large number of routers in the backbone network. These routers are connected to each other to form a huge network, and our network packet is passed through the relay of several routers Is eventually sent to the target Web server. The details are explained in the main text, but the basic principle is the same as that of home and corporate routers. That is to say, whether on the Internet or in the home, Corporate Lan, packets are transmitted in the same way, which is a major feature of the Internet.

However, the router used by the operators is different from the small router we use at home. It is a high-speed large router that can connect dozens of network lines. In the backbone of the Internet, there are a large number of these routers, they are connected to each other in a complex way, and network packets are passing through these routers.

In addition, routers differ not only in size but also in the way they connect to each other. Ethernet cables are commonly used in home and corporate LANs, while the Internet uses older telephony and the latest optical communication technologies to transmit network packets in addition to Ethernet connections. The technology used in this section is the most popular part of today's network, can be said to be the crystallization of the most sophisticated technology.

After passing through the backbone network, the network packet finally arrives in the local Area Network where the Web server is located.

Next, it encounters a firewall, which checks the incoming packets. Think of the firewall as the security guard at the door, who checks all the bags that come in to see if any of the dangerous bags are in there. After the check, the network packet may then encounter the cache server. A portion of the web page data is reusable, and this reusable data is stored in the cache server. If the page data you want to access happens to be found in the cache server, you can read the data directly from the cache server without bothering the Web server. In addition, in large Web sites, there may be load balancers that distribute messages across multiple Web servers, and there may be services that distribute content through caching servers distributed across the Internet. After these mechanisms, the network packets arrive at the Web server.

When the network packet arrives at the Web Server, the data is unpacked and restored to the original request message, which is then handed over to the Web server program. Like the client, this is done by the protocol stack (network control software) in the operating system. Next, the Web server program analyzes the meaning of the request message, loads the data into the response message as instructed, and then sends it back to the client. The process of returning the response message to the client is exactly the opposite of what we described earlier.

When the response reaches the client, the browser reads the data from the web page and displays it on the screen. At this point, a series of operations to access the Web server are complete, and our journey of discovery has come to an end

How the Internet is Connected?

This Network is the Access Network AN (Access Network), which is also known as the local Access Network, or resident Access Network. This is a special kind of computer network. As we explained above, a user must be able to access the Internet through an ISP. Since there are many technologies available for accessing the Internet from a user's home, there are situations where multiple access network technologies can be used to connect to the Internet. The access network itself is neither the core nor the periphery of the Internet. An access network is a network between a client system and the first router (also known as an edge router) on the Internet. From the scope of coverage, many access networks also belong to local area networks. From the point of view of the role, the access network is only to allow users to connect with the Internet "bridge" role. In the early days of the Internet, users used telephone lines to dial into the Internet at very low rates (from a few thousand to a few tens of thousands of bits per second), so the term access network was not used.

Basic Components of Computer Network

No matter which definition can be seen above, the computer network is a complete system composed of some hardware equipment and corresponding software system. The basic components of a computer network include a computer (or a computer terminal with only basic computer functions), network connections and communication equipment, transmission media, and network communication software (including network communication protocols).

These basic computer network components are divided into hardware systems and software systems.

Computer Network Hardware System

Computer Network hardware system refers to the visible physical facilities in the computer network, including all kinds of computer equipment, transmission media, network equipment, these three major parts.

1. Computer Equipment

The purpose of building a computer network is to provide a platform for network communication among users of various computer equipment, such as user access, data transmission, file sharing, remote control and so on. A computer device is a variety of computers (such as pcs, computer servers, computer terminals, laptop computers, IPad and the like) that are controlled and used by network users. The main applications of the network are performed on these computer devices. In fact, now the computer network and the telecommunication network are somewhat overlapped. Many telecommunication terminals can also be connected to the computer network, such as the smartphones we use now Can carry on the data transmission between the USB interface and the computer, even carries on the remote communication.

Note that in the traditional definition of a computer network, a computer network requires at least one fully functional physical computer (others can be terminals). With the rise of Network virtualization technology, the current computer network can be a virtual machine (such as VPC, VMWare, etc.) in a physical computer simulation of a number of independent computer systems, forming a virtual computer network This network can also perform functions that can only be performed in many physical computer networks.

2. Network Equipment

In a computer network system, network equIPment usually refers to equIPment other than computer equIPment Such as network card, bridge, gateway, Modem, switch, router, hardware firewall, hardware IDS (intrusion detection system), hardware IPS (intrusion prevention system) , broadband access server (Bras) , UPS (uninterruptible power supply) , etc. Wlan Network Card, WLAN AP, WLAN Router, WLAN switch, etc.

Network equipment is used to construct the network topology in the "communication subnet", and the communication lines (that is, "transmission medium") together to form the framework of the whole computer network. Of course, the simplest network, in fact, does not need any network equipment, that is, two terminal computers with serial/parallel port cable directly connected to the peer-to-peer network. But this network is not really a computer network, for now, such a computer network does not have much practical significance.

3. Transmission Medium

The transmission medium is simply the network line, is the network communication "road". Without these transmission media, the network communication signal will not know where to transmit, also cannot transmit, just like there is no road ahead, we cannot move forward. Of course, the transmission medium can be physically tangible, such as coaxial cable (which is also used in cable television), twisted pair, optical cable (also known as an optical fiber), etc, or invisible For example, the transmission medium used in various wireless networks is, in fact, electromagnetic waves. Wireless Computer Network (WCN) is to realize the connection of each node in WCN by the electromagnetic wave. Of course, in the coaxial cable, twisted pair, optical cable, and these transmission media.

4. Computer Network Software System

Computer Network communication in addition to the aforementioned various computer hardware systems, but also some computer network communication and application software. These computer network communication and application software refer to the computer program installed in the terminal computer for computer network communication or application. First of all, there is a network application platform, such as computers and servers installed, with the computer network communication functions of the operating system. Operating Systems for computer network communications are also installed on devices such as switches, routers, and firewalls. For example, Windows, Linux, UNIX, CatOS for Cisco Switch/router/ Firewall, IOS for IOS, and Comware for H3C switch/router/ firewall.

In addition to the operating system, the network communication protocols, such as TCP / IP Protocol Cluster, Ieee 802 protocol cluster, PPP, PPPoE, IPX / SPX, and VLAN, STP, RIP, OSPF, BGP, etc. Finally, it is necessary to carry out a variety of specific network applications tool software, such as our common Qq, MSN instant messaging software, Outlook, Firefox, Sendmail and other email software, for dial-up PPP, PPPoE protocol IPSEC, PPTP, L2TP and so on for VPN communication.

How the Internet is given to people?
Internet Communications

Let's take a closer look at how the actual network is constructed. People generally use Internet access services when they connect to the Internet at home or at work. With the Internet, the traffic that converges to the Wireless Lan router and the nearest switch is again connected to the "access layer" mentioned earlier (sometimes directly to the "Edge Network" if the company is large, the network is large, or there is a lot of external access). It is even possible to communicate with the target address through an "edge network" or "backbone".

Mobile Communications

As soon as the phone is turned on, it will automatically communicate wirelessly with the nearest base station. The base station is equipped with a special cell phone base antenna, and the base itself is the "access layer" of the network. When a cell phone terminal sends a signal to another terminal, the request goes all the way to the base station that registers the phone number on the other end. If the other party answers the call, a communication connection is established between the two phones. The communications requests collected by the base station are collected in the Control Center ("Edge Network"), which is then connected to the backbone of the Interconnection Control Center. This mobile network is structured much like an Internet access service.

LTE and Voice Call

His limited data communications. And LTE is regarded as the transition technology from 3G to 4G, which is a kind of mobile communication standard made by 3GPP (the organization that makes the 3rd Generation Mobile Communication Standard made up of standardization bodies in different countries). Depending on the situation, it can achieve up to 300 Mbps down and 75 MBPS UP wireless communications.

In the LTE standard, the use of TCP / IP over the entire network is necessary because the voice is also transmitted as an IP packet. (today, voice communications are also largely digital, using TCP / IP Technology.). However, in reality, it is often impossible to replace all the hardware devices in the network all at once. In this case, the techniques of CSFB (CSFB) can be used. The technology allows voice calls to be transmitted only over cellular networks. Keeps it in line with the original sound process.

Chapter 3: Networking in Detail

The original purpose of a computer network was to connect individual computers to form a more powerful computing environment. In short, to increase productivity. From the age of batch processing to the age of computer networks, there is no doubt that this is the case that computer networks are intended to. Now, however, there seems to be a subtle shift in technology.

One of the primary purposes of modern computer networks can be said to be to connect people. People around the world can connect, communicate and exchange ideas via the Internet. This, however, was not possible in the early days of computer networks. This human-to-human computer network has gradually brought about great changes in people's daily life, school education, Scientific Research, and company development.

This chapter describes in much detail about computer networking architecture in such a way that it can enrich your minds and helps you understand the complex process that goes on in computer networking. A few examples and situations will be used for your better understanding of the topic.

Protocol

In the field of computer network and information communication, people often refer to the word "protocol". The representative protocols in common use on the internet are IP, TCP, HTTP and so on. The protocols commonly used in Lan (local area network) are IPX / SPX (NetWare system protocol developed by Novell) and so on.

Why protocols are needed?

Typically, we send an E-mail, visit a home page to get information and are unaware of the protocol that goes on in the background, which is only possible if we reconfigure the computer's network connection and modify network settings. So as long as the network is set up and connected successfully, people often forget about protocols and things. As long as the application knows how to leverage the protocols, it should be enough to allow people to use the network connection they have built. It is not uncommon for a person to be unable to access the Internet because they do not understand certain protocols. However, in the process of communication through the network, the protocol plays a vital role and as you are keen on knowing about protocols can give you a good overview of the topic.

In a word, the protocol is a kind of "agreement" that the client computer and the server computer realize the communication through the network. This "convention" allows computers that are made up of different devices from different vendors, different

CPUs, and different operating systems to communicate with each other as long as they follow the same protocol. On the other hand, if different protocols are used, communication cannot be achieved. It's like two people speaking in different languages who can't understand each other. There are many types of protocols, each of which clearly defines its code of conduct. Two computers must be able to support the same protocol, and follow the same protocol for processing, so as to achieve mutual communication. Before starting to dwell on the topic of protocols further let us discuss two very basic things that you need to know for better understanding. They are the central processing unit and operating system.

CPU

CPU (Central Processing Unit). It's like the "heart" of a computer, every program Is actually scheduled and executed by it. The performance of the CPU also determines the processing performance of a computer to a great extent. So people often say that the history of the computer is actually the history of the CPU. At present, people often use CPU Intel Core, Intel Atom, ARM CORTEX, and other products.

Operating System

Os (Operating System) Operating System, is a kind of basic software. It integrates the CPU management, memory management, computer perIPherals management, and program management and other important functions. The treatment of

TCP or IP protocols described here, in many cases is already embedded in specific operating systems. Today's operating systems commonly used in personal computers are UNIX, Windows, Mac OS x, Linux, and so on.

The instructions that can be run in a computer vary from one CPU to another and from one operating system to another. Therefore, programs designed for certain CPUs or operating systems may not run directly if they are copied directly to computers with other types of CPUs or operating systems. The data stored in a computer also varies from CPU to the operating system. Therefore, if the CPU and the operating system between different computers to achieve communication, IT needs a party to support the protocol, and follow this protocol for data reading. This is the reason why you can't run an android app in an iPhone.

In addition, a CPU can usually only run one program at a time. In order to make multiple programs run at the same time, the operating system adopts the CPU time slice rotation mechanism to switch between multiple programs and schedule reasonably. This approach is called multitasking.

So What Is An Agreement In Protocol?
Agreements are like conversations between people. Here's a simple example. There's three of them. Sam, Tom, and Jerry. Sam can only speak Chinese, Tom can only speak English, and Jerry can speak both Chinese and English. Now Sam and Tom

need to talk. How should they communicate with each other? What if Tom and Jerry need to talk?

If we: Treat Chinese and English as "agreements. " Use Chat communication"

And Treat what you say as "data. "

I am afraid that Sam and Tom cannot communicate with each other for as long as they speak in one language. Because of the difference in the agreement (language) used in their conversation, neither party is able to transmit the data (what is said) to the other party. (a simultaneous interpreter between the two can facilitate communication, as the gateway does in a network environment.)

Next, we analyze the conversation between Sam and Jerry. By using this "agreement" in Chinese, two people can understand what the other person is trying to say. That is to say, Sam and Jerry use the same protocol in order to communicate smoothly so that they can transmit the desired data (what they want to say to each other).

In this sense, agreements are like the language of ordinary speech. Although language is a human property, when computers communicate with each other over the Internet, it can also be argued that communication is based on something akin to human "language" (similarly, some of the actions we take for granted in our daily lives are in many cases consistent with the concept of "agreement").

Protocols in Computers
Human beings have the ability to master knowledge, and they also have a certain ability to apply and understand knowledge. So in a way, human communication isn't limited by too many rules. Even if there are any rules and the like, people can adapt to the rules naturally through their ability to adapt. However, all of this in computer communication, obviously impossible to achieve. Because the level of computer intelligence has not reached the level of human beings. In fact, everything from the physical connection level of a computer to the software level of an application must be followed exactly.

True communication can only be achieved by a prior agreement. In addition, each computer must be equipped with programs that perform the most basic functions of communication. If you replace Sam, Tom, and Jerry in the previous example with a computer, it's easy to understand why you need to clearly define protocols, and why you should follow established protocols to design software and build computer hardware.

People usually do not need special attention when speaking to be able to naturally enunciate, pronunciation. And on many occasions, human beings can adjust their expressions and what they want to convey according to each other's semantics, voice or expression, so as to avoid misunderstanding. Sometimes even in the course of the conversation if accidentally miss a few words, also from the context and context of the conversation to guess the general meaning of the other party to express, not to affect their understanding. But computers can't do that. Therefore, in the design of computer programs and hardware, we should take full account of the communication process may encounter a variety of exceptions and exception handling. When a problem is actually encountered, the computers communicating with each other must also have the appropriate equipment and programs to deal with the exception.

In computer communication, it is important to reach a detailed agreement in advance and follow it. This kind of agreement is actually "agreement" in the protocol.

Packet Switching Protocol

Packet switching is a method of splitting large data into smaller units called packets for transmission. The bag in question is the same as the one we usually see in the post office. Packet switching is the act of breaking up big data into such packets and handing them off to each other.

When people mail a package, they usually fill out a mailing form, attach it to the package and hand it to the post office. The mailing list usually has the full address of the sender and recIPient. Similarly, computer communications will attach the source host address and the destination host address to each packet sent to the communication line. The sender address, the receiver address, and the part of the packet number written are called the "packet header ".

When a larger piece of data is divided into groups, it is necessary to write the ordinal number of the group into the package in order to identify which part of the original data is. Based on this sequence number, the receiver reassembles each packet into the original data.

In a communication protocol, it is common to specify what information should be written at the beginning of the message and how it should be handled. Each computer that communicates with each other constructs the first part of the message and reads the first part of the content according to the protocol. In order for the two parties to communicate correctly, it is necessary for the sender and the receiver of the packet to keep consistent definition and interpretation of the first part and content of the packet.

So, who regulates the communication protocol? In order to enable computers from different manufacturers to communicate with each other, there is an organization that sets standards for communication protocols and defines international standards. In the next section, we will elaborate on the protocol's standardization process.

The Birth and Standardization of Computer Communications

At the beginning of computer communication, systematization and standardization did not get enough attention. Each computer manufacturer produces its own network products to enable computer communications. No strong sense of systematization, layering, etc. In 1974, IBM released the SNA, which exposed the company's computer communications technology as a systematic network architecture. Since then, computer manufacturers have also released their own network architecture, triggering the systematization of many protocols. However, the various network architectures and protocols of various manufacturers are not compatible with each other. Even if two heterogeneous computers are connected on the physical level, normal communication cannot be realized because of the different network architecture and the different protocols.

This is extremely inconvenient for the user. Because this means that the computer network products of which vendor was used in the first place can only be used from the same vendor all the time. If the relevant vendor goes bankrupt or the product exceeds its service life, the entire network equipment must be replaced. In addition, it is not uncommon for different departments to be unable to communicate even when they are physically connected to each other because the network products used are not the same. The lack of flexibility and extensibility made it difficult for users to use computer communication freely.

With the increasing importance of computers, many companies have come to realize the importance of compatibility. People began to work on technologies that would allow heterogeneous models produced by different manufacturers to communicate with each other. This promotes the openness and versatility of the web.

In order to solve these problems, ISO (International Organization for Standards) has established an International standard, Osi (Open Systems Interconnection reference model), and standardized the communication system. Currently, OSI protocols are not commonly used, but the OSI reference model, which was the guideline of Osi Protocol design, is often used in the development of network protocols.

The standardization of the protocol also enables all devices that follow the standard protocol to no longer be unable to communicate due to differences in computer hardware or operating systems. Therefore, the standardization of protocols has also promoted the popularization of computer networks.

In the real world, there are many good technologies that are not widely available because their development companies do not publish the appropriate development specifications. If companies can make their development specifications public, and more of their peers can use them in time and become industry standards, then there will be more and better products that can survive and be used by us.

OSI reference model

Before ISO standardized Osi, the related problems of network architecture were fully discussed, and the OSI reference model was proposed as a communication protocol design index. This model divides the necessary functions of the communication protocol into 7 layers. Through these layers, the more complex network protocols are simplified. In this model, each layer receives a specific service provided by its lower layer and is responsible for providing a specific service to its upper layer. The conventions that govern the interaction between upper and lower layers are called "interfaces. ". The conventions that govern interactions between layers are called protocols.

Protocol layering is like modular development in computer software. The recommendations of the OSI reference model are ideal. It wants to implement all the modules from the first layer to the seventh layer and combine them to achieve network communication. Layering allows each layer to be used independently, so that even if some of the layering changes in the system, it does not affect the whole system. Therefore, it is possible to construct a system that is both extensible and flexible. In addition, by layering the communication functions can be subdivided, making it easier to implement separate protocols for each layering and to define the specific responsibilities and obligations of each layering. These are all advantages of layering. The downside of layering may be over modularity, making processing more burdensome, and having to implement similar processing logic for each module.

Understanding Layering Through a Simple Example

First, take telephone chat as an example. two people, Adam and Eve, are talking on the telephone (communication device) in English (language protocol). On the surface, Adam and Eve are having a direct conversation in English, but in reality, Adam and Eve are both listening to the voice on the receiver of the telephone, both speaking into the microphone. Imagine what a person who has never seen a telephone would think if they saw this? I'm afraid he must think Adam and Eve are talking on the telephone in networking perspective.

The language protocol they use in an audio input to the microphone is translated into radio signals at the communications device level. Sent to each other's phones, and then converted to audio output by the communications equipment layer, passed to each other. Thus, Adam and Eve actually have a conversation using an interface between the telephone and the voice converted by audio.

People often think that when they pick up the phone to talk to someone, it's as if they're talking to them directly, but if you look closely, it's really the phone that's mediating the whole process, and there's no denying that. What if the electronic signals from Adam's phone were not converted into sounds of the same frequency as those from Eve's? This is similar to the difference in protocol between Adam's phone and Eve's phone. Eve May hear the voice and feel that he is not talking to Adam, but to someone else. If the frequencies are far apart, Eve is more likely to think he is not hearing English.

So what if we change the communication device layer by assuming that the language layer is the same. For example, change the telephone to a radio. If the communication equIPment layer uses the radio, they must learn to use the radio method. Since the language layer is still using the English protocol, users can talk just as normally as they used to when they were on the phone.

So, what if the communication device layer uses a telephone and the language layer changes to English? It is clear that the telephone itself will not be limited by the user's language. Therefore, this situation and the use of English calls exactly the same, still can be achieved call.

The previous example simply divides the protocol into two layers. However, the actual packet communication protocols can be quite complex. The OSI reference model organizes such a complex protocol into seven easy-to-understand layers.

OSI Reference Model

The OSI reference model does a good job of summarizing the necessary functions for communication. Network engineers also often prototype the layers of the OSI reference model when discussing protocol-related issues. For beginners in computer networks, learning the OSI reference model can be the first step to success.

The OSI reference model is, after all, a "model, " a rough set of definitions of what each layer does, without a detailed definition of the protocol and interface. It serves only as a guide to learning and designing protocols. Therefore, if you want to know more details about the agreement, it is necessary to refer to the specific specifications of each agreement itself.

Many communication protocols correspond to one of the seven layers of the OSI reference model. From this, we can get a general idea of the position and function of the protocol in the whole communication function. While it takes a careful reading of the specification to understand the protocol, its general purpose can be found at the corresponding OSI model layer. This is why the OSI model is the first to be studied before learning about each protocol.

The OSI (Reference Model) divides communication functions into seven layers, called the OSI reference model. The OSI Protocol, based on the OSI Reference Model, defines the protocol and interface-related standards for each layer. Products that follow the OSI Protocol are called Osi products, and the communications they follow are called Osi Communications. Do not confuse "Osi reference model" with "OSI protocol" because of their different meanings.

The OSI layers   are presentation layer,   application layer, session layer, transport layer, Network layer, Data link layer, and physical layer. Below we explain all these layers briefly.

Application layer

Provides services to the application and specifies the communication-related details in the application. Including file transfer, email, remote login (virtual terminal) and other protocols.

Presentation Layer

Convert the information processed by the application into a format suitable for network transmission, or convert the data from the next layer into a format that the upper layer can handle. Therefore, it is mainly responsible for data format conversion. Specifically, the device will be inherent in the data format into the network standard transmission format. Different devices may interpret the same bitstream differently. Therefore, making them consistent is the main function of this layer.

Session Layer

Responsible for establishing and disconnecting communication links (logical path of data flow) and data transfer related tubes such as data partitioning manager.

Transport Layer

It acts as a reliable transmitter. Processing is done only on both sides of the communication, not only on the router.

Network Layer

Transfer data to the destination address. The destination address can be a single address that is connected to multiple networks via a router. Therefore, this layer is mainly responsible for addressing and routing.

Data Link Layer

Responsible for the physical level of interconnection, communication between the nodes. For example, communication between two nodes connected to one Ethernet network. The 0,1 sequence is divided into meaningful data frames and transmitted to the opposite end (generation and reception of data frames).

Physical Layer

Responsible for the 0,1-bit current (0,1 sequence) and voltage levels, light flash between the exchange.

After the brief explanation of the reference model, you may be quite confused with new terms. So Here we explain with a small example to make you understand the communication between the OSI layers in detail.

How Do You Modularize Communications in the 7-layer OSI MODEL?

The sender transmits data sequentially from Layer 7, layer 6 to Layer 1, while the receiver transmits data from Layer 1, layer 2 to layer 7 down to each upper layer. At each layer, the data from the previous layer can be processed with the "first" information necessary for the current hierarchical protocol. Then the receiving end of the data received from the "first" and "content" of the separation, and then forward to the next layer, and finally the sending end of the data back to the original state.

Handling above the session level

Suppose that Sam wants to send a "good morning" e-mail to Estella. What exactly does the web do? We analyze it from the top down here to get a clear understanding that goes in the process.

Application Layer

User Sam creates a new e-mail message on the host computer (more usually in a browser), specifies the recIPient as Estella, and enters the message as "good morning". The software that sends and receives emails can be functionally divided into two categories one that is communication-related, and one that is not. For example, the part where user Sam enters "good morning" from the keyboard is a non-communication-related function, while the part where user Sam sends "Good Morning" to recIPient Estella is a communication-related function. Thus, "entering the contents of the e-mail message and send it to the target address" here is equivalent to the application layer.

From the moment the user enters what he wants to send and clicks the "send" button, the application layer protocol is processed. The protocol attaches a header (label) to the front end of the data to be transmitted. The first part identifies the message as "Good Morning" and the recIPient as "Estella ". This data with the first message is sent to host Estella and then the mail-receiving software on that host obtains the content through the "mail-receiving" function. After the application on the host, Estella receives the data sent by host Sam, the data header and the data body are analyzed And will be Saved it into a hard drive or other Non-volatile random-access memory, a storage device where data cannot be lost in a power outage, for processing. If the recIPient's mailbox space on host Estella is full and cannot receive new messages, an error is returned to the sender. The handling of such exceptions is also a problem that the application layer needs to solve.

Presentation Layer

The meaning of "presentation" in the presentation layer is "presentation" and "demonstration" Hence the focus on concrete representations of data (most famously, the way each computer allocates data in memory differently. Typically, large and small entities.). In addition, the use of different software applications will also lead to the performance of different forms of data. For example, some word processors create files that can only be opened and read by a specific version of the software provided by the word processor manufacturer.

So what can you do if you run into this kind of problem in your email? If user Sam and User Estella use exactly the same mail client software, they will be able to receive and read mail without similar problems. But this is unlikely to happen in real life. Getting all users to use the same client software in a cookie-cutter fashion is also a huge inconvenience for users (today, other devices, such as smartphones, besides pcs, are also connected to the Internet. How to make them read each other's communication data is becoming more and more important.

There are several ways to solve this kind of problem. The first is to use the presentation layer to convert data from "A computer specific data format" to "a standard network data format" before sending it out. After receiving the data, the receiving host restores the data in the network standard format to "the computer-specific data format", and then processes it accordingly.

In the previous example, the data was converted to a common standard format before being processed, allowing data consistency between heterogeneous models. This is what the presentation layer is for. That is to say, the presentation layer is a layer that transforms "the uniform network data format" and "the data format specific to a computer or a piece of software".

The text "Good Morning" in this example is converted to "unified network data format" according to its encoding format. Even if it is a simple stream of text that can be encoded in a variety of complex formats. Take Japanese, for example, EUC-JP, Shift, ISO-2022-JP, UTF-8, UTF-16, and many other encoding formats. If you cannot encode in a specific format. Then in the receiving end is the receIPt of mail may also be garbled (in real life when the receIPt and delivery of mail become garbled situation is not It's rare. This is usually because the presentation layer does not run in the expected encoding format or the encoding format is incorrectly set.).

In order to identify the encoding format, the presentation layer and the presentation layer will attach the header information, which will transfer the actual transmitted data to the next layer for processing.

Session Layer

Next, let's analyze how and how to efficiently interact with data between the session layers of the hosts on both sides of data transmission.

ASSUME THAT USER Sam has created five new e-mails ready to be sent to user Estella. These five messages can be sent in a variety of order. For example, you can establish a connection (a communication connection.) And then disconnect each time a message is sent. You can also send 5 emails to each other in a row once you've established a connection. You can even set up five connections at once and send five emails to each other at the same time. It is the primary responsibility of the session layer to decide which connection method to use.

The session layer, like the application or presentation layer, attaches a header or label to the front end of the data it receives before forwarding it to the next layer. These headers or tags contain information about the order in which the data is transmitted.

Handling Below the Transport Layer

So far, we have used examples to illustrate the general process of data written in the application layer is formatted and coded by the presentation layer and then sent out by the session layer tag. However, the session layer only manages when to establish a connection, when to send data and so on, and does not have the function of actually transferring data. It is the "Unsung Heroes" below the session layer that is really responsible for transmitting specific data over the network.

Transport Layer

Host a ensures communication with host Estella and is ready to send data. This process is called "making connections. ". With this communication connection, the e-mail sent by host Sam can reach host Estella, and the final data is retrieved by host Estella's Mail handler. In addition, it is necessary to disconnect the connection when the communication transmission is over.

As above, do the connect or disconnect processing (note here that the session layer is responsible for deciding when to connect and disconnect, while the transport layer does the actual connect and disconnect processing), the primary role of the transport layer is to create a logical communication connection between the two hosts. In addition, the transport layer verifies the arrival of the transmitted data at the destination address between computers on both sides of the communication and retransmits the data if it does not arrive.

For example, host a sends "Good Morning" data to host Estella. During that time, the data may be compromised for some reason Bad, or due to some kind of network exception that only part of the data reaches the destination address. Let's assume host Estella only received "Good Morning If it does not receive the "morning" part of the data, it will be notified of the fact that it did not receive the "morning" part of the data Host, Sam. Host Sam will be informed of this situation will be after the "good" resend to host Estella, and again to confirm whether the other side received.

It's like people saying, "Hey, what did you just say? " In everyday conversation, computer communication protocols aren't as Esoteric as you might think Its basic principle is closely connected with our daily life, much the same.

Thus, to ensure the reliability of data transmission is an important role in the transmission layer. To ensure reliability, a header is attached to the data to be transmitted at this layer to identify the hierarchical data. In practice, however, the processing of transferring data to the other end is done by the network layer.

Network Layer

The role of the network layer is to send data from the sending host to the receiving host in a network-to-network connected environment. Although there are many data links between the two end hosts, the ability to send data from host Sam to host Estella is also due to the network layer.

The Destination Address is critical when actually sending the data. This address is for Communication The unique ordinal number specified in the network. Think of it as a phone number that we use in our daily lives. Once the destination address is determined, the computer that sent the data to the destination address can be selected from a large number of computers. Based on this address, packets can be sent and processed at the network layer. With the address and network layer packet sending processing, data can be sent to any interconnecting device in the world. The network layer also sends the data and address information it receives from the upper layer to the data link layer below for later processing.

The RelationshIP Between the Transport and the Network Layer

Under the different network architecture, the network layer cannot guarantee the data accessibility sometimes. For example, in an IP protocol that is equivalent to the TCP / IP Network Layer, there is no guarantee that data will be sent to the opposite address. Therefore, the data transmission process data loss, the possibility of confusion and other issues will be greatly increased. In a network layer like this, where there are no reliable transmission requirements, the transport layer can be responsible for providing "proper transmission data handling. ". In TCP / IP, the network layer and the transport layer work together to ensure the reliable transmission of packets around the world.

The clearer the role and function of each layer, the simpler the specification of the protocol, implementation (that is, software coding specific protocols to make them work on a computer) will also make the task of implementing these specific protocols easier.

Data Link Layer, Physical Layer

Communication transmission is actually realized through physical transmission media. The purpose of the data link layer is to process data between these devices interconnected by a transmission medium. In the physical layer, o and 1 of the data are converted into voltage and pulse light for transmission to the physical transmission medium, while directly connected devices use the address for transmission. This address is called a Mac (Media Access Control, Media Access Control) address, and can also be called a physical or hardware address. The MAC address is used to identify devices connected to the same transmission medium. Therefore, in this hierarchy, the first part containing Mac address information is attached to the data forwarded from the network layer and sent to the network.

Both the network layer and the data link layer send the data to the receiver based on the destination address, but the network layer is responsible for sending the entire data to the final destination address, while the data link layer is responsible for sending only the data within a segment.

Processing of Host Estella Terminal

The processing flow on host Estella of the receiving end is just opposite to host Sam. IT starts from the physical layer and sends the received data to the previous layer for processing Thus, user Estella can finally use the mail client software on host Estella to receive the mail sent by user Sam, and can read the corresponding content as "good morning". as mentioned above, the reader can think of the functions of a communication network in layers. The protocol on each layer specifies the format of the data header in that layer and the order in which the header and the data are processed.

Classification of Transport Modes

Network and communication can be based on its data transmission methods for a variety of classification. There are many ways to categorize them, and here are a few of them.

Connectable Oriented vs. Connectionless Oriented

Sending data over the network can be divided into two types: connectionless-oriented and connectionless-oriented. connectionless-oriented includes Ethernet, IP, UDP, etc.. connectionless-oriented includes ATM, frame relay, TCP, etc.

Oriented Connected type

Oriented to connected type, in the case of sending data (in the case of connection-oriented data, the data at the sending end does not have to be sent in groups. we will see that TCP packets send data in connection-oriented fashion, circuit switching is also a connection-oriented fashion, but data is not limited to packet transmission.) A communication line needs to be connected between the transceiver hosts (the meaning of the connection may vary in different layered protocols. The connection in the data link layer refers to the connection of the physical, communication line. The transport layer is responsible for creating and managing logical connections.).

Facing connected is like people making a phone call. After typing in the phone number and dialing it out, only the other side can pick up the phone to make a real call. When the call is over, closing the phone is like cutting off the power. Therefore, in connection-oriented mode, it is necessary to establish and disconnect the connection before and after the communication transmission. If there is no communication with the other side, you can avoid sending unnecessary data.

Connectionless Oriented

Connectionless-oriented models do not require establishing and disconnecting connections. The sender is free to send data at any time (more often than not, packet switching is used for unlinked types. At this point, the data can be interpreted as packet data.). Conversely, the receiver never knows when and where it will receive the data. Therefore, in connectionless-oriented situations, the receiving end often needs to confirm that it has received the data.

It's like people going to the post office to mail a package. A postal clerk does not need to confirm that the recIPient's address actually exists, or that the recIPient can receive the package As long as the sender has a mailing address, he can handle the business of mailing parcels. Unlike telephone communication, connectionless communication does not require processing such as making a call or hanging up the phone. Instead, the sender is free to send the data it wants to transmit.

Therefore, in connectionless-oriented communication, there is no need to confirm the existence of the opposite end. The sender can send data out even if the receiver does not exist or cannot receive it.

Connection-Oriented and Connectionless-Oriented

The word "connection" in human society, equivalent to the meaning of "network". At this point, it refers to an acquaintance or a relationship between people. And facing connectionless, in fact, means no relationshIP at all.

In baseball and golf, one often hears the phrase "where to get the ball! ". This is, in fact, typical sender-side processing for connectionless communication. Some readers may consider connectionless-oriented communication to be a bit wonky. But for some special equipment, it is a very efficient method. Because this way can omit some established, complicated procedures so that the processing becomes simple, easy to produce some low-cost products, reduce the processing burden.

Circuit Switching and Packet Switching

At present, there are two kinds of network communication methods-circuit switching and packet switching. Circuit switching technology has a relatively long history, mainly used in the telephone network of the past. Packet switching technology is a relatively new form of communication, from the late 1960s began to be gradually recognized. This book focuses on the introduction of TCP / IP, it is the use of packet switching technology.

In circuit switching, the switch is mainly responsible for data transfer processing. The computer is first connected to the switch, and the connection between the switch and the switch is continued by a number of communication lines. Therefore, when sending data between computers, it is necessary to establish a communication circuit between the switch and the target host.

We call connecting circuits establishing connections. After the connection is established, the user can use the circuit until the connection is disconnected.

If a circuit is only used to connect the communication lines between two computers, it means that only the two computers need to communicate with each other, so the two computers can be exclusive lines of data transmission. But if there are multiple computers connected to a circuit, and these computers need to transfer data to each other, a new problem arises. Since one computer has exclusive access to the entire circuit while sending and receiving information, other computers have to wait until the computer has finished processing the data before they have a chance to use the circuit. And in the process, no one can predict when a computer's data transmission begins and ends. If the number of concurrent users exceeds the number of lines of communication between switches, communication is not possible at all.

To this end, people came up with a new method, that is, let the computer connected to the communication circuit to send the data to be divided into a number of packets, in a certain order and then sent separately. This is called packet switching. With packet switching, data is subdivided so that all computers can send and receive data at the same time, thus improving the utilization of communication lines. Since the addresses of the sender and receiver are written at the beginning of each packet, even if the same line serves multiple users simultaneously, it is also possible to make a clear distinction between the destination to which each packet is sent and the computer with which it is communicating.

In packet switching, a communication line is connected by a packet switch (router). The basic process of packet switching is that the sending computer sends the packet data to the router, which receives the packet data, caches it into its buffer, and then forwards it to the target computer. Therefore, packet switching also has another name: Cumulative switching.

Once the router receives the data, it caches it into a queue and sends it out one by one in a first-in, first-out order (sometimes, it gives priority to data with a more specific destination address).

In packet switching, there is usually only one communication line between computer and router and between router and router. So, this line is actually a shared line. In circuit switching, the speed of transmission between computers is constant. In packet switching, however, the speed of the communication line may be different. Depending on network congestion, the time it takes for the data to reach its destination can vary. In addition, when the buffer of the router is saturated or overflowed, it may even happen that packet data is lost and can not be sent to the opposite end.

Classification By Number of Receivers

In network communication, the communication can also be classified according to the number of the target address and its subsequent behavior. Such as broadcast, multicasting and so on is the product of this classification.

UNICAST

Literally, "Uni" means "1" and "Cast" means "Cast. ". The combination is one-on-one communication. An early example of unicast communication was the landline telephone.

BROADCAST

It literally means to play. So, it means sending a message from one host to all the other hosts that are connected to it.

A typical example of broadcast communication is the television broadcast, which sends the television signals together to non-specific multiple receivers.

In addition, we know that television signals generally have their own frequency bands. Television signals can be received only within the acceptable range of the corresponding frequency band. Similarly, computers that broadcast communications also have their broadcast range. Only a computer within this range can receive the corresponding broadcast message. This range is called the broadcast domain.

Multicast

Like Broadcasting, multicast sends messages to multiple receiving hosts. The difference is that multicast requires a certain set of hosts to be qualified as receivers. Multicasting is best exemplified by video conferencing, a type of remote conference that involves groups of people in different places. In this form, a message is sent from one host to a specific number of hosts. Video conferencing usually cannot be broadcast. Otherwise, there's no way of knowing who's there and where.

ANYCAST

Anycast is a method of communication in which one host is selected as a receiver. Although this approach is similar to multicast in that it targets a specific set of hosts, its behavior is different from that of multicast. Anycast communication. Select the host from the target host group that best meets the network conditions to send the message. Typically, the selected specific host will return a unicast signal, and then the sender host will only communicate with that host.

Anycast applications in real networks have DNS root domain name resolution servers

Address

In communication transmission, the sender and the receiver can be regarded as the communication subjects. They can all be identified by a message called "address". When people use a telephone, a telephone number is equivalent to an "address". When people choose to write a letter, an address plus a name is equivalent to an "address. ".

The real-life "address" is easier to understand, but in computer communications, the concept of this address appears to be more complex. Because in actual network communication, each layer of the protocol used by the address is not the same. For example, in TCP / IP Communications, MAC address, IP address, port number, and so on are used as address identifiers. Even in the application layer, an e-mail address can be used as the address of network communication.
the uniqueness of addresses.

If you want the address to play a role in communication, you first need to determine the main body of the communication. An address must explicitly represent a princIPal object. A communication subject with two identical addresses is not allowed to exist in the same communication network. This is the uniqueness of the address.

So far, the reader may have a question. As mentioned earlier, a communication subject with two identical addresses is not allowed to exist in the same communication network. This is understandable in UNICAST communications, where both ends of the communication are a single host. So for broadcast, multicast, and broadcast communication how to understand it?

Isn't the receiver assigned the same address? In fact, to some extent, this understanding has some rationality. In these communications, there may be more than one receiving device. For this reason, a unique address can be assigned to a group of communications composed of multiple devices, which can avoid ambiguity and explicitly receive objects.

Address Hierarchy

When the total number of addresses is not a lot of cases, with a unique address can be located between the main communication. However, when the total number of addresses is increasing, how to efficiently find out the target address of communication will become an important issue. For this reason, it is found that the address needs to be hierarchical as well as unique. In fact, in the use of telephone and mail communication process, the address hierarchy has long been a concept. For example, a telephone number contains a country area code and a domestic area code, and a correspondence address contains the name of the country, province, city, and district. It is this hierarchical classification that makes it possible to locate an address more quickly.

Both Mac address and IP address are unique in identifying a communication body, but the only the IP address is hierarchical.

Mac addresses are specified by the device's manufacturer for each NIC (Network Interface Card), also known as a Network

Card, which is used by computers to connect to the Internet.).
One can ensure the uniqueness of the MAC address through the
manufacturer's identification number, the manufacturer's
internal product number, and the generic product number.
However, it is impossible to determine which network cards
from which vendor are used in which location. Although the
MAC address has some level of information such as
manufacturer identification number, product number, and
general number, it doesn't do anything to find the address So it
doesn't count as a hierarchical address. Because of this, although
the MAC address is really responsible for the final
communication address, in the actual addressing process, the IP
address is essential.

So how do IP addresses achieve layering? On the one hand, an IP
address consists of a network number and a host number. Even
if the main communication IP address is different, if the host
number is different, the network number is the same, that they
are in the same network segment. In general, the hosts of the
same network segment also belong to the same department or
group. On the other hand, hosts with the same network number
are centralized in the organization, provider type, and
geographic distribution, which makes IP addressing very
convenient). That's why IP addresses are hierarchical.

In network transmission, each node will decide which network
card should send the packet according to the address

information of the packet data. To do this, each address refers to a list of outgoing interfaces. At this point, Mac addressing is the same as IP addressing. But the table referenced in the Mac addressing is called the address forwarding table. The reference in IP address is called the routing control table (currently, the forwarding table and the routing control table are not manually set up on each node in the network but are generated automatically by those nodes. Address forwarding tables are automatically generated based on self-study. The routing control table is automatically generated based on the routing protocol. The actual Mac address itself is recorded in the Mac address forwarding table, while the IP address recorded in the routing table is the centralized network number.

Network Components

Setting up a network environment involves a wide variety of cables and network equipment. Here only the hardware that connects the computer to the computer is described.

Communication Media and Data Links

Computer network refers to the computer and computer connected and composed of the network. So how are computers connected in the real world?

The computers are connected to each other by cables. There are many types of cables, including twisted pair, fiber optic cable, coaxial cable, serial cable, etc. A protocol and its network for communicating between directly connected devices based on data links (Datalink). To this end, there are a number of transmission medium corresponding. Different cable types are used. And the medium itself can be divided into radio waves, microwaves and other types of electromagnetic waves.

Transmission Rate and Throughput
In the process of data transmission, the physical speed at which data flows between two devices is called the transmission rate. In units of BPS (Bits Per Second). Strictly speaking, the flow rate of signals in various transmission media is constant. It's official. Therefore, even if the data link transmission rate is not the same, there will be no transmission speed fast or slow situation (because the speed of transmission for light and current is constant.) High transmission rate does not mean how fast per unit data flow and Refers to the amount of data transmitted per unit time.

In the case of road traffic in our lives, low-speed data links are like too few lanes for many cars to pass through at once The situation. In contrast, a high-speed data link is a road with multiple lanes, allowing more vehicles to travel at once. The transmission rate is also known as Bandwidth. The greater the bandwidth, the greater the network capacity.

In addition, the actual transfer rate between hosts is called throughput. The units are the same as the bandwidth, BPS (Bits Per Second). Throughput is a term that measures not only bandwidth, but also the CPU capacity of the host, congestion on the network, and the share of data fields in the message (not including the header, only the data fields themselves).

The Connection Between Network Devices

Interconnectivity between network devices needs to follow some kind of "law" of norms and industry standards. This is critical to setting up an online environment. If each different vendor uses its own transport medium and protocol when producing various network devices, those devices will not be able to connect to other vendors' devices or networks. To this end, people have developed a unified agreement and specifications. Every manufacturer must produce corresponding network equipment in strict accordance with the specifications, otherwise it will lead to its own products cannot be compatible with other network equipment, or prone to failure and so on.

However, norm-setting is often a long-term process, in this process of technological transition, people will inevitably encounter some "compatibility" problems. This is especially true in the early days of new technologies such as ATM, Gigabit Ethernet, and Wireless Lan. Problems often occur when network devices from different vendors connect to each other. This has improved over time but is still not 100% compatible.

Therefore, when building the actual network, not only should pay attention to the specification parameters of each product,

413

but also should understand their compatibility And more attention should be paid to the actual long-term use of these products in the course of the performance indicators (performance indicators good technology is also known as "mature technology. ". It refers to the market and users over a period of time test, accumulated a considerable amount of practical experience of technology. If you use a new product that doesn't work well without proper research, the consequences can be dire.

Network Card

Any computer connected to the network must use a network card (the full name is the network interface card). The network interface card (Nic) is an integrated device that connects Lan functions. Sometimes it is integrated into the computer's motherboard, or it can be inserted into an expansion slot separately Use. Network Information Center (Network Information Center) is sometimes called a Network adapter, Network card, or LAN card.

Recently, many product catalogs have added the parameter "built-in Lan port", note that more and more computers in the factory settings with Ethernet (Ethernet)1000BASE-T or 100BASE-TX port (computer and external connection interface known as computer port.). A computer that does not have a NIC configured needs to have at least one external socket to plug into the NIC if it wants to connect to Ethernet. By the PC Card standard PCMCIA (Personal Computer Memory Card International Association) unified specifications. Or CardBus compressed flash Memory and USB plug a piece later connected.

Repeaters

Repeater (Repeater) is a device that extends the network at the physical level, layer 1 of the OSI model. The electrical or optical signals from the cable are adjusted and amplified by the waveform of the repeater and transmitted to another cable.

In general, the two ends of the repeater are connected to the same communication medium, but some repeaters can also complete the transfer between different media. For example, signals can be adjusted between the coaxial cable and optical cable. In this case, however, the repeater is simply responsible for replacing the signal between the 0 and 1-bit streams, not for determining whether the data is in error. At the same time, it is only responsible for converting electrical signals into optical signals Therefore, it can not be forwarded between media with different transmission speeds (one 100 Mbps Ethernet and another 10 Mbps Ethernet cannot be connected with a repeater. Connecting two networks of different speeds require devices such as bridges or routers.).

Network extensions via repeaters are not infinitely long in distance. For example, a 10Mbps Ethernet can be connected in segments with up to four repeaters, while a 100Mbps Ethernet can be connected to up to two repeaters.

Some repeaters can provide multIPle port services. This type of repeater is called a relay hub or hub. Therefore, a can also be considered A MULTI-PORT REPEATER Each port can be a repeater.

Bridge / Layer 2 SWITCH

A Bridge is a device that connects two networks at layer 2 of the OSI model, the data link layer. It recognizes data frames in the data link layer (similar to packet data, but more commonly referred to as frames in the data link layer). And temporarily store these data frames in memory, the regenerated signal is then forwarded as a new frame to another connected segment of the network. In addition, data can also be represented in TCP. Because of the ability to store these frames, the bridge is able to connect 10BASE-T and 100BASE-TX data links with completely different transmission rates and does not limit the number of links.

A bit in the data frame of a data link is called FCS (CRC Cyclic Redundancy Check Check) to verify the bit in the data frame. This kind of CRC is used to check whether a data frame has been damaged by the noise that sometimes causes the data signal to get weaker and weaker in the transmission To verify that the data has reached its destination correctly. Bridges Discard corrupted data by checking the values in this field to avoid sending it to other segments. In addition, the bridge can control network traffic (the number of datagrams transmitted over the network) through address self-learning mechanism and filtering function

By address, I mean the Mac address, hardware address, physical address, and adapter address, which is the specific address assigned to the NIC on the network.

When host a communicates with host B, only a data frame can be sent to host A. The bridge determines whether a frame needs to be forwarded based on the address self-learning mechanism.

This is the function of Layer 2(data link layer) of the OSI reference model. For this reason, bridges are sometimes referred to as layer 2 switches (L2 switches).

Some bridges, called self-learning bridges, are able to determine whether or not to forward data packets to adjacent segments. This type of bridge remembers the Mac address of all the frames it forwards and stores them in its own memory table. From this, you can determine which network segment contains devices that hold which MAC addresses.

A Hub (a Bridge-enabled Hub called a switching Hub, and a repeater-only Hub called a Hub), often used in networks such as Ethernet, is now essentially a Network bridge Hub. Each port connected to the cable in the switching hub provides a bridge-like function.

Router / Layer 3 switch

A router is a device that connects two networks at layer 3 of the OSI model, the network level, and forwards packet packets. The bridge is processed according to the physical address (Mac address), while the router / Layer 3 switch is processed according to the IP address. Thus, the network layer address in TCP / IP becomes the IP address.

A router can connect to different data links. For example, connect two Ethernet networks, or connect one Ethernet to an FDDI. Nowadays, the broadband router that people use to connect to the Internet in their home or office is also a kind of router.

The router also shares the network load (since the router splits the data link, the broadcast message at the data link layer will not continue to propagate.), some routers even have some network security features. Therefore, the router plays a very important role in connecting the network and the network equipment.

4 ~ 7 layer switch

Layer 4 ~ 7 switches handle data from the transport layer to the application layer in the OSI model. If the TCP / IP layer model is used (for more details about the TCP / IP Layer Model), layer 4-7 switches analyze the sending and receiving data based on the transport layer of TCP and the application layer above it And do certain things with it.

For example, for an enterprise-level Web site with a high level of concurrent traffic (a server or group of servers connected to the Internet as specified by the URL. At present, according to information content can be divided into game sites, resource download sites and Web sites and other types One server is not enough to meet the front-end access requirements, and multIPle servers are usually set up to share. These servers typically have only one entry address for front-end access (the enterprise only opens a unified access URL to the end user for user convenience). In order to distribute front-end access to multiple servers in the background via the same URL, a load balancer can be added to the front end of these servers. This load balancer is one of the 4-7 layer switches (in addition to load balancing via DNS. By configuring multiple IP addresses with the same name, each customer querying the name gets one of the addresses, enabling different clients to access different servers. This approach is also known as the reuse DNS technique.).

In addition, in actual communications, people want to give priority to communication requests that require more timeliness, such as voice calls, when the network is more congested Slow down the processing of communications requests, such as email or data forwarding, where a slight delay doesn't hurt. This process is called bandwidth control and is one of the important functions of layer 4 ~ 7 switches.

In addition, there are many applications of layer 4 ~ 7 switch. Examples include WAN accelerators, special application access accelerators, and firewalls that prevent illegal access on the Internet.

Gateway

A gateway is a device in the OSI reference model that is responsible for converting and forwarding data from the transport layer to the application layer (by convention, a router behaves like a "gateway"). But "gateways" in this book are limited to devices or components in the OSI reference model that convert protocols at each layer above the transport layer.). Like layer 4 ~ 7 switches, it processes data at the transport layer and above, but the gateway not only forwards the data but also converts it. It usually uses a presentation layer or application layer gateway Two protocols which cannot communicate with each other directly are translated, and the communication between them is realized finally.

A very typical example is the switching service between Internet mail and Mobile Mail. Mobile mail can sometimes be incompatible with Internet mail because of the "e-mail protocol" differences between the presentation layer and the application layer.

So why do computers and phones connected to the Internet send e-mails to each other? There is a gateway between the Internet and the phone. The gateway is responsible for reading various protocols, converting them reasonably one by one, and then forwarding the corresponding data. This allows computers and mobile phones to send e-mails to each other, even if different e-mail protocols are used.

In addition, when using the WWW (World Wide Web), Proxy Server is sometimes used to control network traffic and for security reasons. This proxy server is also a type of gateway, called an application gateway. With the proxy server, there is no direct communication between the client and the server on the network layer. Instead, data and access are controlled and processed from the transport layer to the application layer. A firewall is a communication through the gateway, for different applications to improve security products.

Chapter 4: Advanced Networking

In this chapter, we will expand our knowledge further about reference models and learn in detail about TCP protocol.

Physical layer

When it comes to the "physical layer" of network architecture, the first thing to know is what it does. Compared with other layers, the "physical layer " includes more technologies and procedures because of the types of transmission media, physical interfaces and their communication protocols (that is, "communication protocols") But its main functions are relatively simple, including.

(1) Building a Data Path

"Data Path" is a complete data transmission channel, can be a section of physical media, can also be connected by a number of physical media. A complete data transfer, including the activation of the physical connection, transfer of data, termination of the physical connection three major stages. The so-called "activation of physical connection", is no matter how many pieces of physical media involved, in the communication between the two data terminal equipment must be connected to form a continuous data transmission channel above.

(2) Transparent Transmission

There are many types of transmission media available in the physical layer (such as different types of coaxial cable, twisted pair and optical fiber, et c.), each supported by corresponding communication protocols and standards This determines that different computer networks may have different "paths. ". In addition to repairing these different "paths", the physical layer also ensures that these different "paths" can be "connected" to form paths that eventually carry the bitstream to the "physical layer" on the opposite end the purpose of which is then submitted to the data link layer.

To achieve these functions, the physical layer needs to have the function of shielding different transmission media types and communication protocols, so that the parties communicating on the network can only see that there is a " road" available Regardless of the specific "material" and related standards used to build these "roads" , this is the "transparent transport" function of the physical layer.

(3) Transmission of Data

No matter which layer of the network architecture initiates the communication, the final data has to be transmitted through the lowest "physical layer", which is the only physical channel of the network communication. But the unit of transmission for the "physical layer" is the bit (bit, or "bit", where a Binary 0 or 1 in the data represents a bit). The basic function of "physical layer" is to transmit data in the order of bit stream to the physical layer of the receiver through the physical layer interface and transmission medium.

(4) Data Coding

In order to transmit the data efficiently and reliably on the "physical layer" , the most important thing is to ensure that the data bit stream can pass through the corresponding "channel". This involves the "physical layer" of data encoding functions because different transmission media support different types of data encoding (such as zero-return code, non-zero-return Code, Manchester Code, differential Manchester Code, etc.).

(5) Data Transmission Management

The "physical layer" also has some functions of data transmission management, such as data transmission flow control, error control, activation and release of physical lines, etc.

Datalink Layer

The data link layer is included directly or indirectly in computer network architectures (the functionality of the data link layer in the TCP / IP Protocol Architecture is included in the network access layer). The data link layer and the physical layer below it are essentially the same, that is, they are used to build a channel for network communication and access, only the physical layer builds a physical channel the data link layer builds logical channels that are really used for data transmission. Because of this, in the TCP / IP Protocol Architecture which is widely used on the Internet, the physical layer and the data link layer are divided into the network access layer.

The data link layer is located in the lower layer of the "network layer" (called the interconnect layer in the TCP / IP Protocol Architecture) of the network architecture. So one of its basic functions is to provide transparent, reliable data transfer services to the network layer (in a computer network architecture, the next layer serves the next layer next to the one above). "transparent" means that there are no restrictions on the content, format, or encoding of the data being transmitted at the data link layer This means that some control characters that are intended for special purposes (which are described later in this chapter) can be transmitted as normal data so that the receiver does not mistake them for control characters; Reliable transmission enables data to be transmitted from the sending end to the destination end of the data link without error. Overall, the main functions of the data link layer (in this case, the LLC sublayer) are four: Data Link Management, encapsulation into frames, transparent transmission, and error control.

Network Layer

If we compare the physical layer and the data link layer to intra-city traffic, the network layer described in this chapter can be compared to a transit station, airport, or dock that connects different urban traffic. Just as a transit station, airport or dock can transport passengers from another city to the next stop or to a local destination, the network layer can transfer data from other networks to the next network or to a destination node in this network. When the source and the destination are located in different networks, direct communication is not feasible, then it needs to be solved by the network layer.

Network Layer (called interconnect layer in TCP / IP Architecture) is a very important layer in network architecture, and it is also a very complicated layer in technology It not only solves the problem of route and protocol identification, but also solves the problem of network congestion by route selection strategy, so as to improve the reliability of network communication. The network layer is concerned with routing packets from the source along the network path to the destination. To achieve this goal, the network layer must know the topology of the communication subnet and choose the proper path in the topology. At the same time, the network layer must choose the routing path carefully to avoid the situation that some communication lines and routers are overloaded while others are idle.

The physical layer and the data link layer introduced earlier in this book construct the communication lines within the LAN, which are equivalent to the traffic lines within a city. The network layer described in this chapter is the node used to connect different local area network lines, located at the edge of the different network, is equivalent to the edge of the city, used to connect different urban transit points.

The network layer is the third layer in the OSI reference model (corresponding to the second layer in the TCP / IP Protocol Architecture, the interconnect layer), which is between the transport layer and the data link layer. Generally speaking, the main role of the network layer is to achieve the transparent transmission of data between the two network systems, including routing, congestion control, and Internet interconnection. The network layer is the lowest layer of the end-to-end (that is, between the network and the network) network communication. It is responsible for the connection to the resource subnet above it (Osi / RM reference model transport layer and above four layers) and is the most complex and critical layer of the network communication-oriented lower three layers of the OSI / RM reference model.

The network layer is the product of the development of the computer network, but it is not the product of a computer network. In the early days of computer networks, there was basically a separate local area network, and we know that In the LAN, the communication link constructed by the physical layer and the data link layer can be used to realize the communication access among the users, so there is no need for other layers, including the network layer. Moreover, at that time, the application of computer network was limited, and there was no need to communicate with each other among local area networks, so these local area networks did not need to be connected with each other. But with the popularization and development of computer networks, it is increasingly found that it is very necessary to connect these isolated local area networks one by one to form a larger computer network so that the role of computer networks can be more obvious Enable more people to share server and hardware resources. This involves the interconnection of computer networks.

So why such a network layer? In fact, the reason is very simple, because different networks have different network layer protocols and address specifications, if users in one network cannot identify the other network communication protocols and address specifications, you can't transfer data from one network to another. Just as different cities have different traffic laws and regulations, belong to different traffic police systems, and do not allow random traffic in and out of the city, different networks have different design specifications, belong to different organizations to manage, and must be authorized and special protocols are responsible for communication between the networks.

Usually a computer network is a management boundary, generally belongs to a specific company, by a specific manager responsible. Therefore, when the interconnection of computer networks is carried out, two aspects should be considered at the same time: one is to authorize users to visit each other's network s and share their resources; the other is to maintain the original independence of the management of each computer network So the problem cannot be solved simply by pulling a cable (this does not solve the problem of management independence) . In fact, in many environments, it is not possible for a typical business to connect two computer networks located in different cities or even different countries via a tether.

The main function of the network layer is to route packets from the source node to the destination node, and in most computer networks, packet switching is used Datagram packets go through multIPle hops (that is, how many routers) to reach their destination.

Routing

The routing function is actually a packet switching path selection behavior, is a basic function of the network layer. Routing functions are similar to the way we choose the best (note that "best" doesn't mean the fastest, it's a combination) to travel or transport goods.

There can be multiple routes for sending such a letter. Different routes require different ways of mailing, different length of route and time of mailing, and of course, different transportation costs. The final choice of route should be considered in terms of overall mailing cost, mailing time and reliability of the post office. Routing is the same, it has to consider a number of factors, such as line length, channel bandwidth, line stability, the cost of the port through. Different routing algorithms take into account different factors.

Routing is the act of transferring information from the source node to the destination node via the network. Simply speaking, Routing means that three layers of devices receive packets from one interface and Orient them according to the destination address of the packet And forward it to another interface. But at least one intermediate node needs to be encountered in this routing path, and that is the devices that provide routing functions, such as routers and layer 3 switches. The main difference between routing and bridging is that bridging occurs at layer 2(link layer) of the OSI reference protocol, connecting different segments of the same network or subnetwork, and routing occurs at Layer 3 (network layer) Connected to a different network or subnet.

The realization of the routing function depends on the routing table in the router or three-layer switch. There are two kinds of Routing: Static Routing and Dynamic Routing.

Static routing is something we often need to configure, especially in small Lens, because it is relatively simple to configure and manage

Static routing is feasible for small and infrequently changing networks, such as local area networks. However, for larger Wan, because the topology is more complex and the network structure may change frequently, the static routing is no longer suitable, and the dynamic routing is more flexible and automatic.

One of the most important features of dynamic routing is that the routers included in a route in the network simultaneously start a dynamic routing protocol, after notifying the networks to which they are directly connected These routers will automatically generate routing table entries between the networks to which the routers are directly connected, and administrators do not have to create each one manually. This is the most convenient and simple routing option for larger networks.

IP addresses

The most important protocol of Osi / Rm Network layer and TCP / IP interconnect layer is IP protocol, which is in the transition period of IPV4 and IPv6 So this chapter will be the two versions of the IP address and related knowledge of the system

IPv4 uses 32-bit (4-byte) addresses, so there are 4294967296(2^{32}) addresses in the entire address space or nearly 4.3 billion addresses. However, some of these addresses are reserved for special purposes, such as Lan private addresses (about 18 million addresses) and multicast addresses (about 27 million addresses), in this way can be directly used in the wide area network, the number of public networks IP address routing is even less.

To understand what a subnet mask is, one must first understand the composition of an IPV4 address. The Internet is made up of many small networks, each network has many hosts, thus forming a hierarchical structure. In the design of IPV4 address, each IP address is divided into two parts: a Network ID and host ID, so as to facilitate the addressing operation of IPV4 address. So how many bits are the network ID and host ID of an IPV4 address? If it is not specified, it is not known which bits in the IPV4 address represent the network ID and which represent the host ID at the time of addressing, which is realized by the subnet mask mentioned here.

In the whole network architecture, the bottom three layers of OSI / RM seven-layer model are called communication subnet-oriented layers, which are responsible for the establishment of the communication channel, and the transport layer and above are called resource-oriented subnet-oriented Layers Responsible for data communication between Terminal Systems. There is also a way to divide the "transmission layer" and the following three layers into a communication-oriented layer, in general, responsible for the establishment of communication channels and data transmission The "session layer" , "presentation layer" and " application layer" , which do not contain any data transfer function, are collectively called application-oriented layers.

Application Layer
The application layer is the highest layer of the OSI / Rm and TCP / IP architectures. It provides services directly to users by using the services provided by the following layers. It is the interface or interface between a computer network and users. Just like the services provided by other layers, the service functions of the application layer are realized by specific communication protocols.

Used by users on a daily basis Such as Web Service, e-mail service, DNS (domain name service), DHCP (automatic IP address assignment service), file transfer service, remote login service, etc. With the popularization and development of Internet application, a variety of new network application services emerge in endlessly. This chapter only introduces some of the most commonly used services in TCP / IP Network.

The application layer in TCP / IP architecture solves the common problems of TCP / IP network applications, including the supporting protocols and application services related to network applications. The supporting protocols include domain name service system (DNS), dynamic host configuration protocol (DHCP), simple network management protocol (SNMP) and so on Typical application services include Web browsing service, E-mail service, file transfer access service, remote login service, etc. In addition, there are some protocols related to these typical network application services This includes Hypertext Transfer Protocol, Simple Mail Transfer Protocol, File Transfer Protocol, simple File Transfer Protocol, and remote login (Telnet).

The most popular and frequently used Web application is the World Wide Web (WWW) service or Web service. The core application layer Protocol for Web Services is HTTP (Hypertext Transfer Protocol), which can also be viewed as the "hero behind the Hypertext Transfer Protocol" of Web Services.

The Background and History of TCP / IP

At present, TCP / IP Protocol is the most famous and widely used in the field of a computer network. So how did TCP / IP become so widespread in such a short time? Some think it's because PC operating systems such as Windows and MAC OS support TCPIP. While this is true to a certain extent, it is not the root cause of the popularity of TCPIP. In fact, around the entire computer industry at that time, the whole society formed a popular trend to support TCP / IP, so that various computer manufacturers have to adapt to this change and continue to produce products to support TCP / IP. Today, you can hardly find an operating system that doesn't support TCPIP on the market.

In a literal sense, one might think that TCP / IP refers to both TCP and IP protocols. In practice, it does sometimes refer to these two agreements. However, in many cases, it is only the use of IP communication must be used in the group of protocols collectively. Specifically, IP or ICMP, TCP or UDP, TELNET or FTP, and HTTP are TCP / IP Protocols. They have a close relationship with TCP or IP and are an integral part of the Internet. The term TCP / IP generally refers to these protocols, and therefore, TCP / IP is sometimes referred to as the Internet Protocol Suite (the Group of protocols that make up the Internet Protocol Suite).

The standardization process of TCP / IP Protocol Is Different From other standardization processes, which has two characteristics: one is openness, the other is practicality, that is, whether the standardized protocol can be used in practice.

First, openness is because the TCP / IP Protocol is discussed by the IETF, and the IETF itself is an organization that allows anyone to participate in the discussion. Here, people typically have daily discussions in the form of e-mail groups, which can be subscribed to by anyone at any time.

Secondly, in the process of standardization of TCP / IP, the specification of a protocol itself is no longer so important, but the first task is to realize the technology that can realize communication. No wonder some people quIPped that "TCP / IP is simply to develop the program first, then write specifications. ".

Although that's a bit of an exaggeration, however, TCP / IP does take into account the feasibility of implementing a protocol when developing a protocol specification (implementation: the development of programs and hardware that enable a computing device to perform certain actions or behaviors as expected by the protocol). And while the final specifications for a protocol are in place, some of these protocols already exist in certain devices and can communicate.

To this end, as soon as the general specification of a protocol is determined in TCP / IP, people will experiment with the communication between multiple devices that have implemented the protocol, and once they find something wrong, they can continue to discuss it in the IEFT Modify programs, protocols, or corresponding documents in a timely manner. After so many discussions, experiments, and studies, a protocol specification is finally born. Therefore, the TCP / IP Protocol is always very practical.

However, for those protocols that were not found to be problematic due to the limitations of the experimental environment, improvements will continue at a later stage. The reason OSI is not as popular as TCP / IP, the main reasons were the failure to formulate feasible agreements as early as possible, the failure to propose agreements to deal with rapid technological innovation and the failure to implement late-stage improvement programs in a timely manner

TCP / IP is the most widely used protocol in a computer network. Knowledge of TCP / IP is critical for those who want to build networks, build networks, manage networks, design and build network devices, and even do network device programming.

At the bottom of TCP / IP is the hardware responsible for data transmission. This hardware is equivalent to a physical layer device such as an Ethernet or telephone line. There has been no consistent definition of what it is. Because as long as people on the physical level of the use of different transmission media (such as the use of network lines or wireless), the network bandwidth, reliability, security, delay, and so on will be different, and in these areas, there are no established indicators. In a word, TCP / IP Protocol is proposed on the premise that the interconnect devices can communicate with each other.

The network interface layer (sometimes called the network communication layer by combining the network interface layer with the hardware layer) uses the data link layer in the Ethernet to communicate, so it belongs to the interface layer. That is, think of it as the "driver" that makes the NIC work Prologue doesn't matter. A driver is a software that bridges the gap between the operating system and the hardware. PerIPheral devices or extension cards are not immediately available by plugging them directly into a computer or its expansion slot and need to be supported by a corresponding driver. For example, a new NIC network card, not only the need for hardware but also the need for software to really put into use. As a result, people often need to install drivers on top of the operating system in order to use additional hardware. (There are also many plug-and-play devices because the computer's operating system already has drivers built into the network card, rather than no drivers.).

The Internet layer uses the IP protocol, which is equivalent to layer 3 of the OSI model. A number of IP packets forwarded based on the IP Address. In addition, all hosts and routers connected to the Internet must implement IP functionality. Other network devices that connect to the Internet (such as bridges, repeaters, or hubs) do not necessarily have to perform IP or TCP functions (sometimes they also need to have IP, TCP functions in order to monitor and manage bridges, repeaters, hubs, and the like)

IP is a protocol that transmits packets across a network, enabling the entire Internet to receive data. The IP protocol enables data to be sent to the other side of the Earth During this time it uses the IP address as the identity of the host (all devices connected to the IP network must have their own unique identification number in order to identify the specific device. Packet data is sent to the opposite end based on the IP address.). IP also implies the function of the Data Link Layer. Through IP, the hosts can communicate with each other regardless of the underlying data link.

Although IP is also a packet switching protocol, it does not have a retransmission mechanism. Packets do not resend even if they do not arrive on the end host. Therefore, it belongs to the non-reliable transport protocol.

When an exception occurs on the way to the IP packet and the destination address can not be reached, a notification of the exception is sent to the sender. ICMP is designed for this purpose. It is also sometimes used to diagnose the health of the network.

A protocol for resolving a physical address (MAC address) from the IP address of a packet.

The primary function of the transport layer is to enable communication between applications. Inside a computer, usually, several programs are running at the same time. To this end, it is necessary to distinguish which programs are communicating with which programs. What identifies these applications is the port number.

TCP is a connection-oriented transport layer. It can ensure that communication between the two communication hosts can reach. TCP can correctly handle the transmission process in the loss of packets, transmission order out of order and other abnormal cases. In addition, TCP can effectively utilize bandwidth and alleviate network congestion.

However, in order to establish and disconnect the connection, sometimes it needs at least 7 times to send and receive the packet, leading to the waste of network traffic. In addition, in order to improve the utilization of the network, TCP protocol defines various complex specifications, which is not conducive to the use of video conferencing (audio, video data set) and other occasions

UDP, unlike TCP, is a connectionless oriented transport layer. UDP does not care whether the other end is actually receiving the transmitted data, and if it needs to check whether the other end is receiving packet data, or whether the other end is connected to the network, it needs to be implemented in the application. UDP is often used in multimedia fields such as packet data less or multicast, broadcast communication, and video communication.

In the TCP / IP Layer, the functions of the session layer, presentation layer, and application layer in the OSI reference model are integrated into the application sequential implementation. These functions are sometimes implemented by a single program or by multiple programs. Therefore, a closer look at the application functions of TCP / IP reveals that it implements not only the application layer of the OSI model but also the session layer and presentation layer.

The architecture of TCP / IP application mostly belongs to the Client / Server Model. The program that provides the service is called the server, and the program that receives the service is called the client. In this mode of communication, the service provider is predeployed to the host, waiting to receive requests that customers may send at any time.

The client can send a request to the server at any time. Sometimes the server may handle the exception, overload, and so on when the client can wait a moment to reissue a request.

WWW (worldwide Web, a specification for reading data on the Internet. Sometimes also called Web, WWW or W3.) Can Be said to be the Internet can be so popular an important driving force. Users in a type of browser called the Web Browser (often referred to simply as the browser). Microsoft's Internet Explorer and Mozilla Foundation's Firefox are all browsers. They are already widely used.) With the help of a mouse and keyboard, you can surf the web freely and easily. That means that a single click of the mouse on a remote server will render all kinds of information to the browser. The browser can display text, pictures, animation, and other information, but also play sound and run programs.

The Protocol used for communication between the Browser and the server is HTTP (Hypertext Transfer Protocol). The primary format of the data transferred is HTML (Hypertext Markup Language). HTTP in the WWW belongs to the OSI application layer protocol, while HTML belongs to the presentation layer protocol.

E-mail actually means sending letters on the Internet. With email, no matter how far away a person is, just connect to each other. You can send e-mails to each other over the Internet. The Protocol used to send e-Mail is called SMTP (Simple Mail Transfer Protocol).

Initially, people could only send e-mails in text format (consisting only of text messages. Japanese originally could only send 7- bit JIS encoded text.). But now, the format of an e-mail message is defined by MIME (a specification for the format of mail data that is widely used on the Internet. It can also be used in WWW and web forums. For more details on this point, You can send sounds, pictures, all kinds of information. You can even change the size and color of the message text (some functions may not be fully displayed due to the limitations of the mail-receiving software). The MIME mentioned here belongs to Layer 6 of the OSI reference model, the presentation layer.

File transfer (FTP)

A file transfer is the transfer of a file stored on another computer's hard drive to a local hard drive or the transfer of a file from a local hard drive to another machine's hard drive. The protocol used in this process is called FTP (File Transfer Protocol). FTP has been in use for a long time (the use of HTTP with the WWW for file transfer has been increasing recently) you can choose between the binary or text mode of the transfer. (text-based file transfers between systems such as Windows, MacOS, or Unix change line breaks automatically. This is also part of the presentation layer.). Two TCP connections are established when a file transfer is made in FTP, these are the control connections used to make transmission requests and the data connections used to actually transmit data (the control management of these two connections is a function of the session layer).

Remote Login (TELNET and SSH)

Remote login is the ability to log on to a remote computer, allowing programs on that computer to run. Teletext (short for TELetypewriter NETwork, sometimes referred to as the default protocol) and SSH (short for Secure Shell) are two common protocols for remote login over TCP / IP Networks. There are many other protocols that allow remote Logins, such as the R command for login in BSD UNIX systems and the x protocol in x Window System.

Network Management (SNMP)

When Network Management in TCP / IP, SNMP (Simple Network Management Protocol) Protocol is used. Hosts, bridges, routers, etc. that are managed using SNMP are called SNMP agents, and the segment that is managed is called a Manager. SNMP is the protocol used by this Manager and Agent.

In the agent side of SNMP, the information of network interface, communication data, abnormal data, and device temperature are stored. This Information can be accessed through the Management Information Base, also known as a network-permeable structural variable. Therefore, in the network management of TCP / IP, SNMP belongs to Application Protocol, MIB belongs to Presentation Layer Protocol.

The larger and more complex a network is, the more it needs to be managed effectively. SNMP allows administrators to check network congestion in a timely manner, to detect failures early, and to collect the necessary information for future network expansion.

How are TCP / IP Transmitted over a Medium?

This section describes the flow of data processing from the application layer to the physical media when using TCP / IP.

Packet Header

In each hierarchy, a header is attached to the data being sent, which contains the necessary information for the layer, such as the destination address to be sent and protocol-related information. Typically, the information provided for the protocol is the header of the package, and the content to be sent is data.

The data packet transmitted in the network consists of two parts: one part is the first part used by the protocol, and the other part is the data transmitted from the upper layer. The structure of the header is defined in detail by the specification of the protocol. For example, the domain that identifies the upper layer protocol should start with which bit of the package, how to compute the checksum and insert which bit of the package, and so on. If the two computers communicating with each other are different in identifying the serial number of the protocol and calculating the checksum, they can not communicate at all.

Therefore, at the beginning of the packet, it clearly indicates how the protocol should read the data. Conversely, by looking at the header, you will be able to understand the information necessary for the protocol and what to process. Therefore, looking at the header of the package is like looking at the specification of the protocol.

No wonder people say the first one is like the face of protocol sending packets

Suppose a sends an e-mail to b saying, "Good Morning". In TCP / IP Communication, it is an e-mail from one computer A to another computer B. Let's use this example to explain the process of TCP / IP Communication.

Application Processing

Launch the application to create a new message, fill out the recipient's mailbox, then enter the message content "good morning" by keyboard, mouse click on the "send" button can start the TCP / IP Communication. First, there is coding in the application. For example, Japanese e-mail is encoded using ISO-2022-JP or UTF-8. These codes correspond to Osi's presentation layer functions.

After the code conversion, the actual message may not be sent immediately, because some mail software has the ability to send more than one message at a time there may also be the ability for users to click the "receive mail" button before receiving new mail. Such administrative functions as when to establish a communication connection and when to send data are, in a broad sense, functions of the OSI reference model at the session layer.

The application uses the TCP connection to send data by establishing the TCP connection at the moment the message is sent. The process is to send the application data to the next layer of TCP, and then do the actual forwarding processing.

The Processing of TCP MODULE

TCP is responsible for establishing connections, sending data, and disconnecting according to the application's instructions (which are equivalent to the session layer in the OSI reference model.). TCP provides reliable transmission of data from the application layer to the opposite end.

In order to realize this function of TCP, we need to attach a TCP header to the front end of the application layer data. The TCP header includes the source and destination port numbers (to identify applications on the sending host and the receiving host) , the serial number (which part of the packet to send is the data) , and the Checksum (Check Sum)(to verify that the data is read properly)(to determine whether the data is corrupted) . The packet attached to the TCP header is then sent to the IP.

The Processing of IP Module

IP takes the TCP header and TCP data from TCP as its own data and adds its own IP header to the front end of the TCP header. Thus, the IP header in an IP packet is followed by the TCP header, followed by the application header and the data itself. The IP header contains the receiver IP address and the sender IP address. Immediately following the IP header is the information used to determine whether the following data is TCP or UDP.

After the IP packet is generated, the reference routing control table decides which route or host to accept the IP packet. The IP packet is then sent to the driver that connects to these routers or host network interfaces to actually send the data. If the MAC Address on the receiving end is not known, an ARP (Address Resolution Protocol) lookup is available. As long as we know the MAC address of the opposite end, we can give the MAC address and IP address to the Ethernet driver to realize data transmission.

The Processing of Network Interface (Ethernet Driver)

The IP packet that comes over from IP is nothing more than data to the Ethernet driver. This data is attached to the Ethernet header and sent for processing. The Ethernet header contains the Mac address of the receiver, the Mac address of the sender, and the Mac address of the marked Ethernet type. Ethernet data protocol. The Ethernet packet generated from the above information will be transmitted to the receiving end through the physical layer. The FCS (Frame Check Sequence) in the send processing is computed by the hardware and added to the end of the package. The purpose of the FCS is to determine whether a packet has been corrupted by noise.

Network Interface (Ethernet driver) Processing

After the host receives the Ethernet packet, it first finds the MAC address from the Ethernet packet header to determine whether the packet is sent to itself. Discard data if it is not sent to its own packet (many NIC products can be set to not discard data even if it is not sent to its own packet. This can be used to monitor network traffic.).

If you receive a packet that happens to be sent to you, look for the type field in the header of the Ethernet packet to determine the type of data being transmitted by the Ethernet protocol. In this case, the data type is obviously an IP packet, so it passes the data to the processing IP subroutine, and if it's not IP but some other protocol such as Arp, it passes the data to the ARP handler. In summary, if the type field at the head of the Ethernet packet contains an unrecognized protocol type, the data is discarded.

The Processing of IP Module

The IP module receives the first and subsequent portions of the IP packet and does similar processing. If you determine that the IP address in the header matches your own IP address, you can receive the data and look up the protocol at the next level. If the upper layer is TCP, the portion after the header of the IP packet is passed to TCP; if UDP, the portion after the header of the IP packet is passed to UDP. In the case of Router, the receiver address is often not their own address, at this point, the need to use the routing control table, in the investigation should be sent to the host or router after forwarding data.

The Processing of TCP Module

In the TCP module, the CHECKSUM is first calculated to determine whether the data is corrupted. Then check to see if the data is being received by serial number. Finally, check the port number to determine the specific application. After the data is received, the receiver sends an "acknowledgment receIPt" to the sender. If the return message fails to reach the sender, the sender thinks the receiver is not receiving the data and keeps sending it back and forth.

When the data is received in its entirety, it is passed to the application identified by the port number.

Application Processing

The receiver application receives the data sent by the sender directly. By parsing the data, you can know the recipient location of a message the address is B's address. If host B does not have a mailbox for B, then host B returns an error message to the sender that says "No to this address".

But in this case, host B happens to have B's inbox on it, so host B and recIPient B can receive the body of the e-mail. The message will be saved to the hard drive of the computer. If the save also works, the receiver will return a "process normal" receipt to the sender. On the other hand, if the disk is full and the message is not saved successfully, a "handle exception" receIPt is sent back to the sender.

Thus, user B can use the mail client on host B to receive and read the e-mail sent by the user a -- "Good morning".

SNS (Social Network Service), called Social networking and is a Service for instant sharing and instant messaging to specific contacts within a circle. As described in the previous e-mail communication process, the process of sending or receiving SNS messages with a mobile terminal can also be analyzed. First, because mobile phones, smartphones, tablets and so on are communicating with packet data, the specific IP address is set by the carrier at the moment they are loaded into a battery and turned on. When you start an application on a mobile phone, you connect to the specified server, and the accumulated information from the server is sent to the mobile terminal after the user name and password are verified, and the terminal displays the specific content.

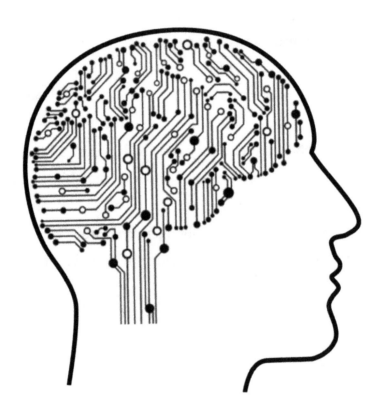

Chapter 5: Machine Learning & Computer Networking

Before going to discuss the use of machine learning in Computer networking there is a need to know in detail about machine learning, deep learning, and Artificial intelligence.

First of all, people are often confused with definitions. Artificial intelligence is a branch of computer science that makes computers work to think like a human. Machine learning is a branch of Artificial intelligence where computers can be made to think like humans with a lot of data given. Deep learning is a branch of Machine learning which uses complex algorithms for text, image and face recognition.

All these three technologies are interlinked and can help computer networks to work better and can act as an intrusion detection system. We will now know briefly about machine learning, artificial intelligence and deep learning for better use of this book content.

In the 1950s and 1960s, with the birth of the computer, artificial intelligence quietly emerged in university labs. Marked by the Turing test proposed by the Alan Turing, the mathematical proof system, Knowledge-based systems, expert systems and other landmark technology and application of artificial intelligence suddenly set off the first wave of researchers.

But at that time, whether it is the computing speed of computers or related programming and algorithm theory, is far from enough to support the development of artificial intelligence needs. In 1951, for example, the Alan Turing, a pioneer in computer science and artificial intelligence, published a paper version of a chess program, but computers of that time could not perform such complex calculations. Like the Explorer Wild China, there's a big difference between setting foot on a new continent for the first time and actually making it flourish. As a result, from the late 1960s, enthusiasm for AI quickly waned among both professional researchers and the general public.

From the 1980s to the 1990s, that's when I invented speaker-independent continuous speech recognition at Carnegie Mellon University and applied it to Apple Computer Systems -- a golden age for AI researchers and product developers. Traditional semiotic-based techniques have been abandoned by me and other contemporary researchers, and statistical-model-based techniques have emerged, making considerable progress in areas such as speech recognition and machine translation Artificial neural networks have also begun to make headway in applications such as pattern recognition, and the 1997 triumph of the deep blue computer over the Human Garry Kasparov has given ordinary people a run for their money.

But the technological advances of that era were not good enough to exceed the psychological expectations of intelligent machines. In the case of speech recognition, the statistical model, while a big step forward for speech recognition technology, is not yet good enough for the average person to accept. At the time, the speech recognition APP I developed at apple was used more for presentations and promotions, with limited practical value. On the whole, that wave of artificial intelligence still has strong academic research and scientific experiment color, although aroused public enthusiasm, more like a bubble before hitting bottom It is far from being in line with the business model and the needs of the masses.

Around 2010, to be exact, since 2006, as deep learning technologies mature, computer computing speeds increase dramatically, and, of course, the wealth of vast amounts of data accumulated in the Internet Age Artificial intelligence is on a different path to a renaissance.

Psychologically, there is a psychological threshold for people to accept something new, just as it is for people to feel an external stimulus. The intensity of external stimuli (such as sound, light, and electricity) is too small for people to feel anything at all; only the intensity of external stimuli exceeds the minimum amount of stimuli a person can perceive People have definite feelings such as "hearing voices" and "seeing things". This minimum amount of stimulus, known psychologically as an absolute threshold, causes a person to perceive and react.

That's exactly what's happening with artificial intelligence. Still, take image recognition. In the early days of artificial intelligence, if a computer program claimed it could recognize a face in a picture, it was only about 50 percent accurate the average person would see the program as a toy, not as intelligent. As technology advances, and as face recognition algorithms improve their accuracy to 80 percent or even close to 90 percent, researchers know that this is not an easy step to take, but the results are still hard for ordinary people to accept Because one out of every five faces is misidentified, this is obviously not practical -- One might say the program is clever, but one would never think it was smart enough to replace the human eye. Only when the accuracy of the computer in face recognition is very close to or even higher than that of ordinary people, the security system will use the computer to replace the human security to complete the identification work. In other words, for face recognition applications, approaching or exceeding the level of the average person is the "absolute threshold" that we care about.

So, when we say "AI is here, " we mean that ai or deep learning can really solve real problems. In Machine Vision, speech recognition, data mining, automatic driving, and other application scenarios, artificial intelligence has continuously broken through the psychological threshold that people can accept, and for the first time in the industrial level "landing" to play and create real value.

How Does Computer Learn?

What kind of laws does the computer come up with? It depends on what kind of machine learning algorithm we use.

There is an algorithm very simple, imitation is a child learning to read the idea. Parents and teachers may have the experience that when children begin to learn to read, for example, when we teach them to distinguish "one" from "two" from "three", we tell them that the word written in a stroke is "one" Two strokes make two characters, three strokes make three characters. This rule is easy to remember and easy to use. However, when it comes to learning new characters, this rule may not work. For example, "mouth" is also three strokes, but it is not three strokes. We usually tell the children that the box is the mouth and the row is the three. The pattern thickens, but the number of words is still rising. Soon, the children found that "field" is also a box, but it is not "mouth. We will tell the children at this time, the box has a "Ten" is the "field". After that, we will probably tell the children, "field" above the head is "by", below the head is "a", above and below is "Shen". Many children are in such a step-by-step enrichment of the characteristics of the law under the guidance of slowly learn their own summary of the law, their own remember new Chinese characters, and then learn thousands of Chinese characters.

Deep Learning

Deep learning is such a machine learning approach that is flexible in its expressiveness while allowing the computer to experiment until it finally gets close to its goal. In essence, deep learning is not fundamentally different from the traditional machine learning methods described above but is intended to distinguish different classes of objects in high dimensional space based on their characteristics. But the expressive power of deep learning is vastly different from that of traditional machine learning.

In simple terms, deep learning is the process of taking what a computer is trying to learn and putting that data into a complex, multi-level data processing network (deep neural network) Then check that the resulting data processed by the network meets the requirements -- if it does, keep the network as the target model, and if it does not, adjust the network parameters Veronica Guerin again and again Until the output meets the requirements.

Suppose the data to be processed by deep learning is the "flow" of information, and the deep learning network is a huge network of pipes and valves. The entrance of the network is a number of pipe openings, and the exit of the network is also a number of pipe openings. The water network has many layers, each layer has many can control the flow of the water flow direction and flow control valve. According to the needs of different tasks, the number of layers and the number of regulating valves in each layer of the water pipe network can have different combinations. For Complex tasks, the total number of regulator valves can be in the thousands or more. In a water pipe network, each control valve in each layer is connected to all control valves in the next layer through a water pipe, forming a front-to-back fully connected layer-by-layer flow system (this is a basic case where different deep learning models differ in the way pipes are installed and connected).

Side note: There are already some visualization tools out there that can help us "see" deep learning on a large scale. For example, Google's famous deep learning framework, Tensor Flow, provides a web version of a gadget that maps out the real-time features of the entire web as it performs deep learning operations using easy to understand diagrams.

Finally, it is important to note that the above concept of deep learning deliberately avoids mathematical formulas and mathematical arguments, and this method of popularizing deep learning with water networks is only suitable for the general public. For Math and computer science professionals, this description is incomplete and inaccurate. The flow control valve analogy is not mathematically equivalent to the weight adjustment associated with each neuron in a deep neural network. The cost function, gradient descent, backpropagation and other important concepts of deep learning algorithm are neglected in the whole description of the water pipe network.

Should professionals learn deep learning, or should they start with a professional tutorial?

Now let us know with a few examples of how machine learning algorithms can be used in computer networking.

Computer networking is a strange field and is often vulnerable to scammers and hackers who try to destroy the otherwise good game into a cruel one with viruses, ransoms, Trojans and certain other weird stuff that can make networks suffer and lose a lot of money, energy and time. Machine learning can be used in intrusion detection systems to secure the network environment. Below we will discuss a few algorithms and its effect on network security.

1. K-Nearest Algorithm
It is a famous machine learning algorithm which can be used to detect network shells and spam content in the network.

2. Decision Tree Algorithm
Decision tree algorithm can be used to detect abnormal operations in the network with a lot of sample data it had collected.

3. Random Forest Algorithm
Random forest machine learning algorithm can be effectively used to detect abnormal operations in the network and can also be used to detect brute force attacks via FTP.

4. Naïve Bayes Algorithm

Naïve Bayes algorithm can be used to detect network shells and DDOS attacks in a computer network.

5. Logistic Regression Algorithm

By using logistic regression algorithm there are huge chances of stopping java overflow attacks that occur often from malicious hackers.

6. Support Vector Machine

Support Vector machine is famous for its detection abilities of Botnets and it can also be used to detect XSS vulnerability in web-based applications.

7. K-Means and DB-Scan Algorithm

Both of these algorithms can be used to detect all types of attacks that occur on computers with an accurate precision rate.

And there are certain deep learning algorithms that can help you detect your employees all the time for any error they may do. By using machine learning and deep learning methods in computer networks we can make networks a lot secure. Machine learning with computer networks has a lot of potential in the coming days.

Conclusion

Thank you for making it through to the end of *Networking for beginners*, let's hope it was informative and able to provide you with all of the tools you need to achieve your goals whatever they may be.

The next step is to learn more about computer networking from various advanced textbooks. Hope you have learned a lot with this module. For further exploration of computer networks try to look at different hardware you encounter in your life.

This module follows up with a layman introduction to machine learning and artificial intelligence. You can check it to improve your expertise in the field.

Just for a quick overview of the material we have seen. We have learned about definition, history, and basics of networking with a thorough overview of a network with a lot of examples. Then we discussed network protocols in detail. And in the end, we discussed Artificial intelligence and machine learning with respect to Computer Networking.

Finally, if you found this book useful in any way, a review on Amazon is always appreciated!